ABOUT THE AUTHORS

Dr. Colm O'Gorman is Professor of Entrepreneurship at DCU Business School. His research focuses on the origins and growth of new firms. He has published extensively in European and US peer-reviewed academic journals, such as *Entrepreneurship & Regional Development, European Planning Studies, Journal of Small Business Management, Organizational Dynamics, R&D Management, Small Business Economics*, and *Venture Capital*. He has completed several European Union research projects and is co-author of the annual *Global Entrepreneurship Monitor*
(GEM) report for Ireland (www.gemconsortium.org), which measures the extent and nature of entrepreneurship in Ireland and benchmarks Ireland against other EU and OECD countries. He has explored the emergence of high-tech firms in the context of cluster dynamics, including a study of the factors that lead to the rapid emergence of a software industry in Ireland during the 1990s (www.nesc.ie). He has co-authored four teaching case-studies on entrepreneurship, published by the European Case Clearing House, including *Abrakebabra: Growing Pains in a Fast-Food Restaurant Chain*, which won the 2007 ECCH case award for Entrepreneurship (www.ecch.com).

Dr. James Cunningham is a senior lecturer in strategic management at the Department of Management, Executive MBA Programme Director and a Research Fellow at the Centre for Innovation & Structural Change at the J.E. Cairnes Graduate School of Business & Public Policy, National University of Ireland, Galway. He has published in international journals, book chapters, and at refereed conferences. He has been awarded three overall best conference paper awards at the British Academy of Management Conference (2002 and 2005) and at the Irish Academy of Management Conference (2003). He has won national and international awards for business case
studies he has written on Irish Ports and Hostelworld.com. His research on technology transfer has been cited in the Government's major strategy document, *Strategy for Science Innovation & Technology*, published in 2006. In December 2006, *Business & Finance* reviewed his co-authored book, *Strategic Management of Technology Transfer: The New Challenge on Campus*, published by Oak Tree Press, commenting that: "... this book should be part of the policy library of entrepreneurs, venture capitalists and top managers in ICT and R&D oriented sectors". His research interests include strategy as practice and technology transfer.

ENTERPRISE IN ACTION

AN INTRODUCTION TO ENTREPRENEURSHIP IN AN IRISH CONTEXT

Colm O'Gorman
James Cunningham

OAK TREE PRESS
19 Rutland Street
Cork, Ireland

© 2007 Colm O'Gorman and James Cunningham

A catalogue record of this book is
available from the British Library.

ISBN 978-1-904887-17-1

Printed in Ireland by Colour Books Ltd.

CONTENTS

FIGURES

ACKNOWLEDGEMENTS

The authors wish to thank Will Geoghegan of the Centre for Innovation & Structural Change at the J.E. Cairnes Graduate School of Business & Public Policy, National University of Ireland, Galway, for contributing the chapter on Creativity & Idea Generation (**Chapter 4**).

The authors also wish to acknowledge the contribution of post-graduate and undergraduate students of the School of Business, University College Dublin and of the J.E. Cairnes Graduate School of Business & Public Policy, National University of Ireland, Galway. Their theses and project work provided the inspiration for some of the chapters. Specifically, our thanks and recognition go to Kevin Dowdall, Joseph Gannon, Geraldine Lavin, Michael Madden, Kevin Marmion, Geraldine O'Loughlin, and Aideen O'Toole.

Finally, the authors would like to thank Brian O'Kane and the staff of Oak Tree Press, for their advice and assistance in developing this edition of the book.

DEDICATIONS

This book is dedicated to
Clare, Tim, Maggie and Neil
Sammi

FOREWORD

As both a practitioner and an academic, I have always found it difficult to get across to people the level of satisfaction, the buzz, of setting up your own business. Taking an idea, a concept or a vision or what many will see as a hare-brained scheme, and turning it into an operating reality, is one of life's pleasures. Even the bad times are good and, believe me, there will be bad times. The fact that the reality often bears little resemblance to the initial idea matters not at all. The heavy levels of work, worry and strain are all part of the package, as are the mistakes that you will make. But you learn, adapt, change, and keep moving forward. Financial success, when it comes, frequently with popular acclaim, is only the icing on the cake. By then, you have done it, you have proven your beliefs to your own satisfaction. That is my understanding of entrepreneurship.

It depends on individuals with a vision willing to take risks to turn the vision into a reality, with the ability to raise the resources necessary by whatever means and the determination and energy to drive the project forward. It is not a career for the many but, for the lucky few with the necessary characteristics, there is a world of opportunity waiting.

How vital are entrepreneurs in society? Critically important. A vibrant, growing economy provides benefits and opportunities for most, if not all, of its people. The vital element in the long-term success of an economy is a group of entrepreneurs creating the industries of the future. These individuals look to the future, dream up opportunities and then, most importantly, make the dreams come true. Often, they fail, but that's how it should be.

For years, it was believed, and it was more or less true, that the Irish were not enterprising. Our culture and society directed people into safe professions. The entrepreneurs emigrated. Business was not a quality career. Attitudes have changed. For those of you with entrepreneurial tendencies, this means that you may now use those scarce abilities in business rather than in some other area.

I am delighted to see the publication of this book. Entrepreneurship in Ireland has long been neglected by academics. The authors not only examine current thinking and research into entrepreneurship but also provide many pen-pictures of Irish entrepreneurs and their ventures. This gives a familiar, comfortable feel to the text.

The book is easy to read. For those of you who already know that you want to run your own business, *Enterprise in Action* will be a valuable companion. For those of you who wonder if you have 'the calling', read the book. It could be the best few hours you will ever spend.

John J Teeling
Founder
Cooley Distillery plc, African Gold plc.

1

PROFILING IRISH ENTREPRENEURS[1]

Do the likes of Colum O'Sullivan, Lloyd Nolan, Jennifer Kinnear, David Walsh, Elaine Coughlan, Fergal Broder, Brody Sweeney, John Concannon, Jan Berg, Ray Nolan, Sean Cronin, Professor Barry Smyth and Paul Cotter, and Angela Hope – all of whom are profiled in this book – have unique advantages that equipped them to succeed as entrepreneurs? Why did these individuals choose to start their own businesses? Are they 'typical' entrepreneurs? What do we mean when we describe them as 'entrepreneurs'? Researchers, investors, bankers and other potential entrepreneurs have always been interested in identifying what it takes to be a successful entrepreneur. This chapter will explore a number of different studies that have sought to identify a 'success formula' for entrepreneurs. The research evidence suggests that there are some personality traits and background characteristics that are common to entrepreneurs but clearly there is no such thing as the typical entrepreneur.

The number and the profile of entrepreneurs in Ireland have changed significantly in recent years. The change has been more pronounced due to the rapid growth of the Irish economy during the last decade. A number of important trends can be identified. The first is the role that small business has played in job creation in the US and in Europe since the 1980s. In both the US and Europe, large companies have been reducing their 'headcount' by investing in technology and reorganising their businesses, while the small business sector has been creating jobs – although, in Europe, where unemployment has remained high, small businesses have been slower to develop. The Irish government has begun to recognise the role that entrepreneurs play in wealth creation and job creation. The second important trend is the increasing importance of the service sector, which includes education, software, tourism, financial services, etc, with many opportunities for small companies and self-employment.

---

[1] The authors acknowledge the contribution of Michael Madden, a Masters of Business Studies student at the Michael Smurfit Graduate School of Business, University College Dublin, whose thesis is *Characteristics & Motives of Entrepreneurs: An Enquiry into the Irish Food Sector* (1996).

FIGURE 1.1: ENTERPRISING IN FINANCIAL SERVICES: DERMOT DESMOND[2]

Dermot Desmond has been involved in many ventures, most of which have a financial flavour. He believes that his success as an entrepreneur can be attributed to his ability to look at things in a different light. He says he never accepts the common wisdom or what everybody else says to be the case without first checking it out for himself. His advice to would-be entrepreneurs is to keep your eyes open at all times, be very patient and do not get frustrated no matter how long it takes.

Some of his successes and business interests are:

◊   In 1981, he founded National City Brokers (NCB), which became Ireland's largest independent stockbrokers. In 1994, he sold his 56% stake in NCB to Ulster Bank.

◊   He has a number of software businesses in Dublin. In 1984, he founded Quay Financial Software (QFS), which today is a leading producer of digital platforms for dealing rooms. In July 1995, he sold his 80% share holding in QFS.

◊   He has a 50% stake in Pembroke Capital, an aviation leasing specialist.

◊   He purchased London City Airport in 1995, developed it into London's business airport for people who preferred convenience and comfort, and sold it in 2006.

◊   He pioneered the development of the IFSC, Dublin.

◊   He has significant holdings in Celtic Football Club, Sandy Lane Hotel, Intuition, International Investment Underwriters, Daon, Barchester Healthcare and the Sporting Emporium Casino.

The third trend is the changing job market. Organisations are redesigning themselves to be more competitive and flexible. This has resulted in outsourcing, short-term contracts, and flexible work practices. As the job market becomes less secure, individuals are more inclined to consider self-employment as a career choice.

The fourth significant trend is the emergence of female entrepreneurship. International research on entrepreneurs has traditionally focused on males. It has been assumed that entrepreneurs are male, and it has even been suggested that entrepreneurship is a way of demonstrating 'maleness'. However, the number of women operating their own business ventures has increased dramatically over the last decade. In the United States, 25% of small businesses are female-owned. Recent evidence suggests that women are now starting enterprises at two to five times the rate of men. Some forecasts suggest that, soon, close to 50% of all businesses will be run by women.

The first part of this chapter examines Irish entrepreneurs. This is followed by a discussion of international research evidence on entrepreneurs, first in terms of background characteristics and then in terms of personality traits. The role of the entrepreneur is considered and entrepreneurs are contrasted with managers. The chapter concludes with a discussion of different ways of studying entrepreneurs.

---

[2]   The authors acknowledge and thank Darren Walsh, a graduate of the Diploma in Entrepreneurial Studies programme, for his help in writing this piece.

RESEARCH EVIDENCE ON IRISH ENTREPRENEURS

THE SECRETS OF SUCCESS: COMMON TRAITS

We profiled a number of leading Irish entrepreneurs.[3] The focus of this research was on the individual entrepreneur, rather than on the businesses they created, and asked a basic question: 'To what do you attribute your success?'. The answers received from this diverse group suggest that there are some common factors associated with entrepreneurial success:

- **Self-belief, passion and vision:** They had the ability to make their own decisions and to ignore what others were telling them, even so-called experts. According to the entrepreneurs, "to be an entrepreneur, you must have an unshakeable belief in your ability, which means you never actually sit down and doubt yourself or your ability to do business". Self-belief is particularly important if you fail – as one entrepreneur commented: "if you are an entrepreneur in this country, you'll get stoned, whereas if you're in India, France, Germany or America, they'll throw flowers at you". All the entrepreneurs were passionate about their business. They all had some vision, dream or goal about their future. For some, these images of the future emerged as they opportunistically identified a new business. For many, starting up a business was not work but rather an opportunity to do something that they enjoyed.

- **Risk-taking:** The entrepreneurs differed in terms of their attitude to risk, some describing themselves as moderately-calculated risk-takers, while others had to risk everything – the greater the risk, the greater the buzz. However, they all believed that the essence of entrepreneurship was about taking a risk. What they have in common is that they took the risk and saw opportunity where others saw risks.

- **Persistence and hard work:** What drove Freda Hayes to set-up House of James after leaving Blarney Woollen Mills and then Meadows & Byrne? For her, starting up a business meant starting at the bottom again. These successful entrepreneurs invested their personal time into their businesses. Aristotle said that "we are what we repeatedly do, excellence then is not an action but a habit". Success rarely came quickly or easily. These individuals refuse to give up or to be set back by the failures that many of them experienced. Denis O'Brien's initial venture, a shopping channel on Sky television, failed, yet he has proved that he "has the ability to pick himself up and run again". Some believed that this ability is the defining characteristic of an entrepreneur.

---

[3] Unpublished research work by students of the Diploma in Entrepreneurial Studies, supervised by Dr. C. O'Gorman.

- **Commitment to people ('Leadership'):** Many described an essential quality
  of entrepreneurship as an ability to win the trust of others, be they
  employees, customers or suppliers. However, these entrepreneurs had little
  time for sentimentality: "if people are not contributing to the organisation, get
  rid of them".

At one level, the entrepreneurs studied appeared to have little in common.
However, the differences identified tell an important story. First, it was clearly
evident that success was not restricted to any one business sector. For many of the
entrepreneurs, the choice of business sector was purely opportunistic. Successful
entrepreneurs are not just found in emerging, changing high-growth sectors, such
as computer software or telecommunications. Success also was achieved in such
diverse product and service areas as fast food, retailing, mineral water,
manufacturing and stockbroking.

Prior experience in the field of entrepreneurial endeavour does not appear to
be a pre-requisite for success. How did his job as a schoolteacher prepare Pat
McDonagh for his Supermac's venture? Conventional wisdom dictates that an
entrepreneur should gain experience in the area before embarking on a new
venture. Many entrepreneurs stumble into a particular area of activity that they
have never worked in previously.

For the entrepreneurs studied, it was never too early nor too late to embark on
an entrepreneurial career. Many of the entrepreneurs had pursued structured
career paths in traditional jobs, only later in life feeling that they were ready to
take responsibility for creating their own wealth.

The qualities outlined above are common to the successful entrepreneurs
studied. Taken together, they describe individuals from all walks of life who have
identified an opportunity and have pursued it with a degree of single-mindedness
that to an outsider may appear obsessive, unbalanced and unhealthy. It is clear
that there is no success formula. Success in business, and success in any other
area of endeavour such as sports, the arts, politics, comes to those who both seek
it and persevere in the pursuit of it: 'An entrepreneur looks for opportunity and
seizes it'.

COMMON BACKGROUND CHARACTERISTICS

Studies of Irish entrepreneurs have explored the background characteristics of
the entrepreneur and suggest that there are commonalities.

Education

Research on Irish entrepreneurs suggests that the level of educational attainment
is high. Education appears to be correlated with high growth and the creation of
ventures producing higher value-added products. A study by O'Farrell (1986)
showed that 22% of manufacturing entrepreneurs had a degree, at a time when

only 9% of males in high population density areas had degrees. Education is more often in the areas of engineering, science and other technical disciplines rather than in commerce and business studies.

Previous Work Experience

Kinsella & Mulvenna (1993) found that over 75% of all individuals who set up their own firms held managerial positions in their employment immediately prior to 'going it alone'.

Overseas experience is an important determinant of new business success in Ireland. Individuals who have experience of working abroad have a far greater propensity to export once they start their own firms. Also they make better use of contacts within the industry. O'Farrell showed that 42% of founders had worked abroad at some time in their career.

Parents' Occupation

Having self-employed parents increases the propensity of individuals to engage in new venture creation. O'Farrell's (1986) study showed that 46% of new firm founders had fathers who were self-employed, at a time when only 27% of the population was self-employed.

Age at Start-up

Irish entrepreneurs are typically aged between 25 and 45 years at the time of new venture creation. The age of start-up in Ireland is less than that of UK entrepreneurs. This may be due to the wide availability of State grants and assistance in Ireland for some categories of entrepreneurship. Grants provide the entrepreneur with the seed capital required for start-up, removing the need for them to accumulate their own. Fast growth ventures are operated by entrepreneurs in the 35-44 age group, whereas slower-growing companies in the same industry are operated by founders mostly in the 45-54 age category.

O'Farrell's research on Irish entrepreneurs in the manufacturing sector is summarised in **Figure 1.2**. These findings were mirrored in many ways by a study conducted in Northern Ireland by Hisrich (1988), who concluded that the predominant entrepreneur in the North is independent, energetic, competitive, self-confident, and goal-oriented. Other characteristics identified are outlined in **Figure 1.3**.

FIGURE 1.2: BACKGROUND CHARACTERISTICS: AN HISTORIC PERSPECTIVE – THE O'FARRELL STUDY

◊   Median age at time of establishment was 32.
◊   Majority of founders (84%) were under the age of 41.
◊   84% were married.
◊   73% had held at least two full-time jobs prior to start-up.
◊   22% held university degrees.
◊   46% came from households where the father was self-employed.
◊   More than half of the sample of entrepreneurs had occupied managerial positions in their last job.
◊   42% had engaged in full-time employment outside Ireland at some point in their career.
◊   Half of all new firms were established as partnerships.
◊   27% of entrepreneurs were self-employed immediately prior to founding their present venture.

FIGURE 1.3: THE HISRICH STUDY: CHARACTERISTICS OF ENTREPRENEURS IN NORTHERN IRELAND

◊   40 years of age.
◊   Married with two children.
◊   25% had degrees, mostly in business and engineering.
◊   Over one-half had previous experience in the business area.
◊   50% had some form of managerial experience.
◊   Manufacturing firms were the most common.

THE MOTIVES FOR START-UP

Why do Irish people choose to be entrepreneurs? O'Farrell's (1986) study of Irish entrepreneurs identified a number of major motivational factors:

- **Desire for independence:** One-third ranked this as their primary reason for start-up. Over 70% identified it as being in the top three reasons for starting a business.

- **Opportunity to exploit a gap in the market**: 30% ranked this as their primary reason for starting up.

- **Frustration:** This motive refers to individuals who felt blocked in their current jobs. They believed their autonomy and social mobility was impeded by the bureaucratic organisation they worked in. One-third of the respondents said 'frustration' was one of the three most important factors in deciding to start-up a business.

1: Profiling Irish Entrepreneurs

- **Money:** To many, this may be surprising, but only 10% ranked money as the number one motive for start-up. About one-third of respondents specified it as the second or third most important motive for start-up.

- Other less important reasons were redundancy, meeting a suitable business partner and a desire to return to work in Ireland.

These motives for starting a business can be classified either as 'push' factors or 'pull' factors. Motives classified as 'push' are mainly negative in nature and include unemployment, frustration in a previous job, redundancy, and lack of promotional opportunities. Motives classified as 'pull' include identifying a market opportunity, desire for independence, meeting a suitable business partner. Often an employee believed that the level of service or quality provided by their employer's business could be improved and decided to leave the business and start-up in competition.

INTERNATIONAL RESEARCH ON ENTREPRENEURS

BACKGROUND CHARACTERISTICS

Do entrepreneurs have common background characteristics? Do the background characteristics of entrepreneurs influence the likelihood of new venture creation? Do these characteristics influence the growth rate of the new business? The research evidence discussed above on Irish entrepreneurs suggests that there may be some characteristics common to all entrepreneurs. International research has suggested that entrepreneurs do share some common characteristics and that these are important in determining whether an individual will consider becoming an entrepreneur.

Researchers have identified five background characteristics that have an important impact on entrepreneurs:

- Level and type of education.
- Previous work experience.
- Parents' occupation.
- Age at start-up.
- Birth order.

When considering the research evidence presented below, it is important that three factors are borne in mind:

- That the characteristics are not important in themselves – what is important is how the characteristics affect the behaviour of an individual.
- A person does not have to have these characteristics to become an entrepreneur.
- These characteristics are strongly associated and interrelated.

Level & Type of Education

Popular literature on entrepreneurship suggests that the entrepreneur attends the 'university of hard knocks', that is, they learn about business by doing it rather than in school and university. This literature also suggests that entrepreneurs develop their managerial and technical expertise from their broad work experiences. Early research literature suggested that the level of education attained by entrepreneurs was lower than that of business executives, creating the myth of the 'uneducated' entrepreneur. However, while the absolute level of educational attainment of entrepreneurs was low, there was evidence in this early research that the entrepreneurs had a higher level of educational attainment than the population as a whole. Recent research has demonstrated a clear link between level of educational attainment and propensity for entrepreneurial behaviour:

- Research studies of high technology ventures established a link between entrepreneurial success and level of education attained by the entrepreneur. However, performance at any given level of education does not appear to correlate with entrepreneurial behaviour.

- A review of 17 studies linking education and subsequent performance suggested that for 10 of them, a positive relationship was found; for six of them, the results were not decisive; and, in the remaining one, there was a negative relationship between education and performance (Cooper & Gascon, 1992). This suggests that a higher level of educational attainment may influence the probability of new venture creation, but it is difficult to isolate education as the independent factor responsible solely for business success.

- The relationship between new venture performance and the education of the entrepreneur may be dependent on the business sector the entrepreneur chooses. In some sectors, education may be the primary route to self-employment while, in other sectors, the opposite is the case. A college education is the primary route to self-employment in skilled services but, in the construction sector, the opposite situation prevails: high school drop-outs are much more likely to enter self- employment than college graduates. A study of high technology venture founders concluded that education does lead to substantially better performance.

- Attendance at college may be more important than the field of study. Attendance at college is important because it is seen as a broadening experience that involves the development of personal skills that would be helpful if a new venture is initiated. The experience of independence and the exposure to new ideas and people may motivate college graduates to start-up a new enterprise. College may be a surrogate for the development of other skills, such as communication skills and time management skills, which are useful to the entrepreneur.

Overall, the research evidence suggests that, in some sectors, the experience of education transfers certain skills and desires to participants. This may increase the propensity for new venture creation. Subsequent performance may also be related to the level of educational attainment, however performance at any given level of education does not affect propensity for new venture creation or subsequent new venture activity.

Previous Work Experience

The previous work experience of the entrepreneur influences the nature and success of the new business venture. Work experience may influence the choice of business sector and the size of the business created. The success of the new venture may be related to breadth of experience, to functional experience, and to the highest level of management experience of the entrepreneur. Prior experience in the business sector of the new venture activity is positively related to both new venture survival and growth. Familiarity with the sector allows the founder to make use of product and market knowledge and contacts.

The entrepreneur's involvement in previous ventures and the extent of the management role the entrepreneur had in such ventures are important determinants of success. Some authors have argued that the more times an entrepreneur has failed, the more likely they will be successful in the future. Entrepreneurs with higher levels of management experience tend to start larger enterprises. Entrepreneurs are frequently successful in their previous jobs. Overall, it appears that a majority of entrepreneurs initiate ventures that are closely related to previous work experiences. Experience increases the likelihood of being profitable, but experience plus education is associated with the greatest success.

Parents' Occupation

Entrepreneurs are more likely to come from families in which their parents owned a business. A household in which one or both parents are self-employed will have exposed the potential founder to certain skills, values and attitudes that will most likely aid them in the business world. Consequently, within the household, there will have been a strong commitment to the ideology of a reward system inherent in self-employment. The potential entrepreneur views their parents as role models, and being 'one's own boss' is perceived as a feasible career. This appears to be regardless of whether the parents were successful or unsuccessful. Over 50% of company founders in the United States have self-employed fathers, while only 12% of the work force are self-employed.

Age at Start-up

Attempts to establish a link between the entrepreneur's age and the performance of the new business have been inconclusive. The age of the entrepreneur at start-up determines the experience of the entrepreneur and may reflect the level of capital saved by the entrepreneur. There is an argument that younger entrepreneurs are more likely to try and grow their business. In trying to establish this link between the age profile of the entrepreneur and the success of the business, it is important to remember that some sectors require a more experienced individual. Age alone may not be a predictor of new venture success, but age may be a measure of experience and wealth accumulation, and therefore a form of milestone that can trigger an individual towards self-employment.

Birth Order of the Entrepreneur

Many studies have suggested that children who are the first-born in a family are more likely to pursue an entrepreneurial career. The reason suggested for this is that the individual is subject to added attention and encouragement from their parents, resulting in the child developing more self-confidence. In a national sample involving over 400 female entrepreneurs, Hisrich & Brush (1984) found that 50% were first-born.

FIGURE 1.4: DENIS O'BRIEN: A 'CLASSIC' SUCCESS STORY?

Denis O'Brien was an Arts student in UCD and completed an MBA in Boston College, USA. During his student days, he was involved in a number of businesses that generated cash for himself. On completing his MBA, he got a job with a bank in Dublin with the intention of learning how banks work. He was determined at this stage that he would start-up his own business. A year later, he left the bank and worked as a Personal Assistant to Tony Ryan of GPA. Denis worked hard with Tony Ryan and gained a lot of business experience. During this time, he learnt a number of important lessons:

Don't invest money without putting in place good top management.

If you go off-piste with investments, you will go bankrupt — don't over-diversify your investments.

Euphoria clouds an entrepreneur's judgement.

O'Brien left Tony Ryan and began a business called E-Sat TV. This company was to launch a shopping channel in the UK. It had a number of investors, including the Grattan Group plc, and over half a million pounds invested. The venture was in trouble from the beginning. Sales did not materialise. He responded quickly by rationalising. Staff were let go and the programme was redesigned. However, due to their own financial difficulties, the Grattan Group had to 'pull the plug' on the venture. E-Sat TV closed and O'Brien wound up the venture.

At the time, the Irish government was advertising for licences for the new private broadcasting sector. He successfully obtained a licence. He hired Australians to run the business because the Australian radio market is very competitive. He organised a very high profile launch for his station, Classic Hits 98FM. The radio station has continued to invest in market research to ensure that it delivers what customers want. Since then, he has opened radio stations in Prague, Stockholm and Vilnius.

The next industry that Denis turned his attention to was telecommunications. He founded Esat Telecom and applied for a licence to lease lines from Telecom Éireann (now eircom). He wanted to sell cheaper calls to corporate customers. After a year of problems and complaints to the Competition Directorate of the EU, he got the licence. One of his biggest ventures was the winning of the second mobile phone licence in Ireland. This was against strong international competition. He subsequently sold Esat to British Telecom, which rebranded the telecoms group Esat BT, while the mobile phone division was rebranded O2.

After exiting the Irish mobile market, O'Brien competed for mobile phone licences in the Caribbean through Digicel and the operations of this company since have expanded to the South Pacific. By 2006, the company has over 4 million subscribers and operations in 22 markets. Through Communicorp Group, O'Brien manages his media businesses in Ireland and in Europe. In 2003, O'Brien chaired the 2003 Special Olympic World Summer Games and he is Chairman and co-founder of Frontline, an international foundation for the protection of human rights defenders.

PSYCHOLOGICAL CHARACTERISTICS

It is more likely that entrepreneurs will have common personality traits than common background characteristics. Most people identify entrepreneurs as risk-takers and as having a strong determination to succeed. It is difficult to measure personality traits, as researchers can never be sure of the measurement or the significance of a personality trait. The most popular personality traits examined in the literature on entrepreneurs are need for achievement, risk-taking propensity, internal/external locus of control, need for independence and type-A behaviour syndrome.

Need for Achievement

A high need for achievement (nAch) has been accepted since the early 1960s as a principal motivator of entrepreneurial behaviour. Entrepreneurs with this trait value excellence, they stay focused and committed to a task, and their burning desire to be a winner sustains their involvement even in uncertain times. McClelland (1961) described the characteristics of high need achievement, which are illustrated in **Figure 1.5**.

Interestingly, entrepreneurs with a high need for achievement view profits as a measure of success, and money as a feedback mechanism not a goal in itself. These individuals remain optimistic even in the most unfamiliar of situations. In choosing advisors, high need achievers select experts rather than family and friends to help them. Other findings associated with high nAch entrepreneurs is that they are more energetic, persistent, realistic and more action-minded than individuals who display other kinds of motivational patterns.

FIGURE 1.5: MCCLELLAND'S CHARACTERISTICS OF HIGH NEED ACHIEVEMENT

◊ Preference for decisions involving risk that are neither very high risk nor very low risk.
◊ Belief that one's efforts will be influential in the attainment of some goal.
◊ Perceive the probability of success in attaining a goal as being relatively high.
◊ Need for feedback.
◊ Capacity to plan ahead.
◊ Desire to take personal responsibility for decisions.
◊ An interest in excellence for its own sake.
◊ Interest in concrete results from decisions.

Locus of Control

The locus of control scale developed by Rotter (1966) measures a person's perceived ability to influence events in their lives. Individuals with an internal locus of control believe that their own behaviour determines their destiny, and give little credence to 'external' forces, such as destiny, luck or 'powerful others'. Individuals with an external locus of control don't believe in their ability to control their external environment and are reluctant to assume the risks that starting a business would entail.

Studies suggest that locus of control is useful for distinguishing entrepreneurs from the general population, but it is not a valid discriminator of entrepreneurs and managers. Managers and entrepreneurs were both characterised as internals. Rotter (1966) argued that an internal control locus of control was consistent with a high achievement orientation. Individuals who portray internal values and beliefs are more likely to have a higher need for achievement.

Risk-Taking Propensity

Much research has been carried out examining the risk-taking propensity of entrepreneurs compared to managers. This research is plagued by measurement problems. It is appropriate to characterise entrepreneurs as moderate to high risk-takers, especially at the outset, but, as the business evolves and grows, these same individuals display calculated tendencies towards risk, preferring to take gambles they feel are within their own ability to control.

Entrepreneurs perhaps are better characterised as opportunity-seekers rather than risk-takers. It seems that the biggest risk an entrepreneur takes is deciding to leave a job in order to start a new venture. Many studies have found that an entrepreneur's tendency to take risks actually reduces as the firm's net worth increases. This is because entrepreneurs then have a substantial asset base to protect. By taking over an existing business rather than starting a new business, the entrepreneur can reduce the element of risk involved.

Tolerance for Ambiguity

Tolerance for ambiguity can be defined as the tendency to perceive ambiguous situations as desirable rather than threatening. Entrepreneurs are capable of sustaining their drive and determination to persist with a course of action even when future outcomes are uncertain. It is this willingness to tolerate uncertainty that separates entrepreneurs from 'would-be entrepreneurs'. This element complements the risk-taking facet previously examined and both are used by researchers in studying potential entrepreneurial subjects. Persons with a high tolerance for ambiguity and a moderate to high risk-taking propensity are the ones most likely to succeed despite the obstacles in their way. They are motivated by a challenge and regard simplicity as uneventful.

Type A / B Behaviour

People can be classified into two different types of behaviours. 'Type A' people are involved in an aggressive struggle to achieve more and more in less and less time, which manifests itself in such tendencies as impatience, time urgency, driving ambition, and competitiveness. 'Type B' individuals are characterised as more easy-going and as less competitive in relation to daily events. Entrepreneurs were found to exhibit a majority of the Type A elements, particularly in relation to the hurried and impatient variables. In some instances, they also can become over-obsessive, which can hinder their capacity to perform efficiently.

Need for Independence

Entrepreneurs are typically characterised as people who prefer to do things on their own, in their own way, and also in their own time. This need mostly stems from a feeling of being blocked and contained in past bureaucratic organisations. Many individuals just can't relate to or adapt to order-taking in an employer / employee relationship. They seek out situations where they can have complete control and personal impact on the results. Research suggests that 'being independent' is the major significant factor for entrepreneurs being glad for having started a business.

FIGURE 1.6: DAVID MCKENNA – FROM PLUMBING TO RECRUITMENT

David left school at 15 and served his time as a plumber in London. In 1993, he set up a recruitment agency with stg£5,000 in capital. This was before the real boom in the Irish economy. By 1997, the company had in excess of 80,000 CVs on file and the future looked bright. This led to the listing of Marlborough International on the Stock Exchange, which netted David in excess of €5 million cash as well as a paper valuation of €12.7 million. He became CEO of the newly-listed company.

Subsequently, the company came under financial pressure due to the consolidation in the recruitment market. Due to this and other factors, Marlborough International was delisted, broken up and sold during the first few months of the new century.

THE ROLE OF THE ENTREPRENEUR

DEFINING THE ENTREPRENEUR

There are numerous definitions of entrepreneurs but it is difficult to identify exactly who is, and who isn't, an entrepreneur. Would you include the owner of a small business as an entrepreneur? Is Michael Smurfit an entrepreneur? Is an investor on the stock exchange an entrepreneur? Is John O'Shea, the founder of the charity GOAL, an entrepreneur? Is your dentist, solicitor or GP an entrepreneur? Can you be an entrepreneur within an existing business? While an exact definition is difficult to reach, there appears to be factors common to many of these definitions. **Figure 1.7** sets out what seem to be the essential elements of entrepreneurship.

FIGURE 1.7: DEFINITIONS OF ENTREPRENEURS

◊ The Irish-born French economist Cantillon is credited as being the first to use the term *entrepreneur*. He defined the entrepreneur as "the agent who purchases the means of production and combines them into marketable products".

◊ The entrepreneur is "the owner or manager of a business enterprise who, by risk and initiative, attempts to make profits" (Collins English Dictionary).

◊ Entrepreneurship: "... is the process of identifying opportunities in the marketplace, marshalling the resources to pursue these opportunities and committing the actions and resources necessary to exploit the opportunities for long-term personal gain" (Sexton & Bowman-Upton, 1991).

◊ The entrepreneur is a person who "... creates a venture and institutes practices intended to increase the firm's size" (Johnson, 1990).

◊ "Entrepreneurs are 'opportunistic decision-makers' who identify and capitalise on opportunities through approaches that emphasise innovation, profitable venture identification, effectiveness, and non-programmed or ambiguous situations" (Olson, 1986).

◊ "The entrepreneur, by definition, shifts resources from areas of low productivity and yield to areas of higher productivity and yield. Of course, there is a risk the entrepreneur may not succeed" (Drucker, 1985).

◊ "Entrepreneurship is the ability to create and build a vision from practically nothing: fundamentally it is a human, creative act. It is the application of energy to initiating and building an enterprise or organisation, rather than just watching or analysing. This vision requires a willingness to take calculated risks — both personal and financial — and then to do everything possible to reduce the chances of failure. Entrepreneurship also includes the ability to build an entrepreneurial or venture team to complement your own skills or talent. It is the knack for sensing an opportunity where others see chaos, contradiction, and confusion. It is possessing the know-how to find, marshal, and control resources (often owned by others)" (Timmons, Smollen & Dingee, 1985).

Opportunity Recognition

Entrepreneurs must identify an opportunity if they are to start-up in business. The source of this idea might be previous work experience, experience of purchasing or using a product / service, the purchase of a franchise, the development or invention of a product. However, identifying an opportunity is not enough; the entrepreneur also must exploit this opportunity.

Uncertainty

Entrepreneurs must deal with market uncertainties. They cannot know the level of future demand for the product / service or whether they will be able to produce the product / service at the required cost. Also a significant uncertainty facing many entrepreneurs centres on obtaining the necessary finance for the venture. Typically, entrepreneurs must commit their own financial resources without any assurance that others will invest in the project.

Risk-taking

The entrepreneur takes a business risk, a financial risk and a personal risk. The business risk is that the entrepreneur does not know whether their new business idea will be successful. There is uncertainty surrounding future demand for the product/service. Therefore, the entrepreneur must make a judgement as to the size of potential demand. The entrepreneur takes a financial risk by investing money in the new business. This begins with the investment of time and money in preparing a feasibility study. This is followed by investment in the purchase of equipment and / or the purchase of a lease for the business. If the business fails, the entrepreneur may be indebted to a bank and may have difficulty in getting business or personal credit in the future. The entrepreneur takes a significant personal risk when starting a new business. If the business fails, it may be difficult for the entrepreneur to get back into paid employment. In addition, failure is still regarded as a social taboo in this country.

Resource-gathering

The entrepreneur has to gather the resources needed for the business, which includes financial resources and others such as human, information and technical resources. The entrepreneur will rarely have all the resources needed in a start-up situation.

Profits /Reward

The entrepreneur engages in the above activities for personal gain. The entrepreneur receives rewards in a number of ways. The first is reward as salary. This is the reward for the time the entrepreneur puts into the business. In most small businesses, the entrepreneur rewards himself with a low salary, preferring instead to keep the money in the business. The second is return on invested capital. Just as an investor expects a return on invested capital, the entrepreneur should expect to receive a return on the money invested in the business. This return may be in the form of a dividend or, more typically, in the form of a capital gain. The third is reward for taking the risk. The entrepreneur should receive a return for the risk taken. The capital gains of the initial investment should reflect the business risk of the investment.

HOW IS ENTREPRENEURSHIP DIFFERENT FROM MANAGEMENT?

The famous economist Joseph Schumpeter (1948) wrote extensively on entrepreneurship as a means of creating something new. He discounted all managers and heads of firms from his definition. His belief was that something innovative had to occur in order for a person or persons to call themselves an entrepreneur. This could include the introduction of a new product, a new method of production, the opening and entering of a new market, or the finding of a new source of raw material. To finance one or more of the above innovations, the entrepreneur must convince money-holders of the worthiness of the innovation. This definition, especially if used in today's context, would lead us to the conclusion that only a small minority of business owners could rightly call themselves entrepreneurs. Most businesses are just clones of other similar operations.

The entrepreneur differs from the manager in their approach to opportunities and resources. The entrepreneur seeks new opportunities, while the manager seeks to protect and build on the existing set of resources. Managers are charged with the stewardship of existing resources; they must protect the resources that a firm owns. The entrepreneur seeks to commit resources to opportunities quickly. They commit resources without knowing whether they will be able to acquire the other resources necessary to make the venture a success. In contrast, the manager will frequently commit resources only after carefully researching an opportunity.

DIFFERENT WAYS OF STUDYING ENTREPRENEURS

There are a number of different ways of studying entrepreneurs. These can be classified into a number of 'schools' of thought (Cunningham & Lischeron, 1991).

The 'Background Characteristics' School

The study of entrepreneurship has traditionally emphasised the background characteristics of the entrepreneur. These studies explore variables such as education, age at start-up, birth order, and parents' occupation. Entrepreneurs are often contrasted with managers and executives in these studies. More recently, entrepreneurs have been compared with other entrepreneurs – for example, high-growth and low-growth entrepreneurs, male and female entrepreneurs. The appeal of this approach is that it is easy to collect the data, but this method is of limited benefit to individual entrepreneurs and public policy-makers.

The 'Personality Traits' School

An alternative approach is to study the personality traits of entrepreneurs. The basis of this school of thought is that an individual's needs, attitudes, beliefs and values are the prime determinants of behaviour. This school believes that entrepreneurs have unique values and attitudes towards work and life, which cause them to act differently to others. Therefore, entrepreneurs can be differentiated according to characteristics such as risk-taking propensity, need for achievement, and locus of control.

The 'Born to Entrepreneurship' School

Some authors believe that individuals are born with the skills and aptitudes necessary for success. Entrepreneurs are considered to be charismatic leaders, to be inspirational, with the ability to communicate ideas and concepts to other people in a way that is interesting, appealing or engaging. These authors believe that entrepreneurs have some sort of natural intuition that enables them to grasp opportunities. Popular literature adopts this perspective by portraying the entrepreneur as a hero and charismatic leader – for example, Lee Iaccoca and Richard Branson.

The 'Process' School

The process school's central tenet is that an entrepreneur is a person who organises or manages a business undertaking, assuming the risk for the sake of profit. It believes that entrepreneurship can be taught, and so it aims to identify the functions involved and to provide training to existing and would-be entrepreneurs. The provision of training in management activities such as marketing and finance should, it is hoped, reduce the number of business failures. As is self-evident from this school of thought, it assumes that entrepreneurs can be 'made', which is in direct contrast to the 'born to entrepreneurship' school.

The 'Intrapreneurship' School

Intrapreneurship involves the creation of independent business units designed to create, market, and expand innovative services, technologies, or methods within the organisation. This approach is appropriate to studying entrepreneurship in large organisations. In these organisations, some individuals are given freedom to act in an entrepreneurial way, without having to take on ownership responsibility. These individuals are referred to as corporate entrepreneurs or, more commonly, as 'intrapreneurs'.

The 'Behavioural' School

Another approach to the study of entrepreneurs is to focus on the behaviours of the entrepreneurs. This school studies the management practices that are associated with successful entrepreneurship. Entrepreneurs are essentially people who make things happen. In this way, they can be classified by their behaviour in how they approach problems, how they delegate responsibilities, and so on. It is a person's behaviour that determines whether they are defined as an entrepreneur and, therefore, it is more appropriate to study entrepreneurial behaviour than background characteristics. It is behaviour, rather than personality, that will best improve our understanding of entrepreneurship. More recent studies have focused on the business that the entrepreneur creates rather than on the entrepreneur who creates the business. These researchers examine the market entry and competitive strategies of the new business.

CONCLUSION

There is an ever-increasing number of entrepreneurs in Ireland. This chapter identified the factors that contribute to the likelihood of an individual considering a 'career' as an entrepreneur. It identified the common background characteristics and the common personality traits of entrepreneurs. There are a number of different ways to study an entrepreneur: studying personality traits and background characteristics are only two of many ways to study an entrepreneur.

QUESTIONS

1. What are the background characteristics of Irish entrepreneurs? Why do entrepreneurs have these characteristics?

2. Identify the common personality traits of successful entrepreneurs.

3. What are the different ways of studying entrepreneurs? Which of these approaches do you consider to be the most useful?

4. In a group, identify the five entrepreneurs you most admire. Now identify the five words that best describe entrepreneurs. Do these words describe the entrepreneurs you identified?

5. Interview an entrepreneur in your locality to establish the reasons for their success. Use this interview to test the ideas presented in this chapter.

6. From sources in your library, write a short history of an entrepreneur that you admire.

PROFILE: COLUM O'SULLIVAN, CULLY & SULLY[4]

Colum O'Sullivan and his friend and fellow entrepreneur, Cullen Allen, were born into enterprising families. Cullen is a grandson of Myrtle Allen of Ballymaloe House and looks after the food end of things and Colum's mum owns the Granary Food Store in Cork, which is where their idea for the Cully & Sully prepared meals range originated.

Cully & Sully is the latest in a long line of trial and error entrepreneurial endeavours that have always been a part of Colum O'Sullivan's life. He was bitten by the entrepreneurial bug from a very early age!

It's simply what I always wanted to do. I set up businesses when I was in school, making tree and bird houses and selling them, then I used to buy golf balls second-hand and sell them to golfers. In college, I used to buy mum's pasta from her and sell it to students, then I started to smoke chickens and sell them to restaurants. While I was at Musgrave's, I was continually 'scamming' – investigating different ideas. I have half-baked business plans for everything from industrial cooking stocks to coffins. I have a wardrobe at home which has more files and statistics about different ideas than I don't know what.

Colum and Cullen, or Cully & Sully as they are known to their friends, spent one year researching the idea, during which time Colum participated in the Genesis Enterprise Programme and benefited from Enterprise Ireland's support under its Feasibility and CORD Programmes.

In September 2004, they launched a range of prepared meals using Ballymaloe recipes into the nation's supermarkets. This was followed by the launch in September 2006 of a patented pub concept, which is now in over 70 pubs throughout the country. Cully & Sully is currently in negotiations with two companies in the Netherlands concerning launching their pies into that market.

Colum emphasizes the support that both he and Cullen received from their families:

We both left our jobs. I had to move back home, after about 10 years of being away. We had to borrow money and they were a big help with aspects of that.

There was support available from other quarters as well:

There is no way we would be where we are without the help of Enterprise Ireland, Genesis and business people generally. We have a policy of talking to everyone. There's lots of grey hair out there, who have tried many things and made plenty of mistakes and they are more than happy to talk to you about it.

---

[4] This profile appeared in Fitzsimons, P. & O'Gorman, C. (2006).

People are very, very supportive of people trying to set up a business and this general attitude is a really fantastic trait of the Irish. EI have been excellent to us, not just financially, but in things like providing a mentor, which is worth way more than a few thousand Euro grant. Joe O'Keeffe – ex-MD of Apple Europe is our current mentor and is excellent. Drew O'Sullivan in Genesis in Cork is super. Us 'entrepreneurs' are stubborn and are dreadful at being told what to do. Drew is excellent at this and works phenomenally hard helping us to sort out problems like tax, patenting etc. He's a really good guy!

Asked what the greatest challenges were that he had to face in setting up the business, Colum does not underplay the difficulties involved:

To be absolutely honest, there were many mountains and there are many more. It's incredible, you think you've sorted one thing out and that just leads to the next challenge. You have to be constantly innovating. Getting the Ballymaloe approval was probably the biggest challenge and took the longest time.

Colum describes the last two and a half years as *'a phenomenal roller-coaster ride with lots of highs and lows'* but, despite all the difficulties encountered along the way, when asked would he do it all again, he replies immediately:

Absolutely! I wouldn't change it for the world. I love it. It does have its bad days, but then I say to myself 'would I prefer to be back working for someone else?' and the answer is simple. It's tough at the start, as you're borrowing a lot of money. Then some months, you make money and, other months, you lose money. You lose a fortune in your first year, and it's a battle to get through this. It's very rewarding and, once you start becoming recognized and respected, it does make life easier.

2

ENTREPRENEURIAL
ACTIVITY IN IRELAND:
GEM EVIDENCE[5]

Ireland is an interesting case study of entrepreneurship and economic growth. During long periods of low economic growth, analysts emphasized the relative poor development of Irish industry as a major contributory factor. The Telesis Report (National Economic Social Council, 1982) highlighted the poor performance of Irish industry in terms of low levels of profitability, over-dependence on the domestic and UK markets, and the production of commodity products that compete on cost. Barry, Bradley and O'Malley (1999) demonstrated the striking differences between indigenous and overseas industry in Ireland in terms of innovation, exporting, productivity, and sector composition, with indigenous industry having low levels of innovation, low levels of exporting, much lower levels of productivity, and tending to be concentrated in traditional rather than modern sectors. Despite this historical entrepreneurial deficit, Ireland has experienced significant economic growth during the last decade.

In describing the factors that account for the 'Celtic Tiger', indigenous entrepreneurial activity is rarely mentioned. For example, Barry (2003) argued that, broadly speaking, many factors explain Ireland's economic growth in the 1990s. First, a new fiscal strategy was adopted by the government in 1987. While the expected economic effect of the strategy was a contraction in the economy, factors such as growth in world demand, the inflow of foreign direct investment (FDI), and improvements in competitiveness allowed the economy to grow. The second factor was the development of a model of 'social partnership'. The third factor that explains the 'Celtic Tiger' were Structural & Cohesion Funds that transferred money from the EU to Ireland. These funds accounted for 3% of the

---

[5] This chapter is an edited version of an article published in the *Irish Journal of Management Studies*: O'Gorman, C. & Fitzsimons, P. (forthcoming). 'Entrepreneurial Activity in Ireland: Evidence from the Global Entrepreneurship Monitor'.

economy for the decade 1989-1999, allowing investment in infrastructure and capital projects, which had been put on hold in the 1980s. These funds were spent on three areas: human resource development, physical infrastructure, and production and investment aids to the private sector. In terms of industrial policy, explanations of the 'Celtic Tiger' typically refer to high levels of inward FDI by multi-national enterprises (MNEs) into Ireland to produce goods and services for overseas markets. During the 1990s, there was a rapid growth in such investment, particularly from US firms. In contrast, there is little mention of indigenous entrepreneurial activity.

However, increasingly, entrepreneurship is seen as an important component of industrial development in developed economies for a number of reasons. First, entrepreneurial activity is important because increased entrepreneurial activity is associated with economic growth (Austretch, 2004) and because the shortage of entrepreneurial talent is associated with low levels of economic development in developing economies (Kilby, 2004). Second, entrepreneurial activity is an important component of knowledge-intensive clusters, as entrepreneurial activity is an important mechanism through which new innovation is brought to market (Austretch, 2004). Third, entrepreneurial activity may also be important in attracting inward FDI in knowledge-intensive sectors, as 'asset-seeking' FDI may seek a dynamic environment where entrepreneurs are active in creating new knowledge. For example, while multinational firms played an important role in the development of the indigenous software sector in Ireland, indigenous firms also played an important role in attracting MNEs to Ireland (O'Malley & O'Gorman, 2001). Specifically, indigenous firms acted as sub-suppliers to MNEs involved in software translation, and indigenous software firms have played an important role in developing and up-grading the labour skills in the sector – a factor that MNEs cite as a reason for locating in Ireland. Fourth, entrepreneurial activity contributes to overall competitiveness and productivity improvements.

This chapter explores entrepreneurial activity in Ireland by asking the question: Does Ireland has enough entrepreneurs? To answer this question, the chapter first examines both the level and the nature of early-stage entrepreneurial activity in Ireland and how this compares with other countries. If, as is argued here, Ireland needs more entrepreneurs, then it is necessary to identify what aspects of the environment in Ireland facilitate entrepreneurial activity and in what areas there are barriers to entrepreneurial activity: that is, what factors affect the supply of, and demand for, entrepreneurs. The findings of the *Global Entrepreneurship Monitor* (GEM) for Ireland are used to explore these issues.

THE *GLOBAL ENTREPRENEURSHIP MONITOR*

The *Global Entrepreneurship Monitor* is a cross-country comparison of early-stage entrepreneurial activity that seeks to identify the level of entrepreneurial activity within national economies and then to identify what aspects of the socio-economic institutional environment might be associated with higher levels of entrepreneurial activity. The project is an annual assessment across a range of participating countries.

This chapter draws on the GEM databases (Acs *et al.*, 2005, Reynolds *et al.*, 2004) and the analysis presented each year in the Irish GEM report (see, for example, Fitzsimons & O'Gorman, 2005).[6] Based on a population survey in each participating country, the GEM project seeks to identify levels of entrepreneurial activity, including nascent entrepreneurial activity, by directly asking people whether they are engaged in such activity (for a more complete description of the GEM model and methodology, see the Irish GEM report (Fitzsimons & O'Gorman, 2005) and Reynolds *et al.*, (2005)).

In Ireland, the annual population survey is a telephone survey of approximately 2,000 adults. This survey provides measures of entrepreneurial activity and informal investment activity for the adult population. In addition, it captures attitudes towards entrepreneurship of the adult population that are used to create a measure of the national cultural context. It also provides data on aspects of the personal context of the population that are important in determining entrepreneurial activity. Further, the entrepreneurs and informal investors identified in the survey are asked additional questions.

Within GEM, a nascent entrepreneur is someone who responded positively to the following statement: 'you are, alone or with others, currently trying to start a new business, including any self-employment or selling any goods or services to others', provided they have not yet paid themselves a wage for more than three months. A new firm entrepreneur is someone who has started a new business, of which they are part-owner and manager, in the previous 42 months. Informal investors are those who have, in the previous three years, provided funds for a new business started by someone else.

A second source of data collected for GEM is the opinions of experts and entrepreneurs, selected to represent critical aspects of the environment that influence entrepreneurial activity, who are asked each year to complete a questionnaire. All of them have been interviewed, using a semi-structured interviewing format, at least once as part of the GEM research cycle.

---

[6]   The Irish GEM reports, the Executive Global GEM reports, a study of women entrepreneurship, and an annual GEM Finance report are available to the public free at www.gemconsortium.org.

GEM RESULTS FOR IRELAND

EARLY-STAGE ENTREPRENEURIAL ACTIVITY

The level of early-stage entrepreneurial activity (Total Early-Stage Entrepreneurial Activity or TEA rate) in Ireland has averaged at 9.1% for the period 2001 to 2006 (**Figure 2.1**). The TEA rate in 2001-2006 was 7.4%, and has decreased each year since 2001. Extrapolating from the 2006 GEM survey to the population suggests that there are approximately 200,000 individuals in Ireland active as early-stage entrepreneurs. Of these, 122,000 are active in planning to start a business, though many of these are still in employment. Approximately 80,000 people have started a business in the previous 42 months, which is approximately 20,000 *per annum*.

FIGURE 2.1: TOTAL ENTREPRENEURIAL ACTIVITY IN IRELAND 2001-2006[7]

Measure of Entrepreneurial Activity	2001	2002	2003	2004	2005	2006
Total Early Stage Entrepreneurial Activity	12.2%	9.1%	8.1%	7.7%	9.8%	7.4%
Total Early Stage Entrepreneurial Activity	12.2%	9.1%	8.1%	7.7%	9.8%	7.4%
Nascent Entrepreneurs	7.3%	5.7%	5.1%	4.4%	5.7%	4.5%
New Firm Entrepreneurs	4.9%	4.2%	3.8%	3.6%	4.7%	2.9%

Compared to the 42 countries that participated in GEM in 2006, Ireland is ranked 21st in terms of TEA rate. A more meaningful comparison is to compare Ireland with countries that have a similar level of economic development or that operate in similar economic contexts. For the 22 OECD countries, Ireland ranks seventh and, for the 15 pre-accession EU countries, Ireland ranks second (**Figure 2.2**).

---

[7] The level of nascent entrepreneurial activity and new firm entrepreneurial activity sums to greater than the TEA rate, as some individuals are both nascent and new-firm entrepreneurs. In calculating TEA, such individuals are only counted once.

FIGURE 2.2: TOTAL ENTREPRENEURIAL ACTIVITY [TEA PREVALENCE] 2006

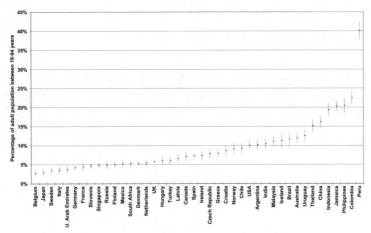

Source: *Global Entrepreneurship Monitor: 2006 Executive Report.*

IRISH ENTREPRENEURS: GENDER, AGE, EDUCATION, WORK STATUS & MOTIVATION

TEA rates are significantly higher for males than they are for females. The average rate of early-stage entrepreneurial activity for males for the period 2002-2006 was 12.0%. In comparison, the average rate for females is 4.8%. Internationally, participation rates by men tend to be 50% higher than those for women; though in high-income countries the difference tends to be smaller at only 33%. The difference in the TEA rate between men and women in Ireland is particularly high.

The mean age for early-stage entrepreneurs is 35. The distribution of entrepreneurs across age categories is as follows: 19% of entrepreneurs are in the 18-24 age group, 33% in the 25-34 age group, 28% in the 35-44 age group, 12% in the 45-54 age group and 7% in the 55-64 age group.

Irish entrepreneurs are relatively well-educated. The distribution of entrepreneurs by education category is as follows: 12% of entrepreneurs have not completed secondary school, 32% have completed no more than the Leaving Certificate, 41% have completed third level education, and 15% have post-graduate education.

The vast majority of new-firm entrepreneurs are working full-time in their new business (85%). For nascent entrepreneurs, the majority are still in employment prior to starting-up (full-time 64%, part-time 12%), though 17% report that they are 'not working' ('not working' 14%, 'homemaker' 3%), while 6% are either retired or students.

The vast majority of Irish entrepreneurs are motivated by positive factors, such as the desire to exploit an opportunity (85%). A small number of all Irish entrepreneurs (15%) responded that they are entrepreneurially active because they have 'no better alternative'.

NEW VENTURE FINANCING

The majority of entrepreneurs planning new businesses in Ireland typically require relatively small amounts of money to start their new businesses – the average cost of start-up is €20,000 (**Figure 2.3**). Almost two-thirds (64%) of entrepreneurs expect to start with less than €100,000, although one in three entrepreneurs (36%) anticipate that their new business will need more than €100,000.

FIGURE 2.3: FINANCIAL REQUIREMENTS OF EARLY-STAGE ENTREPRENEURS IN 2006

	Total finance required (median)	Entrepreneurs own investment (median)	Median owner investment as a percentage of median total finance required
All early stage entrepreneurs	€40,000	€20,000	50%
Entrepreneurs requiring less than €100,000 (64% of all entrepreneurs)	€20,000	€6,000	30%
Entrepreneurs requiring €100,000 or more (36% of all entrepreneurs)	€263,000	€71,700	27%

Source: Fitzsimons, P. & O'Gorman, C. (2007).

NEW VENTURES: SECTOR, EXPORT-ORIENTATION & GROWTH-ORIENTATION

Entrepreneurial activity is most frequent in three sectors: business services; retail, hotels and restaurants; and consumer services. Combined, these sectors account for 53% of entrepreneurial activity (**Figure 2.4**). Manufacturing accounts for only 7% of all entrepreneurial activity. Compared to other high-income countries, the distribution of entrepreneurial activity in Ireland is different. In particular, Ireland appears to have a lower level of entrepreneurial activity in business services (including such activities as computer and related activities, and research and development).

FIGURE 2.4: ENTREPRENEURIAL ACTIVITY BY SECTOR

Standard Industry Code (1 digit)	Ireland (2002-2004)	High Income Countries (2004)
Agriculture, forestry, fishing	6%	6%
Mining, construction	11%	7%
Manufacturing	7%	7%
Transportation, communication, utilities	8%	5%
Wholesale, motor vehicle sales and service	6%	5%
Retail, hotel, restaurants	17%	22%
Financial, insurance and real estate	3%	6%
Business services	21%	30%
Health, education, and social services	7%	1%
Consumer services	15%	12%

High income countries are Australia, Belgium, Canada, Denmark, Finland, France, Germany, Iceland, Ireland, Italy, Japan, Netherlands, Norway, Sweden, UK, US.

GEM 2006 data suggests that Irish entrepreneurs are active in terms of exporting and in growing their new businesses. Although 56% of all Irish entrepreneurs expect to have no export customers; 24% expect to have between 1% and 25% of their customers in export markets; while 19% expect to have more than 25% of their customers in export markets.

In terms of growth, most entrepreneurs (61%) expect to stay small (employing fewer than five people). That said, GEM reports that an average of 18% of all Irish early-stage entrepreneurs expect to grow to employ at least 20 people within five years.

THE CONTEXT FOR ENTREPRENEURIAL ACTIVITY IN IRELAND

Cultural Context

GEM provides a unique cross-country index of whether there is an environment supportive of entrepreneurial activity. This index measures the attitudes of the population in terms of whether entrepreneurship is considered a good career choice, whether successful entrepreneurs are held in high regard and whether there is much media attention devoted to entrepreneurial activity.

GEM suggests that Ireland has one of the most positive cultural contexts for entrepreneurship. In 2006, successful entrepreneurs were perceived to have a very high status by 82% of the Irish adult population. Seven out of 10 (70%) of the adult population considered becoming an entrepreneur to be a good career choice. The Irish media was also perceived by Irish adults to be highly supportive of entrepreneurship and to reflect it in a good light (84%).

Personal Context

GEM research has shown a strong positive correlation between the rate of entrepreneurial activity in a county and the personal context of individuals in that country. To illustrate the personal context, GEM measures the proportion of those who perceive good opportunities to start new businesses, those who believe that they have the skills to start and successfully run new businesses, and those who know recent entrepreneurs within their social network – personal role models, as it were. Besides these positive predispositions to entrepreneurial activity, GEM also measures the inhibitors, in particular, the fear of failure.

In 2006, the percentage of Irish people who perceive 'good opportunities to start a new business' was 44%; those who know an entrepreneur, who recently set up a new business, was 39%; and those who believe that they have the necessary skills was 51%. These are all positive influences on entrepreneurial activity. Fear of failure, however, would deter 35% of the population from becoming active as entrepreneurs.

The Availability of Finance

The most important external source of finance (that is, finance not provided by the founder) is access to informal investors. Informal investors are typically family, friends, and occasionally, so-called 'fool-hardy' investors. While the absolute amount of informal investment in Ireland might be high (GEM estimates that over €1 billion was invested in 2002-2004), the level of informal investment in Ireland is comparatively low.

In Ireland in 2006, just over two out of every hundred adults (1.7%) in the past three years have personally provided funds for a new business started by someone else (excluding any purchase of stocks or mutual funds). This rate of involvement as informal investors, while higher than in the UK (1.6%), is relatively low. The rate of informal investment among the adult population in the US, for example, is three times what it is in Ireland.

The low level of informal investment activity means that the overall amount of funds available to new businesses in Ireland is comparatively low. Comparing the amount of external finance nascent entrepreneurs expect to require with the amount of finance available from informal investors suggests that, in most countries, nascent entrepreneurs require more finance than is available (**Figure 2.5**) (Bygrave, 2005). However, this may be expected, as not all nascent entrepreneurs start new business. In Ireland, the amount of informal investment invested would fund only 14% of nascent entrepreneurs. This figure is low when compared to other countries.

FIGURE 2.5: PERCENTAGE OF NASCENT BUSINESSES THAT COULD BE FUNDED WITH AVAILABLE INFORMAL INVESTMENT IN 2004

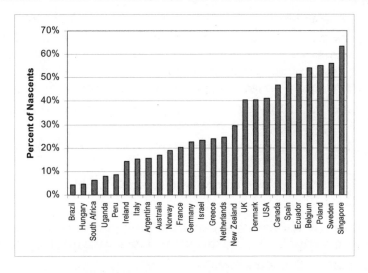

Source: Bygrave (2005): *GEM 2004 Financing Report.*

THE VIEWS OF IRISH ENTREPRENEURS & EXPERTS

According to the experts and entrepreneurs interviewed and surveyed as part of the GEM Ireland study, Ireland has many positive features. These include:

- A positive cultural context, in which entrepreneurs and entrepreneurial activity are held in high regard.
- Very positive media coverage within the country.

- Many aspects of government policy that are supportive of entrepreneurs and entrepreneurial activity – for example, a pro-business attitude, continuing low interest rates, and a fiscal regime that does not penalize success.
- Government programmes that support entrepreneurs.
- A range of benefits flowing from the strong high-tech FDI presence in the country.
- A buoyant economy.
- A highly skilled workforce.
- A vibrant capital city.
- A growing range of networks and advisors.

Set against these very positive features in the environment, however, are other less positive features. In particular, the negatives noted included:

- Difficulties in accessing finance.
- The lack of a champion for entrepreneurship within the government.
- Shortcomings in the development agencies related to their coordination, the appropriateness of the background and experience of many of their executives, and the time and effort required to access their support are considered to impose unnecessary difficulties on entrepreneurs.
- The increasing regulatory burden flowing from the EU and Government, which is adding to the cost and difficulties for new firms.
- A skills deficit in entrepreneurs with regard to sales, internationalisation, and growth.
- Difficulties in accessing information on entrepreneurship.
- The high cost economy.
- An educational sector that is not particularly supportive of entrepreneurship or effective in equipping entrepreneurs with the skills that they need.
- The limited size of the home market.
- Physical infrastructure deficits that impact on international trade.
- Skills gaps in the labour force.

DISCUSSION

DOES IRELAND NEED MORE ENTREPRENEURS?

Ireland has experienced high levels of economic growth, high levels of employment creation, and, compared to European economies, has a relatively high rate of early-stage entrepreneurial activity. As such, it could be argued that Ireland does not need more entrepreneurs. However, the GEM reports for Ireland have consistently argued that Ireland needs more entrepreneurs. In arguing that Ireland needs more entrepreneurs, it is important to recognise that not all entrepreneurial activity has the same economic impact. As such, the argument advanced here is that Ireland needs more entrepreneurs who will positively impact on economic development.

One reason for the need for more entrepreneurs in Ireland is that there is increasing evidence that entrepreneurial activity is associated with economic growth and, in particular, that the relationship between the level of entrepreneurial activity and economic growth depends on a country's stage of development. GEM research suggests that the extent and nature of entrepreneurial activity varies depending on the stage of economic development. In developing countries, high rates of entrepreneurial activity, motivated to a large degree by necessity, reflect the relatively few alternatives available for paid-employment in those countries. As a country develops, the rate of necessity entrepreneurial activity declines, as greater economies of scale become possible. The growth of larger firms is facilitated by better transportation and communications systems and by the emergence of more sophisticated credit markets. The emergence of larger firms means that fewer entrepreneurs can provide more employment to others, thereby lessening the need for a high proportion of the population to make a livelihood through self-employment, as had previously been the case. For countries within this income group, therefore it can be expected that fewer people will need or will want to start new businesses. However, with the emergence of the 'new economy', as a country becomes wealthier and its economy further develops, there is a shift away from larger firms and the importance of entrepreneurial activity increases. Ireland appears to be at a stage of economic development for which the theory suggests that increased levels of entrepreneurial activity will be associated with increased economic growth. So, while the rate of entrepreneurial activity in Ireland is favourable when compared to European economies, it is much less favourable when compared to other high income countries such as the US. Furthermore, the rate of entrepreneurial activity in Ireland has decreased in recent years.

A second reason for advocating that Ireland needs more entrepreneurs is that entrepreneurs are critical to knowledge economies. Irish Government policy is directed towards developing Ireland as a knowledge-intensive economy, with clusters of economic activity in sectors such as software, bio-technology, and financial services. Entrepreneurship is a central component of knowledge-intensive regions and clusters. As part of its strategy to build a knowledge economy, the Irish Government has committed to funding research in the third-level education sector. To maximize the economic benefits of such research, entrepreneurs will need to commercialize the outputs of such research and bring these to the market. GEM data suggests that entrepreneurial activity in the business services sector is under-represented in Ireland and that Ireland needs entrepreneurs to commercialise R&D.

One component of the policy to develop Ireland as a knowledge economy is to attract inward FDI by MNEs in higher valued-added activities, such as R&D and marketing, and to encourage MNEs already located in Ireland to up-grade their activities. Extant theory and emerging research suggests that, in many ways, large MNEs increasingly depend on the strength of the supporting cast as much as their own strengths (Gomes-Casseres, 1996). As such, the ability to attract higher-valued added inward FDI will depend on the success of indigenous entrepreneurial activity.

A third reason for increasing the number of entrepreneurs in Ireland is that entrepreneurial activity contributes to the overall competitiveness of the Irish economy, through increased competition in both locally- and internationally-traded products and through increases in productivity. Reports by the OECD and the Competition Authority have demonstrated that some Government regulations reduce competition and, in doing so, have reduced the competitiveness of the Irish economy (for examples, see the Competition Authority's website, www.tca.ie, for reports on various sectors of the economy) (OECD, 2001). While GEM research does not systematically capture the 'demand' for entrepreneurial activity, beyond a measure of the population's perception of opportunity for entrepreneurship, the Irish GEM reports have argued that there are systematic barriers to entrepreneurship across a range of sectors, due to barriers to entry that typically result from Government regulation.

A fourth reason for advocating that Ireland needs more entrepreneurs is that entrepreneurial activity among women entrepreneurs is particularly low in Ireland (when compared to other high-income economies). In particular, there appears to be a much lower number of women who have recently set-up a business, yet there is a pool of well-educated women who are considering starting new businesses. Why are rates of entrepreneurial activity low for Irish women? GEM suggests that the reasons for this may be the personal context of women in the Irish population. Compared to Irish men, women are much less likely to perceive opportunities, have much lower perceptions of having the required knowledge, skills and experience necessary to start a business, and are much less likely to have an entrepreneurial role model (in that they are less likely to personally know an entrepreneur who has recently started a new business). Added to this, women entrepreneurs are less likely to have been engaged recently in full-time employment. Presumably, full-time employment provides access to market opportunities and to networks of contacts.

INCREASING THE LEVEL OF ENTREPRENEURIAL ACTIVITY IN IRELAND: POLICY CHALLENGES

There are two main thrusts to industrial and economic policy for entrepreneurs in Ireland. First, there are measures that improve the environment for entrepreneurs and, second, there are specific supports for entrepreneurs. Supports for entrepreneurs in Ireland have generally been focused narrowly on firms that export, typically manufacturing firms and internationally-traded services such as software. These firms are generally referred to as 'high potential start-ups' (HPSUs). The following is a brief review of the policy challenges for increasing the level of entrepreneurial activity under these two policy domains.

The Environment for Entrepreneurs

GEM research suggests that there are many aspects of the environment in Ireland that are supportive of entrepreneurial activity. In particular, it suggests that there is a very positive cultural context for entrepreneurial activity – one of the best in the world. GEM research also suggests that Irish adults in general have a personal context that is positively associated with entrepreneurial activity. The current and projected growth in the Irish population and the age structure of the Irish population suggest that Ireland should be able to increase its rate of entrepreneurial activity. However, there are a number of aspects of the environment that are not supportive of entrepreneurial activity.

First, Ireland has a low level of informal investment activity. While entrepreneurs typically find it difficult to access finance in all countries, GEM research suggests that the availability of funds for entrepreneurs in Ireland is low. Specifically, GEM research suggests that there is a relatively low level of informal investment activity among Irish adults. It also suggests that the availability of informal investment is particularly low as a percentage of the funding requirements of all nascent entrepreneurs. For most entrepreneurs, such investment is the most important external source of finance after their own personal investment (both savings and borrowings). International evidence suggests that many high growth firms rely on such funding during their early stages of development.

GEM research suggests that there are a large number of entrepreneurs (over 30% of nascent entrepreneurs) expecting to need in excess of €112,000. Such entrepreneurs may need to access funds from business angels and, for a small number of entrepreneurs, from venture capitalists. The formal venture capital market in Ireland is relatively small. The amounts invested in firms are also relatively small, particularly when compared to US firms. The US market is an important market for many high tech firms that receive venture capital in Ireland, and they may expect to compete with many firms, including new firms that are much better resourced. However, the view of many venture capitalists is that there is a shortage of attractive investment prospects rather than a shortage of venture capital.

Second, according to the entrepreneurs and experts surveyed as part of the GEM research, there is an increasing regulatory burden on entrepreneurs, stemming both from Irish Government policy and EU policies. The burden of regulation impacts entrepreneurial activity in several ways. First, regulations can increase the time and cost of doing business, thus making it more expensive to start a new business. Second, regulations can restrict entry into markets, reducing opportunities for entrepreneurs. Third, comparably speaking, many Irish adults perceive that they lack the knowledge, skills, and experience required to start a new business. This is an important aspect of personal context that is associated with entrepreneurial activity. Many experts and entrepreneurs suggested that the educational sector does not recognize the importance of entrepreneurship or does not prepare individuals for an entrepreneurial career. In particular, women have a poor personal context.

Supports for Entrepreneurs

To the extent that policy directly supports entrepreneurs, the focus of support has been targeted support for HPSUs, firms considered to be innovative and to have the potential to grow rapidly in international markets. Typically, HPSUs are in newer sectors of the economy, such as ICT and biotechnology. Such firms have been the focus of policy, because of the contribution they can make to economic growth and because it is assumed there are a number of market failures that impact on the emergence of such firms. Such a targeted approach is probably appropriate to Ireland's stage of economic development. Indeed, it is one that many developed economies are seeking to emulate.

However, GEM evidence suggests that the remit of the Government development agencies may be too targeted and that there are many other entrepreneurs who can deliver high growth and export activity. GEM suggests that there is a much larger cohort of Irish firms that are growth- and export-orientated than are typically supported by Irish development agencies.

GEM also suggests there are many entrepreneurs who achieve some growth in that they employ more than 20 people. Few, however, attain significant competitive scale when compared to international competitors. In the opinions of the experts and the entrepreneurs, this inability to attain scale reflects a skills deficit. Entrepreneurs and their new firms often lack the skills to build sales in international markets and to grow the business.

GEM suggests that there are a number of deficiencies in the delivery of Government programmes targeted at entrepreneurs, including a lack of coordination of the efforts of separate State agencies, a lack of market or sector experience among agency executives, and too much agency bureaucracy.

CONCLUSION

In this chapter, we have reported the results of the GEM study for Ireland. GEM suggests that the level of early-stage entrepreneurial activity in Ireland is relatively high when compared to other developed European Union economies, though it is relatively low when compared to some high-income economies such as the US and Australia. The typical early-stage entrepreneur in Ireland is a well-educated male in his mid-30s. Most entrepreneurs require relatively small amounts of money to start their new business. Typically, the entrepreneur provides most of this finance (through savings and borrowings). In seeking external finance, most entrepreneurs seek funds from informal investors, such as family members. The level of informal investment in Ireland is relatively low. Most entrepreneurs expect their new business to remain small, though as many as 15% expect to grow to employ 20 people within five years. Over two-thirds of all entrepreneurs (73%) expect that their new business will have some customers in overseas markets.

This chapter argues that there is a clear need for an entrepreneurship policy in Ireland. Developing such a policy requires a systematic review of existing fiscal, educational, financial, and advisory supports for entrepreneurs and for encouraging entrepreneurship. If, as argued here, Ireland needs more entrepreneurs, what should policy makers do? Suggestions include:

- Gaps in availability of pre- and start-up seed capital for different types of businesses' needs should be should be addressed, as should the relative risk / reward attractiveness for investors of investing in early stage enterprises.

- More women must be actively encouraged and supported to become entrepreneurs.

- Means of transferring the significant research, technological development and innovation (RTDI) investment, currently being implemented, into new entrepreneurial initiatives should be actively encouraged and any barriers to its transfer should be identified and removed.

- The government should seek to facilitate easy, low cost, market entry across all sectors of the economy.

- Skills deficits in entrepreneurship need to be addressed.

Does Ireland need more entrepreneurs? This chapter suggests the answer is 'yes'. However, not all entrepreneurs have the same economic impact, and as such, this chapter has argued that Ireland needs more entrepreneurs who might be expected to impact on economic growth, by developing new knowledge-intensive activities, to attract higher value-added inward investment projects; and to increase Ireland's overall competitiveness.

QUESTIONS

1. What is the *Global Entrepreneurship Monitor*?

2. What is a nascent entrepreneur?

3. According to the GEM research, what are the characteristics of Irish entrepreneurs?

4. According to GEM research, what types of businesses are started in Ireland?

5. Does Ireland need more entrepreneurs? Why / why not?

6. Find the most recent GEM report for Ireland (see www.gemconsortium.org) and identify how the scale and nature of entrepreneurial activity has changed in Ireland during recent years.

7. Compare entrepreneurship in Ireland with entrepreneurship in any other country of your choice (see www.gemconsortium.org for other national reports and the *Global Executive Report*).

PROFILE: LLOYD NOLAN, COMMERCIAL INFORMATION TECHNOLOGY[8]

A graduate of University of Limerick with a Bachelor in Technology, Lloyd Nolan had always wanted to become his own boss and had been considering the idea of creating a business for some time.

I have always wanted to work for myself, for several reasons. I am not averse to managed risk - I work better without a boss and enjoy being empowered to build my own livelihood. I am also motivated by money and felt that my career path in the PAYE sector would never allow me to reach my financial goals.

Travelling in connection with his work, he was yet another travel-weary transient passing briefly through Hong Kong in the autumn of 2004. Killing time, he was attracted to a golf simulator, which was one of the most sophisticated he had ever seen. Quickly, he realised that he had the basis on which a new business might be built, because he was fairly sure there was nothing of this quality available anywhere within Europe. Much intensive after-work research was needed to check out his idea further, before obtaining the European distribution rights for the GolfPro simulator and swing analysers.

Full of enthusiasm, in May 2005, Lloyd left the security of his well-paid position in a US blue chip company in the South West of Ireland to join the ranks of the self-employed. The first major challenge that he faced was to try to find a means of offsetting his immediate loss of income and to pay ongoing personal expenses, including a hefty mortgage. He quickly realised that he would need to bring in outside investors and give away part of the new company to create the conditions necessary to allow him time to concentrate full-time on getting the new business off the ground.

The challenge here was to make contact with people with the right background and, more importantly, with people I could trust - for what would hopefully turn out to be a long-term proposition.

Lloyd decided that the VCs were less attractive an option for him as an outside source of equity than business angels, as he wished to retain full control over the decision-making within the company, while prepared to give up part of the ownership. He found the informal investors that he was looking for within the circle of close family and friends.

During this time, Lloyd attended the Venture Start programme, which is run on a part-time basis in the Innovation Works by Shannon Development. He found this

---

[8] This profile appeared in Fitzsimons, P. & O'Gorman, C. (2006).

course most useful in helping him to crystallise his thoughts about the new businesses.

In particularly, it helped my self belief, because it dispelled any perceived 'special circumstances' around starting a business and it broke through the sense of isolation that I was the only one facing the challenges of starting businesses as it gave me an opportunity to meet with and exchange ideas with others in the same boat as myself.

By September 2005, Lloyd Nolan's new company, Commercial Information Technology Ltd (CIT), was ready for business.

The next challenge was how to target my potential customers. I had never managed any type of marketing campaign before, and I quickly learned that ROI on advertising is something of a dark science that can simply eat money!

He has learnt through this initial experience and is more cautious today, spending more time doing initial research himself before hiring consultants to tell him what he could find out himself with a little effort and for a fraction of the cost.

Lloyd quickly learned that his best route to winning customers was not with advertisements but with referrals. By the time CIT's software is installed, the product is entirely customised to a particular club's needs. The challenge was less about convincing prestige clubs about the product itself, as its integrated nature held its own appeal. The real challenge was convincing them that the new company would be around in the future to cater to their service needs. Within six months of setting up, CIT was able to claim Fitzwilliam Lawn Tennis Club, the Kildare Street Club, and Luttrellstown Golf Club among its client-base.

Lloyd is now leading the pressurised life that most entrepreneurs encounter, in which multitasking and long hours are a feature:

Multitasking is a skill that requires a steep learning curve, and it can be challenging to concentrate to completion on single tasks knowing that several others require your immediate attention. I have had to cancel booked weekend trips, be away from home for several days on end, cry off from social events and, even when I am home, I am still very much focused on work. Because the new business dominates every aspect of my life, it can be challenging to refrain from burdening friends and family with the latest success when we do meet on social occasions.

Lloyd stresses that his wife's Helena's support and understanding has been essential to him over this period:

Without her support, I simply could not have given up a well-paid position and followed my ambitions to set up and run my own business. Friends and family can also be counted on for much-needed words of encouragement.

3

THE ENTREPRENEUR'S STORY[9]

There is evidence to suggest that entrepreneurship has a high degree of popular support in Ireland and that such support has contributed to increased levels of entrepreneurial activity in Ireland. Recent reports support the view that entrepreneurs in Ireland are perceived as 'local heroes', in recognition of the important role that they play in creating wealth and employment (Goodbody, 2002). This has not always been the case. Historically, the regard for entrepreneurship as a career option has been relatively low, and Irish entrepreneurs were viewed with jealousy as newly-rich 'upstarts' (Ardagh, 1994). However, as the economy has grown, begrudgery towards successful entrepreneurs in Ireland has diminished (McCarthy & Leavy, 2000). The *Global Entrepreneurship Monitor* indicates that entrepreneurs now have a higher status throughout the island of Ireland compared with many other developed countries, including the USA.

Increased popular support for entrepreneurial activity may reflect the increased media coverage of entrepreneurs and, in particular, of entrepreneurial success stories. Entrepreneurial stories are considered important, because reported accounts of heroic individual innovations may act as a stimulus to latent entrepreneurial activity. In areas where there appears to be less popular support for entrepreneurs, such as Northern Ireland, it is not uncommon for policy-makers to advocate the profiling and promotion of 'success stories'. For example, Government policy for the promotion of enterprise in Northern Ireland places the task of changing attitudes and culture as a top priority; as part of this strategy, stories of successful entrepreneurs will be promoted as role models.

By examining newspaper articles on entrepreneurs in the UK, Nicholson and Anderson found evidence that British entrepreneurs were portrayed 'as giants' in 1989 but, by the year 2000, 'they were discovered to have feet of clay' (2005). In

---

[9] This chapter is an edited version of an article published in the *Irish Journal of Management Studies*: Garvan, W. & O'Gorman, C. (forthcoming). 'The Schumpeterian & universal hero myth in stories of Irish entrepreneurs'.

Ireland, the opposite appears to have occurred: hitherto, entrepreneurs were previously demonised but, more recently, they have been celebrated (Goodbody, 2002).

Why do stories of entrepreneurs attract attention in popular media in Ireland? How are stories of entrepreneurs presented in the Irish media? In what way might the presentation of the entrepreneur's story influence how entrepreneurs are understood in society? This chapter seeks to address these issues by presenting an analysis of the stories of three Irish entrepreneurs. Analysing and interpreting the stories of entrepreneurs can help in the understanding of how entrepreneurs are perceived by society, and how the entrepreneurial story can be used to encourage innovative activity.

The chapter proceeds as follows. First, the chapter clarifies the meaning of the terms 'Schumpeterian' and 'universal hero myth'. We then examine the stories, as portrayed in the popular media, of three well-known Irish entrepreneurs, and seek to identify elements of the Schumpeterian and universal hero myth. The case studies presented are based on a review of publicly-available sources of biographical material. A discussion of the three cases is presented in terms of the recurring themes from the Schumpeterian and universal hero myth. The chapter concludes by considering the implications of the analysis for policy-makers and others concerned with the portrayal of entrepreneurs in Ireland.

THE 'SCHUMPETERIAN HERO MYTH'?

The 'Schumpeterian hero myth' is a romantic vision of the entrepreneur as a great individual who carries out acts of innovation that are vital for economic development. Schumpeter asserts that entrepreneurs are unique individuals, insofar as they engage in a special type of conduct that is 'accessible in very unequal measure and to relatively few people' (Schumpeter, 1934). Schumpeterian entrepreneurs carry out new combinations and are prepared to step outside the 'boundaries of routine, where many people can go no further' (Schumpeter, 1934).

According to Schumpeter, these unique individuals who bravely go beyond these boundaries must overcome a number of difficulties. Firstly, since they are venturing into areas outside the 'accustomed channels', entrepreneurs must deal with uncertain situations that may lead to failures and setbacks. Therefore, the individual who dares to embark upon the entrepreneurial journey must be prepared to make mistakes and to commit 'other kinds of errors than those occurring in customary action'. Another difficulty outlined by Schumpeter refers to the special 'effort of will' required to conceive of the new combination 'as a real possibility' as opposed to 'merely a day-dream'. A third difficulty is the reaction by the wider 'social group' against the individual 'who wishes to do something new'. This will most likely be initiated by 'the groups threatened by the innovation' and can manifest itself in different forms of 'pressure on the individual', including 'social ostracism'. However, the entrepreneur will overcome these adversities, and will even use the 'social opposition' as a stimulus to continue on with the 'special kind of task' or innovation. In summary, Schumpeter views the entrepreneur as a unique individual who exercises the 'mental freedom' to conceive of a new way of doing things, is brave enough to follow this vision, even if it means risking the possibility of failure and incurring the ridicule of other members of the social group – business or otherwise.

This romantic view of the entrepreneur as an individual hero in the world of business came to prominence in Europe and North America in the late 19th century. Examples include the story of Henry Ford as a poor Irish immigrant, who achieved business greatness through individual effort and the ability to organise others, and reports of the 'Thomas Edison-like drama of the lonely inventor struggling for a breakthrough' (Weiss, 2003). Historically, entrepreneurs in America have been held in high regard, and are often portrayed as heroes. Shapiro has remarked that this hero status for entrepreneurs is based on the mythic figure of the cowboy who was a loner and who focused on 'individual accomplishments' (Shapiro, 1993). Schumpeter's works also provide the foundation for entrepreneurial stories, whereby individuals who overcome adversity against all the odds are portrayed as heroes.

THE UNIVERSAL HERO MYTH

What is the 'hero myth'? The term 'myth' is generally taken to mean a story containing imaginary or exaggerated events. In everyday usage, the term has negative connotations. Leach notes that some use the word as if it meant 'false history', whereas the usual anthropological and cultural view is that myth is a 'sacred, traditional tale' (Leach, 1970). He claims that the idea that history is true and myth false is 'whimsical' and observes that any body of social tradition starts with a creation story, followed by tales of the adventures and achievements of its cultural heroes (Leach, 1970).

Tales of heroic deeds have endured through the ages because the need for heroes is a 'fundamental part of the human condition'. They are communicated through stories that are 'told through the ages'. Joseph Campbell, in his book *The Hero with a Thousand Faces,* reports on the findings from his review of stories and myths from different countries and historical time periods. He noted that these stories contained similar, recurring themes and moral lessons 'valid for all of mankind' (Campbell, 1949).

The purpose of this 'ubiquitous myth of the hero's passage' is to provide a 'general pattern' or blueprint for dealing with life's difficulties and hazards (Campbell, 1949). Campbell also explains that, for the archetypal hero, symbolic rites of passage and the theme of a perilous journey are typical in such stories. The dangerous journey itself has three common motifs: *separation, initiation,* and *return.* The initial call to adventure is usually precipitated by a chance circumstance and the most dangerous part of the journey may be overland or on water but fundamentally it is *inward*, into the deepest recesses of the self, where the demons of fear lie in wait. Then the hero emerges transformed, possessing the power to bestow great benefits on humanity. Upon return, however, he or she is faced by 'uncomprehending opposition' to the message before it is eventually accepted (Campbell, 1949).

This universal mythic journey is similar to the pattern of entrepreneurial behaviour identified by Schumpeter. He observed that the fundamental difficulty faced by any person who is contemplating an innovative act 'lies *in the psyche*' of the individual entrepreneur. This individual must overcome a fear of unknown situations that will arise as a result of stepping outside 'a boundary beyond which the majority of people' will not venture. While Campbell was concerned with universal themes that can be identified in stories and myths from different cultures throughout the ages, Schumpeter's observations (unwittingly?) refer to those same universal themes in the context of economic and business behaviour in the Western industrialised nations in the early part of the 20th century. From this, one could conclude that Schumpeter's insights pertain to the archetypal behaviour that follows a pattern identified by Campbell as the journey undertaken in the universal hero myth.

THE 'TEAM' AS A HERO?

Schumpeter's conceptualisation of the heroic individual entrepreneur has popular appeal, and his influence on researchers in the field of entrepreneurship has been overwhelming. Some writers have been critical of the widespread acceptance of the Schumpeterian view of entrepreneurship. Some have pointed out that the vision of the lone individual hero may not be appropriate for a high-tech business environment that requires high levels of collaboration and teamwork. For this reason, the (early) Schumpeterian view of the entrepreneur with its emphasis on individual innovations has been labelled as 'myth' (that is, as false history). This is partly justifiable, since many innovations do take place in a team setting. In his later work, Schumpeter himself recognised that the majority of innovation was being carried out by 'teams of trained specialists' (Schumpeter, 1942). Reich observed that firms operate in a global networked economy with greater emphasis on co-operation within and between groups (Reich, 1987). He proposed that the concept of 'the team as a hero' as an alternative to the popular myth of the entrepreneur as a lone hero.

Based on the above literature, it could be anticipated that stories of Irish entrepreneurs will contain extensive reference to the recurring themes of the universal hero myth, and as such will emphasise individual rather than team efforts. These recurring themes can be summarised as follows:

- The hero's humble or obscure background.
- The hero's need to leave the group and embark on a journey.
- The hero overcomes adversity, setbacks, and temporary failures.
- The hero takes on a formidable enemy, usually in the form of a giant.
- In the final stage of the heroic journey, the hero returns to popular acclaim and is honoured for individual accomplishments.

CASE STUDIES OF IRISH ENTREPRENEURS

The stories of the three entrepreneurs studied are presented below. These stories are constructed from the secondary material reviewed and are presented to illustrate how elements of the hero myth are common in the telling of the story of an entrepreneur. The purpose of each of these cases is to illustrate how the published material can be presented around the recurring themes of the universal hero myth.

CASE HISTORY: MOYA DOHERTY

Moya Doherty was selected, along with her business partner, John McColgan, as Ernst & Young Irish Entrepreneur of the Year in 1999 to honour their achievement in developing 'Riverdance'. Moya, the daughter to two teachers, was born in Donegal, but grew up from an early age in Clontarf, Dublin. As a teenager, she considered herself to be somewhat of a rebel. After completing school, Moya opted for a course in drama instead of attending university. She spent a year touring as an actor, and then she joined RTÉ, the state television broadcasting company, as a production assistant. While she enjoyed the work in RTÉ, she was never content as an employee in a large bureaucratic organisation. In 1982, she left RTÉ and moved to London, where she spent five years working in various roles for breakfast television in London. In 1987, Moya returned to RTÉ on a producer training course, which included a two year producer's contract.

In the same year, Moya started Tyrone Productions, a small independent television production company, with John McColgan, whom she had met in London. However, competition for contracts in Ireland was intense and the first four years were very lean times for the new business. Both Moya and John teetered on the brink of giving up and returning to England. Moya and John started a family around this time. Moya found this period of her life very difficult, because she had two children under the age of two and was working very long hours. The couple struggled with the business until, in 1994, Moya was given the task of producing the Eurovision Song Contest final. The budget was tight, but she was determined to make an impact and channelled much of her energy into the interval act – a new piece of music by Bill Whelan and a troupe of Irish dancers led by two Irish-Americans, Jean Butler and Michael Flatley. With a story based on Irish myth and legend, it was a visual spectacle that embraced speed, sound, and rhythm. The seven-minute interval act, titled 'Riverdance', brought the audience to their feet.

While John and Moya had no experience of large-scale theatrical performance, and she had no business training, they re-mortgaged their house to help fund the initial investment required to put the Riverdance show on the road. Moya expanded the original Riverdance piece into a two-hour show and adapted it to suit an international audience. The show proved to be very popular, but there were many problems along the way. For example, for the second run of the show in London, Michael Flatley, the star attraction, withdrew, and Jean Butler, the other star, pulled ligaments in her leg the day before opening night. Riverdance had to survive opening night with neither of their headline acts. Furthermore, there was extensive litigation between Riverdance's original performers and the Riverdance show developed by Moya and John. Nonetheless, Riverdance went on to become an Irish success story that has been universally acclaimed. It has been staged in 27 countries across four continents and the worldwide television audience is over 1.5 billion.

In 1997, Moya and John became involved in another venture, Radio Ireland, a new national radio broadcasting station. The investment in radio got off to a bumpy start. They were the front members of the consortium that won the licence to be the national broadcaster but, in its first incarnation, Radio Ireland was a commercial and critical failure. The investors were called on a number of times to invest more. The schedule was changed, new presenters were hired, and the station was re-launched as Today FM. The ratings increased. In total, Moya and John invested €3 million in this venture, and five years later they sold their shares to Scottish Radio Holdings for €17 million.

Moya Doherty has won many awards and accolades over the years. She has been named Veuve Clicquot Business Woman of the Year, *The Sunday Business Post* named her as one of the leading role models for women achievers, and she has been bestowed with honorary doctorates. While she has received financial rewards for her ventures, she measures success on a different scale. Moya claims that the most satisfying part of her career is the enjoyment she gets from being involved with a team that works well together, regardless of the size of the project.

CASE HISTORY: PÁDRAIG Ó CÉIDIGH

Pádraig Ó Céidigh was selected as the Ernst & Young Irish Entrepreneur of the Year in 2002 for revitalising and then growing an 'island-hopping' air travel service into a new marketspace and developing a business model to deliver a 'regional superhighway' air travel service in Ireland.

Ó Céidigh came from a working class background in rural Ireland. At the age of 10, the Connemara-born Pádraig was picking periwinkles from a beach in Spiddal and travelling to Galway to sell them to fish exporters. From an early age, he learned to work hard and graft for any kind of rewards and, in hindsight at least, it was probably obvious to those who knew him in his younger days that he would become an entrepreneur. After secondary school, Pádraig attended university in Galway, completed a commerce degree and then worked for a period with KPMG Accountants. In his early 20s, he took a career break and went teaching for approximately 10 years.

In the 1980s, he started to study law at night and set up his own legal practice in 1992. In May 1994, he became part-owner of Aer Arann, a Connemara-based airline that served the three Aran Islands (which are popular tourist destinations off the coast of Galway). At that time, the airline was running at a loss, Pádraig had no track record in the airline industry, and the industry was considered highly competitive, with a large number of failures in the preceding 10 years. With an acute sense of its business potential, Pádraig steered Aer Arann from its situation as a small Irish domestic carrier to its current position as one of the fastest growing regional airlines in Europe. In 2006, it employed over 400 people, reached a turnover in excess of €94 million per annum and carried over 1 million passengers over 600 flights per week in Ireland, the UK and France with its 14 ATR fleet. From its tiny origins, Aer Arann is now competing for business with Aer Lingus and Ryanair. Following the takeover of CityJet by Air France in 2003, and the collapse of JetGreen in 2004, Padraig is now the 'last man standing' when it comes to small Irish airlines.

Pádraig Ó Céidigh attributes the success of his company to its culture of using cross-functional teams in formulating policy and strategy. He involves the teams in all main decision-making points. He states that the teams are very focused and supportive of each other, that everybody in the company has a passion for success, and that the company's ethos is based on openness and flexibility and a commitment to continually improve customer service.

Pádraig Ó Céidigh has also started a number of other businesses. For example, in 1995, the Irish-speaking Pádraig set up *Foinse*, which became one of the best-selling Irish language newspapers. He is also the owner of a printing company, *Clodoirí Lurgan Teo*, based in Connemara, as well as a local summer language school.

In 2006, he stepped down as CEO, and Garry Cullen was appointed as CEO, with Ó Céidigh assuming the role of executive chairman.

CASE HISTORY: DR PETER FITZGERALD

Dr Peter Fitzgerald was named as Ernst & Young Irish Entrepreneur of the Year in 2004 in recognition of the international success of his company, Randox Laboratories, a business that specialises in medical diagnostics. Randox Limited is a private company (Peter Fitzgerald owns 98% of the shares), with annual revenues of £48 million and 600 employees (including 185 research scientists) in Ireland and another 130 worldwide. Peter Fitzgerald was born in south Antrim, and he attended school in Lisburn. He went to university in Glasgow, where he graduated in 1973 with a degree in biochemistry. After that, he completed a PhD in the National Institute of Medical Research in London. He was very keen on medical research, as he wanted to help improve medical healthcare. He returned to Northern Ireland to Queen's University in Belfast, where he carried out research on multiple sclerosis and other medical conditions.

Peter always had an urge to create something and to improve society. While working as a researcher, he looked around for ideas on how to start a business that would help improve healthcare and contribute to society by generating employment. In 1982, he came across a medical field called diagnostics. He set up a small laboratory in the back of his parents' house in a building that was previously used as a stable and hen-house. Peter started on a very small scale. Working in the evenings and at weekends, he developed his first products. They were evaluated at the local hospitals and performed well. Peter decided to go into business full-time and started Randox Laboratories Limited.

It was a tough time to start a business in Northern Ireland, as 1982 was one of the worst years of the 'Troubles', with bombings and shootings taking place almost every week, and a political process that was in stalemate. His colleagues at Queen's University thought he was mad to leave a safe, secure position in order to start up his own company. When he approached Government agencies for assistance, they were very reluctant to help since he had no knowledge about starting his own business. Peter had already spent his own savings and his parents' money in developing the new products. He approached a number of banks for a loan, but was turned down on the grounds that he had no profits or cash-flow. Furthermore, he had no assets to offer as security. Eventually, he came across a bank manager who believed in what he was trying to achieve. Peter received a £30,000 unsecured loan. His next task was to find customers. He received very little support from organisations in Northern Ireland in the early stages. Peter later reflected that 'often a prophet is never accepted in his own land'. In England, it was difficult to convince hospitals that a small company in the outback of County Antrim in Northern Ireland could manufacture and deliver quality clinical diagnostic products. He travelled throughout Ireland looking for business. The hospitals in the southern part of Ireland and those in Scotland and Wales were more supportive. Gradually, he grew the business as customers came to realise that his products were technically superior and could be delivered faster. In the past 20 years, the company's average revenue growth has been 60% *per annum*.

Peter is aware that his success means that multinationals such as Roche, Abbott, and Bayer will see him as a potential takeover target. However, he is confident that with self-belief, hard work, and teamwork, his company will prevail over his major competitors. In so doing, Peter will have achieved his twin goals: improving medical healthcare, and making a contribution to society by creating wealth and jobs in Northern Ireland.

Dr. Peter Fitzgerald's success has been recognised by a series of other awards – he is a four times winner of the Queen's Award for Export Achievement; in 2003, on behalf of Randox, Peter accepted the MacRobert Award which is the UK's most prestigious engineering award (other finalists for the prize included Rolls Royce Plc).

DISCUSSION

Do the stories of Irish entrepreneurs contain the recurring themes of the universal hero myth? Having reviewed published material of three Irish entrepreneurs, and summarised these in the three case studies outlined above, these cases, which are drawn solely from published accounts of the stories of these entrepreneurs, contain the elements of the universal hero myth. Evidence was also found that, in telling their stories, and in the telling of their stories by others, references were made to events and outcomes that illustrate that the entrepreneurial story is frequently retold in terms of the Schumpeterian and universal hero myth. Indicative elements from these stories are presented and categorised under the themes found in hero myths, for each of the three entrepreneurs, in **Figures 3.1**.

In terms of the entrepreneurs' background, stories of two of the entrepreneurs, Pádraig Ó Céidigh and Peter Fitzgerald, emphasise how they came from obscure backgrounds. Pádraig Ó Céidigh tells how he was reared on a small farm in Galway, illustrating his up-bringing with reference to 'picking and selling periwinkles' as a youngster. Peter Fitzgerald also makes use of the 'humble background' metaphor by pointing out that his company started out in a converted stable/hen-house at the back of his parents' house, although he came from what could be described as an ordinary but comfortable middle-class background. The 'obscure origin' image is also found in his story in the emphasis that is frequently placed on the rural and isolated location of his business. Moya Doherty also came from what could be described as a reasonably comfortable middle-class background, though the telling of her story often suggests that she was somewhat of an 'outsider' in her choice of study (drama), which, it is suggested, was an atypical choice when compared to her socio-economic peers.

The second common theme in the hero myth is the hero's need to leave the group and embark on a journey – what Schumpeter describes as the decision to 'swim against the stream' (Schumpeter, 1934). The story of each of the entrepreneurs tells how they left secure and comfortable jobs to start their businesses. Moya Doherty tells how she had a yearning for independence; that she was 'a bit of a rebel'; and that she could not be 'a corporate person'. Pádraig Ó Céidigh tells how he moved from secure professional jobs in accountancy into teaching, and then how he left teaching to start his legal practice, and eventually became involved with Aer Arann and a number of other ventures. Peter Fitzgerald recalls that his colleagues could not understand how he could leave a 'safe, secure position' in a university to establish a new firm. He also remarked that he had to travel out of Northern Ireland to generate sales, citing that 'a prophet is never accepted in his own land'.

The third common theme in the hero myth is that the hero overcomes adversity, setbacks, and temporary failures. Moya Doherty recalls how she had to make sacrifices along the way, how they 'teetered on the brink of giving up', the difficulties in staging a live performance, and how the failure of Radio Ireland was at first 'dismal' but is now seen as 'a great learning experience'. Pádraig Ó Céidigh is described as 'the last man standing' in the small to medium-sized airline category by *The Irish Times*, thus evoking an image of one who has battled successfully against enemies and adversaries. Peter Fitzgerald tells of his difficulties in convincing hospitals that a high-tech firm from rural Northern Ireland could deliver quality products on time.

The fourth common theme in the hero myth is that the hero takes on a formidable enemy, usually in the form of a giant. This is not a strong theme in the story of Moya Doherty, though there is a reference to 'a contest within a contest', when she 'fought very hard' against the 'old guard' in the European Broadcasting Union in a successful effort to scrap the 'antiquated' telephone-based voting system for the Eurovision Song Contest. In contrast, the stories of both Peter Fitzgerald and Pádraig Ó Céidigh emphasise on a number of occasions how their companies competed against larger organisations. For instance, writing in the *Sunday Business Post*, Catherine O'Mahony hints at a 'David versus Goliath' scenario, when she summarises the growth of Pádraig Ó Céidigh's company: 'from its tiny origins, Aer Arann is now competing for business with Aer Lingus and Ryanair'. Peter Fitzgerald speaks of 'endeavouring to sell our products *against* multinational organisations such as Roche, Abbot, and Bayer'. He describes them as 'dinosaurs', who are not responding quickly enough to changing market conditions and he predicts that his company 'will prevail' over the larger multinationals.

The fifth common theme in the hero myth is that, in the final stage of the heroic journey, the hero returns to popular acclaim and is honoured for individual accomplishments. The entrepreneurs selected for this study had received such recognition and it is therefore unsurprising that their stories contain references to such accolades. Frequently, the context of the story is the presentation of an award, and the award partly explains why the entrepreneurs received widespread media attention. That said, references can be found – in many news stories about these three entrepreneurs – not only to the Ernst & Young Entrepreneur of the Year Award, but also to other awards and accolades that the entrepreneurs or their firms have received.

FIGURE 3.1: HERO MYTH THEMES

Hero Myth Themes	Moya Doherty	Padraig Ó Céidigh	Dr. Peter Fitzgerald
The hero's humble or obscure background	Daughter to two County Donegal teachers 'Somewhat of a rebel.'	Working class background in rural Ireland: 'picking periwinkles from a beach in Spiddal and travelling to Galway to sell them to fish exporters'.	Remoteness of Northern Ireland. Starting the business in a hen house/stable.
The hero's need to leave the group and embark on a journey	Choosing a course in drama instead of attending University. Leaving RTÉ, and moving to London.	Leaves accountancy, then leaves teaching, and then leaves his legal practice.	Leaving Queen's University 'safe, secure position' to start his own company. Seeking business outside Northern Ireland: 'a prophet in his own land is never accepted'.
The hero overcomes adversity, setbacks and temporary failures	The early years of Tyrone Production 'teetered on the brink of giving up'. Running the new business and starting a family. Difficulties in staging show, e.g.: surviving opening night with neither of the headline acts. The radio station venture.	Aer Arann is making losses prior to involvement of Pádraig. Pádraig is the 'last man standing' when it comes to small Irish airlines.	1982 was a bad time to start a business in Northern Ireland due to the 'Troubles'. Government agencies reluctant to support his business but Peter uses own and parents' money, and then finds a banker to back his firm. Overcomes customer reluctance to deal with small start-up from Northern Ireland.
The hero takes on a formidable enemy	Successfully challenged the 'old guard' of the European Broadcasting Union.	Aer Arann competing with Aer Lingus and Ryanair. A small Irish domestic carrier grows to be one of the fastest growing regional airlines in Europe.	Describes multi-national competitors (Roche, Bayer, etc.) as 'dinosaurs'. Claims that his company will 'prevail' over these larger firms.
The hero returns to popular acclaim and is honoured for individual accomplishments.	Ernest & Young Irish Entrepreneur of the Year. Veuve Clicquot Business Woman of the Year; the Sunday Business Post named her as one of the leading role models for women achievers. Awarded honorary doctorate by NUI Maynooth, and by the University of Ulster.	Ernest & Young Irish Entrepreneur of the Year. Member of judging panel for the National Small Business Awards Guest on Ireland's leading television talk-show.	Ernest & Young Irish Entrepreneur of the Year. Queen's Award for Export Achievement. MacRobert Award for engineering excellence.

Do stories of Irish entrepreneurs emphasise great individual achievements rather than the importance of team work? The choice of entrepreneurs studied meant that the chapter focuses on stories of individuals who have been recognised for their outstanding individual achievements, although, in the case of Moya Doherty, the award was to both herself and her partner John McColgan. However, the primary interest is the telling of the stories in the media: do the stories told by, and of, these entrepreneurs emphasise the individual achievements or do they recognise the role of a wider team?

Moya Doherty is accorded iconic status when she is described as 'Queen of the Dance', and one journalist headlined a profile of Doherty with the phrase: 'Moya's Midas touch'. It is widely acknowledged that Moya Doherty provided the inspiration and motivation for Riverdance and, in so doing, she carried out the Schumpeterian act of innovation by combining the elements of Irish dance, tap dancing, flamenco, and other artistic traditions to produce Riverdance. In 2005, the *Sunday Business Post* listed Moya Doherty as one of the top two role models for Irish women achievers. However, Moya herself refers to the importance of her collaboration with John McColgan, and she maintains that she derives most satisfaction from coordinating the many elements of a project into a coherent completed show. So, while the story of Moya Doherty emphasises her individual accomplishments, she also refers to the importance of a wider team in her success.

Pádraig Ó Céidigh is typically portrayed as a 'local hero', and has been described as a 'high-flying entrepreneur' in the local Galway press, where his achievements are commented upon favourably. At a national level, Pádraig was one of the invited key speakers at a conference with the theme, 'Being Brave in Business', organised by the Marketing Institute of Ireland. In August 2005, Padraig appeared as the main guest on Ireland's leading television talk show, The Late Late Show. The introduction to the show noted that '*he* dreamed the impossible dream' and made that dream come true because '*he* runs' the world's fastest growing regional airline. Also in 2005, Pádraig was a judge on the panel for the National Small Business Awards organised by the Small Firms' Association. However, in explaining his success, Pádraig Ó Céidigh tells how he incorporated the concept of teamwork into his style of management and claims to use cross-functional teams in key business decisions, including those at a strategic level.

In a similar vein, various commentators have praised Peter Fitzgerald for the phenomenal growth of Randox Laboratories. In the stories, there is very little evidence of Peter Fitzgerald's individual heroic status. This may be due to the collaborative nature of developing new products in the medical diagnostics business, or possibly because of his reticence regarding personal publicity. Peter Fitzgerald credits the success of his company to the extraordinary efforts of his staff and cites 'team-building' as an essential part of a successful business start-up.

CONCLUSION

This chapter examined the stories of three Irish entrepreneurs, based on material published between 1999 and 2005, seeking to identify the themes of the universal hero myth in these entrepreneurial stories. We also examined the data for evidence of the Schumpeterian hero, with its emphasis on the entrepreneur as an individual, as opposed to the more modern emphasis on the team as a hero (Reich, 1987). It was found that the stories of the three entrepreneurs from different parts of the island of Ireland are generally consistent with the structure of the universal hero myth, but with less weight attached to Schumpeterian individual accomplishments in some of the stories. This may be due to a growing recognition of the importance of teamwork in a complex business environment.

The Schumpeterian hero myth views the entrepreneur as an economic hero who carries out individual acts of innovation. This romantic vision of the entrepreneur appears to be central to the popular understanding of entrepreneurs in Ireland. There is some evidence from the data in this chapter to suggest that the story has been up-dated to include references to the importance of teamwork. A view of entrepreneurship that blends individual acts of innovation with the necessary collaboration of other parties is recognised in the stories. The support provided by business partners, family, and bank officials was recognised by the entrepreneurs as playing an important role in the entrepreneur's individual achievements.

One interpretation of the hero myth is that it is only the special, chosen few who possess the extraordinary set of personality traits required to achieve success. However, another interpretation that takes into account the various elements of the hero myth is to view these stories as a roadmap for a journey that anyone could embark upon, to a greater or lesser extent, provided that they had sufficient determination to overcome the various obstacles that are encountered along the way. This is why hero myths emphasise the main character's ordinary background; it *could* be anyone. As Campbell noted, in the mythic journey, the hero 'ventures forth from the world of common day' (Campbell, 1949).

The deep-rooted need for heroes is reflected in the words of W. B. Yeats: 'children play at being great and wonderful people' (Yeats, 1904). If government agencies wish to promote increased entrepreneurial activities through the use of role models and the publication of their stories, then misleading aspects of the myth, such as the misconception that it takes a person with unique personality traits to become an entrepreneur, should be downplayed. On the other hand, the notion that many successful individuals started from relatively modest backgrounds and learned to treat initial failures as temporary setbacks, as well as the importance of teamwork and collaboration are features of a successful venture that should be highlighted in the stories that publicise entrepreneurs as role models.

QUESTIONS

1. What are the elements of the 'universal hero myth'?

2. Review the story of one of the three entrepreneurs discussed in this chapter and prepare notes for a short talk that you would present to an audience interested in learning about entrepreneurship. Emphasise aspects of the story that might encourage others to be entrepreneurs.

3. Identify similarities and differences in how Moya Doherty, Pádraig Ó Céidigh and Dr Peter Fitzgerald started their new businesses.

4. Identify an entrepreneur you consider as a good role model and collect their story (from secondary sources, such as newspapers, or by interviewing them). Does his / her story contain elements of the Schumpeterian hero myth?

5. What was Joseph Schumpeter's contribution to the study of entrepreneurship? (You will need to source material from your library or the web to answer this).

PROFILE: JENNIFER KINNEAR[10]

In college, Jennifer Kinnear studied Sports, Recreation & Leisure Management. At that time, few of her fellow students could have realized that some years later, Jennifer's jewellery designs would be sold in 35 shops throughout the country, and that she would have her own flagship store in Temple Bar, Dublin where she showcases her jewellery collections.

Jennifer was always creative and had a great interest in the fashion world. This interest brought her to work for a fashion clothing company after college and to attend evening courses in jewellery design in the National College of Art & Design. She loved these classes and, while working in a variety of jobs, continued to experiment with jewellery design and manufacture, reading every book she could lay her hands on in this area. Friends and family all raved about her designs and gave Jennifer the determination to make a career for herself as a jewellery designer.

Jennifer's drive was to create stunning jewellery: she became an entrepreneur by default. In 2002, Jennifer started selling in the Blackrock market and then moved to Cow's Lane market in Temple Bar, where she found a ready interest and many customers for her jewellery. At the same time, she started to sell on a wholesale basis to a variety of shops and galleries.

During this initial start-up phase, she had the benefit of a mentor from the Dublin City Enterprise Board, which was just as well as she had to absorb a great deal of information in a relatively short time in order to set up the new business. As she says herself:

The learning curve was so steep, it was almost vertical!

The commercial realities of managing a business meant that she would not be able to dedicate herself full-time to designing, but would have to strike a balance between all the conflicting demands of a new business. One of the earliest lessons was that cash is king and that watching the cash flow is fundamental.

Jennifer now showcases her work in JK Retail Studio & Showrooms. Located in Temple Bar, the shop was opened in December 2004, and displays the three distinct ranges, *Kink Bijoux, Vanilla* and *Jenny Wren* that Jennifer designs and makes. She also works *in situ*, designing custom-made, 'one off' pieces for the commission client, who wants to partake in the design process.

Jennifer Kinnear comes from a line of entrepreneurs, her father and grandfather both had their own businesses. She believes that an entrepreneur, be they a man or a woman, needs tenacity and resilience:

---

[10]   This profile appeared in Fitzsimons & O'Gorman (2006).

The ability to keep hold of the vision and when the knocks come along, as they invariably will, to bounce back and get straight back into it.

Jennifer's family gave her great support and urged her to follow her dream. Without a network of support from friends and family, she believes that becoming an entrepreneur would not have been possible. Her partner, Simon, particularly fuelled her sense of self-belief whenever it started to flag, and they brainstormed over many cups of coffee, as he was also setting up a new business, in a totally different area, at the same time as Jennifer was starting out.

At the beginning, Enterprise Ireland was not convinced that the new business was a viable proposition. Looking back on this now, Jennifer laughs as she says this was not particularly surprising as they were faced:

... with a young designer with plenty of creativity and drive but with no formal design or commercial training.

Once Jennifer, as she says, could prove her worth, the agency backed her with research and development grants. These allowed her to develop a further collection of her jewellery and underpinned her securing sales in the US market and an agent in Japan. Jennifer meets buyers at Showcase Ireland, run by the Crafts Council of Ireland, which she says proved invaluable as a way of giving a platform to the jewellery and meeting major buyers from Ireland and from overseas.

Asked if she would do it again, Jennifer hesitates and then says she would. The hesitation comes from a greater awareness of what is involved in the whole process of starting up a new business. She would have loved to have known back in 2002 what she knows now.

I have learnt so much along the way and have acquired new skills in many areas that I would never have acquired if I had not taken the plunge and become an entrepreneur.

Jennifer is now looking to further grow sales of her jewellery in the US, get her sample collection out to Japan where she has just landed an agency deal and to break into the UK market. It seems a long way from a stall in the Blackrock Saturday market.

4

CREATIVITY & IDEA GENERATION[11]

When one thinks about creativity and idea generation, images that are evoked involve artistic people and masterpieces of art. One thinks of the Sistine chapel and *The Creation of Man*, the kiss of the muse, the Eureka moment and the light bulb suddenly brightening over the head of a cartoon character. However, one does not usually associate business and entrepreneurial endeavours with creativity. One might be slow to recognise the creative ability of entrepreneurs such as James Dyson, Steve Jobs or even Michael O'Leary, when it involves cost cutting and marketing ploys.

Creativity and idea generation are becoming more and more important in the globalised, flat world that companies operate in. More firms than ever are focusing on creativity as a key success factor for the environment in which they work. This, allied to shorter product life-cycles and the increased speed of change, has lead to a concerted effort to understand and structure creativity for entrepreneurs and companies.

---

[11] This chapter was written by Will Geoghegan, a Research Fellow at the Centre for Innovation & Structural Change at the J.E. Cairnes Graduate School of Business & Public Policy, NUI, Galway.

FROM IDEA GENERATION TO CREATIVITY

The idea generation and creativity stage is associated with the early stages of the innovation process. In the linear model of innovation (**Figure 4.1**), creativity and idea generation are mainly present in the first stage.

FIGURE 4.1: IDEA GENERATION TO CREATIVITY

Idea $\Longrightarrow$ Evaluation $\Longrightarrow$ Development $\Longrightarrow$ Market

Within this process, the entrepreneur firstly comes up with the idea, which will emerge from market pull or technology push. 'Market pull' signifies that society is in need of a product or service – for example, support services for Microsoft's new operating system, Microsoft Vista. 'Technology push', on the other hand, is when one attempts to solve a problem that society is not aware exists – for example, VOIP (voice over Internet protocol), where Skype is a VOIP provider that has become popular as a substitute to calling people by telephone.

Often overlooked is that many successful creative ideas stem from commonsense and an ability to recognise that an opportunity exists, as these quotes show:

- *This 'telephone' has too many shortcomings to be seriously considered as a means of communication. The device is inherently of no value to us.* (Western Union internal memo, 1876)

- *The bomb will never go off, and I speak as an expert in explosives.* (Vannevar Bush, US Presidential Advisor, 1945)

- *So many centuries after the Creation, it is unlikely that anyone could find hitherto unknown lands of any value.* (Advisory Committee to Ferdinand & Isabella of Spain, 1491)

- *The Japanese auto industry is not likely to carve out a big slice of the US market for itself.* (Business Week, August 2, 1968)

- *We don't like their sound. Besides, guitar groups are on the way out.* (President of Decca Records, on turning down the Beatles, 1962)

CREATIVITY & IDEA RECOGNITION

Creativity and idea recognition are often confused with innovation, although there is a subtle difference between the two concepts. Creativity involves the ability to develop new ideas and to explore novel ways of looking at problems and opportunities. Innovation is more involved with the application process, as it involves an ability to apply creative solutions to problems and opportunities so that they enrich people's lives and add value to society. Theodore Levitt (1983) highlighted that:

> ... *creativity is thinking new things, and innovation is doing new things.*

Amabile *et al.* (1996) talked of the iterative nature:

> *All innovation begins with creative ideas ... creativity by individuals and teams is a starting point for innovation; the first is necessary but not sufficient condition for the second.*

Creativity has become a necessity for survival in the globalised world. Companies and entrepreneurs must now out-create and out-innovate their competition, as traditional factors of competitive advantage are being eroded. Many tasks can be outsourced to areas of cheap labour and as conditions become less and less prevalent to the success of businesses, creativity and innovative ability will be the deciding factors as to whether a company will be successful or not. Warren Bennis (1999) summed it up by saying that:

> *Today's successful companies live and die according to the quality of their ideas.*

CREATIVITY & INNOVATION

So what is the link between creativity and entrepreneurs? Entrepreneurship entails exploiting an opportunity or gap in the market, as George Bernard Shaw said:

> *Other people see things and say 'Why?'... But I dream things that never were and say 'Why not?.*

The opportunity usually exists due to a change in one of realms: technological, social, political, economic or psychological. Of course, these are not mutually exclusive and an opportunity may exist due to a change in more than one. An opportunity can be defined as 'a desired future state that is different from the present'. For it to be considered an opportunity, though you must believe that this future state is achievable – for example, there is not yet an opportunity to sell commercial space travel to Mars, as the capability to travel to Mars does not exist as yet.

The opportunity also depends on a number of factors, including:

- The person.
- The environment.
- Access to the required resources.
- Timing.

The skills to identify opportunities can be learned and are not seen to be innate. Edward de Bono (1973), for example, highlighted the behavioural nature of the exploitation of opportunities:

> *Creative thinking is not a talent, it is a skill that can be learnt. It empowers people by adding strength to their natural abilities which improves teamwork, productivity and where appropriate profits.*

Drucker (2002) said that:

> *Innovation is a discipline, with its own fairly simple rules and so is entrepreneurship. Neither of them require geniuses. Neither of them will be done if we wait for inspiration and for the 'kiss of the muse'. Both are work.*

Wycoff & Wycoff (2003) said that:

> *Every person can be taught techniques and behaviours that help them generate more ideas.*

One of these techniques to discover innovations is the seven sources of innovation (see below) detailed by Drucker (2002). His contention is that entrepreneurs must 'search purposely' for innovations; he believed that most innovations are brought about not by inspiration and Eureka moments but by hard work and the purposeful search through his seven sources of innovation. He said (Drucker, 2002) that:

> ... despite much discussion these days of the 'entrepreneurial personality', few of the entrepreneurs with whom I have worked during the past 30 years had such personalities. But I have known many people – salespeople, surgeons, journalists, scholars, even musicians – who did have them without being the least bit entrepreneurial. What all the successful entrepreneurs I have met have in common is not a certain kind of personality but a commitment to the systematic practice of innovation.

He further said (Drucker, 2002) that:

> Innovation is the specific function of entrepreneurship, whether in an existing business, a public service institution, or a new venture started by a lone individual in the family kitchen. It is the means by which the entrepreneur either creates new wealth-producing resources or endows existing resources with enhanced potential for creating wealth.

Drucker notes that the first four of the seven sources of innovation (unexpected occurrences, incongruities, process needs, and industry and market changes) exist within a company, while the other three (demographic changes, changes in perception, and new knowledge) are present outside the boundary of the firm in its social and intellectual environment. We now explore each of these seven sources in more detail.

THE SEVEN SOURCES OF INNOVATION

- **The unexpected:** Be it the unexpected success or failure or event.
  - ◊ An example of an unexpected event that lead to innovation was that of Bulmer's Cider in the mid 1990s, when the company decided to launch the pint bottle of cider, mainly with the intention of it being used in nightclubs. What actually transpired was that customers began to use the pint bottles with ice on warm summer days. Bulmer's immediately saw what was happening and concentrated its marketing on the new use for the product. Now, 15 years later, you can even buy Bulmer's with the ice already in the bottle (see Bulmer's Iced - the new iced age innovation from Bulmer's: http://www.bulmers.ie/latest-news/article10.asp)
  - ◊ An example of an unexpected failure is that of the padlock company that sold its product to India, where they were used primarily as bicycle locks. With sales increasing, the company decided to improve the quality of its padlocks. What happened was that, when it improved the lock, the company found that fewer and fewer people were buying the new improved lock. The lock had become 'too good' – customers preferred the old lock, as it could be broken into more easily using hairpins when the owners lost their original key. This lead to innovations such as the key-coded bicycle padlock.

- **The incongruity:** Between what actually happens and what was supposed to happen.
  - ◊ Ryanair is an example of an incongruity between expectations and results. Ryanair was not supposed to be successful in the European airline industry, since everyone 'knew' that what people wanted on their trip from Dublin to Brussels was a free meal and a copy of *The Irish Times* and that people would not travel with 'uncomfortable Ryanair', no matter what the price. However, what actually transpired was that people did not value the added extras that they had to pay more for and only wanted to get from point A to B safely and as cheaply as possible. Hence, the success of the so-called 'no frills' airline.

- **Innovation based on process need:** The inadequacy in underlying processes, things that are taken for granted but can be improved or changed.
  - ◊ An example of process need is that of the old-style telephone switchboards often seen in old movies, where you call an operator, who then takes out a connection and puts it in somewhere else. At the rate that telephone usage was growing, it was estimated that, by 1930, every woman aged between 16 and 65 would have to be working as a switchboard operator.

- **Changes in industry structure or market structure:** This can take everyone by surprise.
  - ◊ Several Irish industries have changed their structure, due to the privatisation of previously State-run companies – for example, the deregulation of the telecoms industry has lead to more innovative opportunities for firms and entrepreneurs.

- **Demographics:** Population changes caused by changes in birth rates, wars, medical improvements, etc.
  - ◊ The Irish demographic is changing quickly: we have become more aware of the need for a pension, with the State advertising this necessity at every opportunity; external and blended learning offer opportunities for busy executives, who ordinarily would not have the time to come into college 20 hours a week.

- **Changes in perception, mood, and meaning:** These can be brought about by the ups and downs of the economy, culture, fashion and so on.
  - ◊ Although our generation is less prone to illness than any other before, we exhibit the highest use of medical facilities. Anecdotally, our grandparents would have been on their deathbed before the doctor was called, while we are prone to attacks of near-hypochondria. This can lead to innovations in self-diagnosis and the use of medical staff, as well as trends such as healthy eating.

- **New knowledge:** Both scientific and non-scientific knowledge.
  - ◊ This is the source that we often associate innovation with. The huge breakthrough, like the cure for cancer or the new form of travel that will take us to the moon in 30 minutes. However, this is the most problematic and has the longest lead-time. Take chemotherapy as an example: it was invented in 1907, but it was 1936 before it was used extensively in hospitals – not unlike the digital computer, where the technical knowledge was available in 1918 but it was 1946 before it first appeared.

CREATIVITY: LEFT & RIGHT BRAIN

The entrepreneur must be aware that he / she must use both sides of the brain, if they are to be successful. From the middle of the last century, people began to discover that each hemisphere of the brain is used for different functions, these functions need to act together for successful entrepreneurship.

The left side of the brain accounts for verbal, analytical, abstract, rational, linear and logical thoughts and actions. The right side helps with the non-verbal, synthesising, processing analogies, non-rational, spatial, intuitive and imaginative thoughts and actions that the brain processes. Although one may assume that the two sides of the brain have differing responsibilities, they are integrated through a group of connecting nerve fibres called the *corpus callosum*, hence each hemisphere reinforces and aids the other actions.

We tend to use one side of our brain more than the other, however, and the dominant side of the brain is the one that will process the stimulus and information. However, the thinking and learning process is improved when we use both sides of the brain in tandem, in an equal manner. **Figure 4.2** below outlines how the two hemispheres of the brain process information.

FIGURE 4.2: HOW THE BRAIN PROCESSES INFORMATION

Left Hemisphere	Right Hemisphere
Linear	Holistic
Sequential	Random
Symbolic	Concrete
Logical	Intuitive
Verbal	Non-verbal
Reality-based	Fantasy-based

In order for someone to be creative, they cannot have an over-reliance on one side of the brain. The creative process, although it has been popularised as the eccentric 'rain man'-type abstract thinker, needs structure and logical, analytical thinking if it is to succeed.

FIGURE 4.3: LEFT / RIGHT BRAIN TEST

The following is a sample indicative test to see which hemisphere of the brain you rely most on. On a sheet, write down the numbers 1 through to 30. As you read the statements below, circle the numbers of the statements that you think apply to you; if the statement does not apply to you, then leave the number uncircled.

1.   I prefer to be helped individually.
2.   If I buy a new iPod or digital camera, I read the directions first.
3.   I like the company of others.
4.   I like to be spontaneous and for things to be unplanned.
5.   I can spell very well.
6.   I can tell intuitively by looking at people whether they are guilty or not.
7.   When I have to drive to a place in Ireland I use AA route planner or a map.
8.   I like lists and construct a list whenever possible.
9.   I am rarely punctual.
10.   I gesture and am quite animated when talking.
11.   I prefer when the lecturer gives us very well-structured notes and doesn't allow extra input or thinking from the student.
12.   When someone asks me how to get somewhere, I usually prefer to draw a map instead of explaining it verbally.
13.   I don't consider reading as one of my hobbies.
14.   I prefer to go to a lecture, rather than read the chapter of a book.
15.   I have thought about a career as a poet, artist, actor, politician, architect, or dancer.
16.   I have thought about a career as a banker, lawyer, trader, accountant, mathematician, laboratory scientist, or doctor.
17.   If I lose something, I am methodical about retracing my actions until I find it.
18.   If I have a big decision to make, I write down the pros and cons.
19.   I am organized most of the time.
20.   I get good grades at mathematics.
21.   I have thought about running with the bulls in Pamplona.
22.   The same food every Sunday would disinterest me.
23.   I daydream a lot.
24.   I find it easier to remember faces than names.
25.   I try to test out new things and ideas, rather than staying with what is tried and tested.
26.   I try to have a Lonely Planet book or another type of guide book when I go to a new country.
27.   I can't study while listening to music.
28.   I wear a watch.
29.   I start a lot of tasks that I never finish.
30.   I am not imaginative when I do assignments.

You should have a list of 1 to 30, some with circles, some without. Go through the list now putting and 'R' (right) or a 'L' (left) next to the corresponding number that you have circled – for example, for the first statement, 'I prefer to be helped individually', if you think it applies to you and have circled it, then put an L next to it in accordance with the list below.

1:L, 2:L, 3:R, 4:R, 5:L, 6:R, 7:L, 8:L. 9:R, 10:R, 11:L, 12:R, 13:L, 14:R, 15:R, 16:L, 17:R, 18:L, 19:L, 20:L, 21:R, 22:R, 23:R, 24:R, 25:R, 26:L, 27:L, 28:L, 29:R, 30:L

Now count up all the L's and R's. If you have more L's than R's, you are more reliant on the left side of your brain; if you have more R's than L's, you are more reliant on the right side; if you have an equal number, then you are equally reliant on both hemispheres. This test is by no means conclusive and only gives you an indication of which side you rely on more.

BARRIERS TO CREATIVITY

Roger von Oech (1990) identified 10 'mental locks' that limit individual innovation:

- **Searching for the one right answer:** In our education system, since we are taught to find the one correct answer and then to stop our search, most of the time we assume that this is the optimum solution. Creativity experts such as Edward de Bono suggest that we should continue to search, even when we have found a correct answer. He calls this thought process 'lateral thinking'.

- **Focusing on being logical:** Sometimes, logical thought processes stifle creativity. If Roald Dahl had stopped to think logically before he wrote *Charlie & the Chocolate Factory*, a book that millions of children the world over love would never have been written.

- **Blindly following the rules:** We are all guilty of this one – so many times, we do things because 'everyone else is doing it'. When we were children, most of us coloured in our colouring books very carefully so as not to get any crayon outside of the lines. What would have happened if Picasso had approached his colouring book in this manner?

- **Constantly being practical:** Creativity can be greatly enhanced by imagining completely impractical answers to 'what if' questions. Thomas Edison, acknowledged as the most prolific inventor of all time, when hiring a new employee would tell them 'Walk through the town and list 20 things that interest you'. When he / she returned from town, Edison would ask the employee to split the list into two columns and see how many potential inventions could be obtained from the list. One can learn a lot from impracticality that may spur you on to novel ideas and creations. Try a word association game at: http://www.wordassociation.org/

- **Viewing play as frivolous:** Several authors suggest that one should seek inspiration in relaxation and play; 'Ha Ha' often turns into 'Aha!'.

- **Becoming overly-specialised:** An overly-specialised person silos themselves into an area where cross-fertilisation is not possible. One should not be myopic in one's search for creativity and should try to embrace as many other disciplines as possible. Read Eric von Hippel's *Democratizing Innovation*, for examples of how people have combined their hobbies with aspects from their jobs for innovative results (download a free PDF copy http://web.mit.edu/evhippel/www/democ.htm).

- **Avoiding ambiguity:** Ambiguity is seen as a major stimulus for creativity. Things are rarely black and white, so allowing yourself to recognise the inherent vagueness and the lack of clarity of meaning often leads to a creative approach.

- **Fearing looking foolish:** Sometimes being creative entails looking silly. The first guys to snowboard, for example, strapped their self-made boards to their feet and used their skills on a completely different surface.

- **Fearing mistakes and failures:** Mistakes and failures are part of the creative process. Walt Disney tried to borrow from over 300 banks before he received funding for Disney. Stevens & Burley (1997) studied the success rate of raw ideas and found that it takes 3,000 raw ideas to have one commercial success.

- **Believing that I'm not creative:** The human psyche will allow you to achieve only what you believe is possible. As Vincent Van Gogh famously said, 'If you hear a voice within you say 'you cannot paint', then by all means paint, and that voice will be silenced'. Confidence can be a key barrier, if you do not believe yourself that you can be creative then it is highly unlikely you ever will.

ENHANCING ORGANISATIONAL CREATIVITY

A range of methods can be used to enhance the creativity within an organisation – for example:

- **Expecting creativity:** Firms should proactively seek creativity from their workforce, whether through suggestion boxes or by offering incentives for the most creative idea that may produce results. 3M for example, allow their employees 10% of their time to think creatively.

- **Expecting and tolerating failure:** To innovate successfully, or to be creative, you must be willing to accept failures. It took Edison 8,000 attempts to perfect the Edison Battery. When questioned about all the time and effort wasted, he famously commented that 'At least, we know 8,000 things that don't work'.

- **Encouraging curiosity:** The 'Seven Whys' framework is a classic example of this and was developed as part of Toyota's quality push. It involves starting with the problem and asking 'why?' seven times in a row, until you have reached the root of the problem, helping you better understand it and framing it clearer in your head.

- **Viewing problems as challenges:** A lot of the time, we view things as impossible or unachievable. Framing problems as challenges allows employees to gain the intrinsic motivation to allow them to strive to overcome. For example, can the following letters be made into an English word: AAEIIOY DLNRRRTX?

- **Providing creativity training:** It helps to get an expert on creativity to make sure that you have the structure and the policies in place to fully allow for creativity to grow. It can also be helpful for employees to go on creativity workshops and seminars to help them explore the topic fully.

- **Providing support:** Support can be key to endorsing creative behaviour. Allowing people time and resources to pursue their ideas can make or break the potential for creativity in your firm.

- **Rewarding creativity:** Rewards should be in place so that creative behaviour does not go unnoticed. One should reward employees both intrinsically and extrinsically for creative behaviour.

- **Modelling creative behaviour:** Best practice in the area of creativity should be modelled. Increasingly, innovative work environments are modelled for the successful generation of creative ideas – for example, Google's headquarters, referred to as the Googleplex, located in Mountain View, California, is seen as the utopia for the creative person.

ENHANCING INDIVIDUAL CREATIVITY

Research suggests that most successful entrepreneurs have the capacity to be creative; this ability can be enhanced in non-entrepreneurs too. Some ways to enhance your own personal creativity are listed below; they represent the converse of the barriers to creativity already outlined above:

- **Allow yourself to be creative:** Confidence is closely related to competence. If you allow yourself to be creative, then it will flourish organically.

- **Give your mind fresh input every day:** Giving your mind fresh input helps to stimulate thinking and learning. Change the radio station you listen to on your way to work, change your perfume or aftershave, or the food you eat at lunch – these all give your mind fresh input. Use Nintendo's handheld DS console and the game called *Brain Age* to improve your mental activity through word and number puzzles, connect-the-dots exercises and other challenges. Afterwards, it issues you a 'brain age', which is best when the same or below the player's actual age.

- **Keep a journal handy to record your thoughts and ideas:** Some of your best ideas can come to you at the strangest times and places, so it can be very useful to have a journal or notebook no matter where you are at or what you are doing to enable you to jot down any potential creative ideas.

- **Read books and takes classes on stimulating creativity:** Reading books and taking classes that are designed to help increase your creativity allow for techniques and methods to be learned, so you can improve your creative ability.

- **Take some time off:** It is very hard to be creative, if you have no time to yourself and are constantly stressed or exhausted. Like the 3M example mentioned earlier, Google allows its engineers 20% of their time to research projects that interest them, which was held to be the catalyst for products such as Gmail, Google News, and AdSense.

CONCLUSION

Idea generation and being creative is an essential ingredient to being an entrepreneur or being entrepreneurial in any professional context. By thinking – and acting – differently, entrepreneurs may challenge the industry's conventional wisdom. Every day, as consumers, we buy products and services in many ways we didn't do 10, or even five, years ago. Coffee, travel and music are just three examples of this change but they also illustrate that, by being creative, entrepreneurs can alter industry competitive dynamics and dominant business models. Creativity and idea generation are essential capabilities for all workers, particularly as economies become more knowledge-dependent.

QUESTIONS

1. Describe the differences between creativity and innovation.

2. Outline the seven sources of innovation and discuss Drucker's contention that entrepreneurs must 'search purposely' for innovation?

3. Describe the functions of the left and right brain and discuss the barriers to creativity.

4. How can firms enhance organisational and individual creativity?

PROFILE: DAVID WALSH, NETWATCH[12]

For David Walsh, the desire to become an entrepreneur came before he had identified the specific opportunity that would turn his aspiration into reality. He explains that he had always wanted the freedom of working for himself and had looked at a number of ideas previously. It was, he says, a matter of timing and trying to identify a winning business proposition.

The idea for NetWatch, the brainchild of David Walsh and his partner, Niall Kelly, arose following an attack on a friend of the founders, who had been called out to answer a traditional alarm activation at his business premises. The NetWatch founders felt there had to be a better way to protect both key-holders responding to an alarm and the premises itself from intruders.

As no system was available in Ireland, David and his partner looked abroad for the answers. Together, they travelled to Australia to meet a company that specialises in video transmission for military installations. This system they considered to be far better than the traditional alarm and CCTV systems, and more cost-effective than employing full-time security guards. Rather than seeking to develop an entirely new solution, they discussed the possibility of customising this technology to meet the needs of Irish businesses, which led to the development of the NetWatch system.

NetWatch uses modern communication technologies to provide remote visual monitoring security systems to businesses. This intelligent security system allows the NetWatch command centre to watch in real-time any intrusion at a client premises and more importantly, to speak directly to the criminals, clearing them from the site, thus preventing theft and damage to property.

Asked about the greatest challenges that he had to face in deciding to become an entrepreneur, David immediately mentions the lack of financial support systems for those who decide to leave a secure job and set up their own business, particularly if that new business is in the services sector:

> *The financial support systems are less than satisfactory, particularly for service-based companies such as ours. A good example is the Seed Capital Scheme, which is aimed at manufacturing or export companies, despite the fact that it is the services sector that forms the backbone of Ireland's economic success.*

Another challenge that had to be overcome before NetWatch could be rolled out was accessing the necessary telecommunication infrastructure. This proved unnecessarily difficult:

---

[12] This profile appeared in Fitzsimons & O'Gorman (2006).

We also had difficulties in actually securing telecoms service and broadband service to enable us to deliver the NetWatch system to our clients. The roll-out of broadband is positioned by Government as key to our continued economic success but, unless you are in Dublin, you are going to meet with difficulties in obtaining broadband. This impacts on all businesses and needs to be seriously addressed.

From the outset, David recognised the need to build a balanced team with complementary skills:

Like any new start-up, financing and finance management was a major challenge. My own background is in sales, and Niall's is in technology. We knew we could build and sell the NetWatch system, but could we make any money from it? Our first appointment was a financial controller who helped us put the processes in place to actually secure financing and make the business earn money.

In common with most entrepreneurs, David recognises that a strong network of support is essential to getting even the best of ideas off the ground. That support needs to be personal as well as professional and advisory:

The belief and support of my wife Beatrice – who had more to lose than anyone if the business failed – was very important to me in starting the business.

Many entrepreneurs make bad business managers. The Carlow Enterprise Board ran an excellent training course for owner-managers, which gave us incredible insight and knowledge into running a business and the importance of internal systems and controls. Later on, the South East Business Innovation Centre (SEBIC) were invaluable in helping us to develop our business plan and to identify the strategy to take us to the next level. They not only helped us to identify our mission and plan, but more importantly, they helped us to clearly identify the sectors we should avoid.

Asked if he would do it all again, David replies without hesitation:

Most definitely! My advice to people who are thinking of setting up their own business would be to research the market place thoroughly before you start, make sure you have the expertise on board and just go for it.

5

START-UP STRATEGIES

There are many different ways to start a new business. Richard Branson began his entrepreneurial career in the music business with no experience and few resources. However, his entry into the cola business, the airline business and renewable energy business were very different. In these businesses, he sought to become a significant competitor from the start. Though he continued to lack industry-specific experience, he had the resources to make large investments and to seek market share quickly.

There are many business opportunities and most start-ups never make it into the headlines. The start-ups that receive most popular attention tend to be either highly successful and innovative products, for example, the iPod or Tetra-Pak, or novelty products. The choice of how to become an entrepreneur will depend on the nature of the business opportunity that interests the entrepreneur and the resources and experiences of the entrepreneur. This chapter reviews the strategies that entrepreneurs pursue when starting a new business. It examines the start-up period and identifies problems that are common to many new businesses.

STARTING A NEW BUSINESS

There are several alternative routes to becoming an entrepreneur.

COPY AN EXISTING BUSINESS IDEA

This is by far the most common route into entrepreneurship. Most new businesses copy an existing business and apply it to a new geographic area. Most service-type businesses such as hairdressers, video shops, restaurants, builders and most professional businesses such as solicitors, opticians and electricians are examples of an entrepreneur copying an existing business idea. A more successful variant of this approach to new business start-up is to copy a business opportunity from an overseas market. Many new business ideas in Ireland originate from the US and the UK.

   The advantage of this approach is that the business has a proven product / service idea. Also it may be easy to identify potential customers, who are the people using the product / service of competitors. This is also a disadvantage, in that it may be difficult to develop any competitive advantage and to persuade existing customers to change supplier. Competitors may be able to react quickly to any innovations that the new business introduces.

DEVELOP A NEW PRODUCT / SERVICE

Most people consider that it is essential to do something new if they are to start a new business. However, this entrepreneurial route has the highest risk and the highest failure rate. For every new idea that is commercially successful, there are a large number that fail. International evidence suggests that one in three new business fail within the first three years. The advantages of developing a new product / service are that there may be an opportunity for rapid market penetration. Also, by being first into the market, the new business may get some 'first mover' advantages – the development of a brand image, acquiring the best locations and distribution outlets or patent protection, if the product is a technical innovation. However, being first to the market does not guarantee success. Many new ideas are copied by existing businesses that may have a brand image or better access to distribution outlets. Often the first-mover carries the cost of developing both the product and the market, allowing later entrants to pursue a lower cost strategy – 'pioneers get arrows in their backs'. In many industries, it is possible to be too innovative, too far ahead of what the market and customers are prepared to accept.

FIGURE 5.1: JILL HOLTZ & MICHELLE DAVITT SET UP
MYKIDSTIME.IE

Mykidstime.ie was formed in January 2007 by Jill Holtz, who has over 15 years' experience in business analysis and customer relationship management, and Michelle Davitt, who has 15 years' experience working in publishing and is a qualified Montessori teacher. As parents, Jill and Michelle found it difficult to get information about kids' activities in Galway, as there was no website or publication bringing together in one place information on activities, classes, events and / or services for parents. So busy parents had to look for information in different formats and in different places, finding often that it was neither up-to-date nor accurate. mykidstime.ie is an information website aimed at parents which lists children's activities, classes, events and services in their local area, as well as other useful features for parents such as notice-boards and other services. The uniqueness of the company lies in its emphasis on quality content and innovation in the technology and functionality offered to service providers and the end-user, the parents.

BUY / FRANCHISE AN EXISTING BUSINESS

There are a number of variants to this strategy. These include franchising a business, licensing a product from an inventor or company, and acquiring an existing business.

Franchising is where the entrepreneur purchases the right to operate a business. Examples of successful franchises are McDonalds, Abrakebabra and Supermac's. Franchising accounts for one-third of all US retail sales.

Licensing is different from franchising, in that the entrepreneur buys the right to manufacture or distribute a product in a region. The entrepreneur pays the inventor or developer a royalty for every product sold. Inventors and businesses license their products because they may not have the skills, resources or time to develop the product in all markets. Licensing is very common in the computer software business and among developers of computer games.

The advantage of these strategies is that the entrepreneur gets a proven business idea. In the case of a franchise, the entrepreneur gets a complete package that may include business training (**Figure 5.2**). However, these strategies can be very expensive. Franchises require an up-front investment and an on-going payment of a percentage of sales revenues or profits to the franchiser (**Figure 5.3**). Also, growth opportunities for franchise holders may be limited.

Buying an existing business has the added advantage of giving the entrepreneur an established customer base.

FIGURE 5.2: ADVANTAGES & DISADVANTAGES OF FRANCHISING

For the Franchiser (seller of the franchise):

◊ **Advantages**: Rapid expansion of the business; Increased income; Less time spent operating the business; Access to more capital.

◊ **Disadvantages**: Have to identify suitable franchisees; Difficulty in keeping control.

For the Franchisee (buyer of the franchise):

◊ **Advantages**: Business format tested and proven; Often a recognised business name, therefore existing brand loyalty; Advice available from franchiser and other franchisees.

◊ **Disadvantages**: Initial up-front costs; Fees increase as business grows; Limited autonomy to change or improve the business.

FIGURE 5.3: FINANCIAL CONSIDERATIONS FOR THE FRANCHISEE

◊ **Initial franchisee fee**: Usually 5 to 10% of start-up costs.

◊ **Franchise package**: The cost of fixture and fittings, initial stock, etc.

◊ **Management services fee**: Ongoing costs for rights to the franchise. Average of 3 to 15% of turnover.

◊ **Advertising levy**: Contribution to central advertising fund. Usually 2.5 to 5% of gross turnover.

◊ **Exclusive purchase of product**: May have to purchase goods from franchiser or nominated supplier.

THE NEW VENTURE CREATION PROCESS

THE START-UP PERIOD

How does an entrepreneur feel during the launch of a new business? The problems and experiences of entrepreneurs who have started their own business are surprisingly similar. Research into the process of starting a new business attempts to identify and categorise these common events.

Common emotions experienced by an entrepreneur at start-up are:

- **Relief**: The difficult decision to start-up the business has been made and attention is now directed at running the new business.

- **Stress**: The entrepreneur is under constant pressure.

- **Time pressure**: Starting a business is very time-consuming. The entrepreneur is doing everything for the first time. Most entrepreneurs work day and night, seven days a week, during the early days of the business.

- **Uncertainty**: The entrepreneur does not know whether the business will succeed or fail.

- **'Out of control'**: The entrepreneur is dependent on others for the success of the business. Customers, bankers, investors, staff and suppliers are all putting pressure on the entrepreneur to 'deliver the goods'.

- **Under-resourced**: The entrepreneur does not have the financial, managerial and personnel resources to cope with all the demands on the business.

- **Excitement**: The start-up period is an exhilarating period for most entrepreneurs. Usually there will be a sense of commitment and enthusiasm among employees with everybody trying to help get the business up and running.

Not all start-up businesses follow the same pattern. Some start small and grow and develop very slowly. In some sectors, entrepreneurs might start working on their new business at weekends. As demand for the business develops, the entrepreneur may consider leaving full-time employment and devoting all their time to the business. In many cases, these businesses may never be very profitable but the entrepreneur prefers to be self-employed rather than an employee.

Other businesses grow very quickly, because the entrepreneur has developed a successful product or service. Some businesses must grow quickly if they are to earn enough to repay the large amounts of capital invested.

These alternative start-up patterns are described below.

'Improvised' New Businesses

'Improvisation' is 'when the design and execution of novel actions converge' (Baker *et al.*, 2003). It refers to entrepreneurs creating businesses without any prior 'planning'. In an improvised new business, the entrepreneur starts a new business in a short period of time in response to some unanticipated opportunity. Improvisation is contrasted with the 'design-precedes-execution' process, which is when the entrepreneur uses a linear process that starts with an idea, that is then researched and developed into a plan, which is eventually implemented.

The 'Bootstrapped' New Businesses

'Bootstrapping' describes start-ups that are characterised by a period of a constant and almost daily struggle for survival. These businesses start small and develop slowly. Due to a lack of resources and a lack of time, the entrepreneur is continually problem-solving and 'fire-fighting'. To cope with this situation, the entrepreneur tries to leverage the scarce resources available. Anita Roddick's decision to refill customers' bottles, because she could not afford to purchase enough bottles when she started The Body Shop, is an example of an entrepreneur bootstrapping by turning a disadvantage into an advantage. Often, entrepreneurs will rent premises and plant rather than purchase them. Staff will be hired on a part-time basis until the business can afford full-time staff. The entrepreneur may seek help from family and friends.

'Boom or Bust' Businesses

'Boom or bust' businesses require a large up-front commitment of resources and often expenditure on specialised assets. It is not possible for the entrepreneur to start small and gradually develop the business. These businesses must develop enough sales to fund the large capital investments made at start-up. If targeted sales are not achieved, the business fails; however, if the business is successful, it will normally be quite large and profitable. An example of this type of business would be building a whiskey distillery or the development of a large-scale tourist attraction. These projects require large capital investments and therefore must achieve large sales to cover the investment.

MANAGING A START-UP

The overall objective of the entrepreneur at start-up is to establish the business in the market. The entrepreneur will spend all of the start-up period managing and solving short-term problems. A well-prepared business plan can be an essential guide to the entrepreneur during this period. The business plan provides the entrepreneur with a set of objectives and actions. Additionally, it provides a mechanism for comparing actual performance with expected performance. The main areas of activity that the entrepreneur needs to pay particular attention to during the launch period are:

- Resource acquisition.
- Getting ready for business.
- Producing the product / service.
- Getting customers and establishing a market presence.
- Managing finance and monitoring performance.

Resource Acquisition

The entrepreneur will spend most of the time prior to start-up acquiring the resources that are needed. In some businesses, these must all be in place prior to start-up — for example, a restaurant must be fully fitted and staff must be hired and trained prior to opening. Entrepreneurs may rent or borrow equipment rather than purchase it.

Getting Ready for Business

The day-to-day problems associated with getting ready to do business will take most of the entrepreneur's time. The entrepreneur will have to deal with issues such as getting the telephone connected, buying stock and supplies, and equipping the premises. Many problems will be encountered and often the entrepreneur will fall behind schedule. This can be very costly, as the business will be incurring costs without producing any revenues.

Producing the Product / Service

The entrepreneur must begin production of the product/service. During the first few months of business, it is essential that the entrepreneur manages both the cost of producing the product / service and the quality of the product/service. As the business expands and sales increase, the attention that each individual order receives may decrease and quality may slip.

Getting Customers & Establishing a Market Presence

The objective of the launch period is to get the business established. The most essential element of this is to inform potential customers of the business and to get them to try the product or service. Where possible, the entrepreneur should make use of free publicity associated with the launch of the business. The entrepreneur faces a number of challenges in trying to build up a customer base. During the initial few months of a new business, sales may be satisfactory due to friends and business contacts supporting the start-up. These initial customers are referred to as 'soft' customers. These initial orders will have to be developed into repeat orders. In most businesses, it is repeat orders and purchases that keep the business alive. Having got the customer to buy the product / service, the entrepreneur must ensure that payment is received. Additionally, the entrepreneur should monitor the price of the product / service and how competitors have reacted. Competitors may react by putting pressure on suppliers, distributors and buyers not to deal with the new business.

Managing Finance & Monitoring Performance

Cash management is the most important issue during start-up. Cash is the lifeblood of a new business. Most businesses fail due to poor financial management. Many good ideas that have been proven in the marketplace have failed due to poor cash management. Monitoring performance during start-up is critical. Most entrepreneurs are weak in this area and get so caught up in the day-to-day running of the business that they lose sight of the overall direction and performance of the business. In an effort to get sales, many entrepreneurs ignore the necessity of managing the credit process. The entrepreneur must pay close attention to the management of cash and, in particular, the generation of cash. The performance of the business should be compared to the budgets in the business plan. Computerised accounting packages can help the entrepreneur to control the performance of the new business.

BARRIERS TO A SUCCESSFUL LAUNCH

Despite all the planning done prior to start-up, many things will go wrong. The problems that the start-up is likely to experience include:

- **Lack of resources**: The new business will only survive if it acquires the financial, human and physical resources it needs. Failure to secure all the funding needed may create cash flow problems for the business. Some businesses find it difficult to acquire the premises and equipment they need. In particular, getting the right mix of human talent to execute the business plan can be a major barrier to successful launch.

- **Overcoming customer inertia**: Customers will usually have an existing supplier. Changing supplier and / or trying a new product / service involve a risk. The power of existing brands and brand image can make it difficult for entrepreneurs to persuade customers that the new product / service is better. Satisfied customers may not be interested in investing time to consider a new product / service. Even if customers can be persuaded to try the product, the entrepreneur may have to change a buying pattern and habit.

- **Overcoming competitors**: Most markets are supplied by a number of competitors. Competitors may react to a new entrant by reducing prices or increasing expenditure on sales and promotion. Alternatively, existing competitors may try to restrict access to distribution channels or access to suppliers.

- **Achieving satisfactory margins**: Inevitably during start-up, costs overrun budgets. There are many costs that the entrepreneur did not anticipate. A combination of higher costs and lower sales prices due to the reaction of competitors may result in lower margins.

- **Getting paid**: Sales will be slow to develop and converting credit sales into cash may be a very slow and difficult process. The entrepreneur may be slow to put pressure on customers for payment because of a fear that subsequent business may be lost. Also, the entrepreneur may not have a credit control process or payment collection procedure in the company. The lack of these systems may slow down the flow of cash into the business.

- **Time**: The entrepreneur will find that there is not enough time to get everything done and that things take longer than planned. Delays can be costly for a new business. Delays may be the result of poor and unrealistic expectations about the business. The preparation of a business plan should help the entrepreneur overcome these problems. Inevitably, there will be some time delays that the entrepreneur cannot anticipate or control.

A seminal study by O'Farrell (1986) identified the main problems that Irish manufacturing businesses experienced at start-up in the mid-1980s. More recent research for the UK suggests that these problems persist:

- **Obtaining working capital**: Working capital problems arise due to bad debts, slowness of payments, high interest rates.

- **Obtaining medium- and long-term finance**: Difficulty in getting access to finance at a reasonable interest rate. Most entrepreneurs are resistant to the idea of selling equity to raise finance for the business.

- **Obtaining suitable premises**: Difficulty in getting suitable premises at an acceptable price.

- **Obtaining payment**: Entrepreneurs find it difficult to get payment from customers.

- **Getting credit from suppliers**: Suppliers may be slow to extend credit facilities to a new company. Cash on delivery requirements put added strain on the cash flow of a business.

- **Lack of demand**: Interestingly, this was not high on the list of problems.

CHOOSING A STRATEGY

A new business should have both a competitive strategy and a market-entry strategy. These decisions should be based on an understanding and an analysis of customers and competitors. The strategy of the business should be explained and justified in the business plan.

MARKET-ENTRY STRATEGY

The market share and market coverage of a company such as O2 is very different from that of a new local video store or an online gift company. Market-entry strategy refers to how the new business will enter the market. A new business may choose to enter only one market segment or one geographic market, or alternatively it may choose to enter the whole market. The decision on which market-entry strategy to use is determined by a number of factors:

- **Resources**: New businesses with limited resources will usually choose to concentrate these resources in a limited number of market or geographic segments. They will enter one market segment and, over time, develop into other segments of the market.

- **Capital investment and scale requirements:** Industries that have large economies of scale favour larger businesses. A new entrant must attempt to get sufficient volume quickly. Often this volume will only be achievable if the whole market is entered.

- **Product life cycle:** If the product/service has a short life cycle, the entrepreneur will need to grow the business quickly and may be more likely to enter with a broad market-entry strategy. The software industry is an example of a sector where the entrepreneur will probably have to maximise sales of the product quickly.

- **Proprietary protection:** If the product/service lacks any proprietary protection such as patents or trade secrets, the entrepreneur will seek to get maximum sales before competitors imitate the product/service.

- **Market structure and competition**. The more competitive and saturated a market, the more difficult it is for a new entrant to achieve sales.

FIGURE 5.4: COOLEY DISTILLERY – ENTERING THE WORLD WHISKEY INDUSTRY

Cooley Distillery was set-up by two Irish entrepreneurs in September 1987 to produce and sell an independent Irish whiskey. Prior to this, the production and sale of Irish whiskey had been monopolised by Irish Distillers Group, owned by the international drinks company, Pernod-Ricard. Despite a long tradition as a whiskey-producing country, Irish whiskey has only a 1% share of the world whiskey market. Under Irish law, whiskey must be matured for three years before it can be called 'Irish whiskey'.

Due to lack of financial resources, Cooley Distillery ceased production of its whiskey in February 1993. Cooley's worsening financial situation persuaded the original investors and management to abandon their dream of creating an independent Irish whiskey brand. John Teeling began negotiations to sell out to Irish Distillers Group. IDG launched a €27.93 million bid for Cooley and publicly announced its intention to close down the company. IDG justified the proposed closure on the grounds that the Cooley Distillery might 'damage the reputation of Irish whiskey' in overseas markets. In March 1994, the Irish Competition Authority blocked the bid on the grounds it was anti-competitive. Teeling put together a €2.41 million rescue package and faced up to the challenge of breaking into the world whiskey market.

As Ireland's only independent Irish Distillery, like its other competitors in this competitive market, Cooley has to be innovative not alone in terms of its business model but also with the introduction of new products. In 2005, Cooley developed its private label business, whereby it acts as the distiller or distributor for existing drinks companies. On the new product front, the company launched in 2006 'Greencore', a single grain Irish whiskey brand and, in partnership with Sidney Frank Importing Co, the 'Michael Collins' Irish whiskey was introduced in a blend and a single malt. Cooley won 12 medals at the 2007 International Wine & Spirits Competition.

'Niche' Market-entry Strategy

A niche market-entry strategy involves the entrepreneur targeting the product / service at specific market segments. The advantages of such a strategy are that the entrepreneur can conserve limited resources and ensure that all attention is given to the chosen market segment. The dangers of a niche strategy are that the entrepreneur may not achieve sufficient sales to support the business and / or the chosen market niche may be too small for the business to survive. The choice of a niche strategy may be a factor that limits the growth of a business in a small domestic market like Ireland. Small Irish businesses may have to become involved in risky and expensive export markets at an early stage.

The entrepreneur should pursue a niche strategy, only if it confers a competitive advantage on the business. Otherwise, a more broadly-based strategy is preferable. For example, the market for carbonated orange drinks is unlikely to be a niche market. Customers do not identify this product as any different from other soft drinks. Competitors supplying a wider range of products – for example, lemon drinks, cola drinks, apple drinks – will have an advantage due to lower overall production, distribution and promotion costs.

'Broad' Market-entry Strategy

The entrepreneur might try to gain a large share of the market from start-up. New businesses such as Apple's iPhone or Disneyland-Paris entered the market with very high market share objectives. The advantage of a broad market-entry strategy is that, if the business is successful, it will be large from the beginning. A broad market-entry strategy is often more attractive to distributors, retailers and consumers, as it suggests that there will be continuity in the business. Most new businesses do not have the resources to pursue such a strategy and therefore start on a small scale. Some new businesses must pursue a broad entry strategy because of the large capital investment required at start-up. A business may pursue a broad market-entry strategy by licensing or franchising the business. Some businesses will out-source manufacturing so that resources can be concentrated on marketing and sales.

COMPETITIVE STRATEGY

Competitive strategy refers to how the new business will compete with existing suppliers of the product / service. A new business must either provide a better service than competitors or the same service at a lower cost. There are numerous ways in which a business can deliver a better service. Many entrepreneurs fail to understand their market and customers and, as a consequence, don't develop a strong competitive advantage. They adopt a 'me-too' strategy. This means that they replicate what has been done before without improving it.

'Lower Cost' Strategy

A 'lower cost' strategy involves offering a product / service to consumers at a price less than competitors. Most entrepreneurs believe that this strategy will be successful. Their logic is that customers should be willing to pay less for the same product / service. The advantage of this strategy is that the new business should be able to attract customers. The lower price should encourage customers to try the product / service and may encourage new customers into the market. To pursue this strategy profitably, the new business must have a lower cost base than competitors. However, this strategy is not that easy to pursue and many entrepreneurs fail to pursue it successfully with the result that the business achieves low profits. There are a number of reasons why this strategy may not work for the small business:

- **Miscalculating costs and overheads:** The entrepreneur may not have identified all of the overheads that the business will incur. Many small businesses achieve lower overheads by operating outside the tax system or by not costing their own time at the market rate. As the business grows, overheads will increase and prices may have to be increased.

- **Customer perceptions:** For many products, the price charged is assumed by customers to be a reflection of the quality of the product. Low prices may be interpreted by customers as a lower quality service rather than as a more efficient supplier. To overcome this problem, it might be necessary for the entrepreneur to inform customers why they are cheaper, for example, 'cheaper because we buy direct from the factory'.

- **Customer requirements:** For many products, customers are more interested in better quality and better service. Increasingly, consumers are prepared to pay premium prices to businesses that will deliver high quality.

- **Failure to advertise:** The entrepreneur may incorrectly assume that a low cost strategy means not investing in marketing and selling costs. The net effect of this is that the customer is unaware of the lower cost alternative and the new business remains small. Many small businesses fail to generate revenues to invest in advertising and promotion because of their low prices and low turnover. Ryanair successfully pursues a low cost strategy by ensuring that the cost of providing its service is minimised, yet it spends heavily on advertising and promotion.

- **Competitor response:** New competitors with lower costs may enter the market. Often, these are overseas competitors that operate in low wage countries or new businesses that do not understand the full cost of operations.

'Better Service' Strategy

A 'better service' strategy involves offering a better product or service to consumers at an acceptable price. There are many ways in which a business may have a better product / service. These include superior product / service performance, faster delivery service, better location, wider product range, personal advice and after-sales service, longer credit terms, more flexible service, personalised attention. It is important that the entrepreneur tries to maximise the number and the extent of these advantages.

This strategy is often not successful for several reasons:

- **Customer requirements:** Often the 'better' product / service that the new business offers is not of value to customers.

- **Poor pricing:** To get the benefits of a better product / service, the new business should be able to charge a similar or higher price. Most new businesses claim that they offer a superior product / service than their competitors. However, despite this better product / service, these businesses will claim that they are also more price-competitive.

- **Poor promotion:** Often new businesses fail to communicate their better product/service to their customers. This may be because promotion, advertising and sales support expenditures are often wrongly considered by the entrepreneur to be a luxury.

STRATEGIES FOR SUCCESS IN IRISH SMEs[13]

This survey of successful Irish companies revealed that they pursue common strategies. The study analysed 131 small and medium-sized manufacturing and services businesses. Success was defined as the ability of the company to grow consistently over a five-year period. The study suggests that those small companies that wish to be successful must pay special attention to the decisions they make with regard to market choice (industry, sector, segment) and competitive strategy. The results of this research suggest that the first key managerial choice is 'where to compete', but that this is followed by a second key choice, which is about 'how to compete'. It is the combination of these that results in success.

Some important implications flow from this:

- Market choice is a critical managerial decision. It is not, however, a choice that is, or can be, subject to frequent change. Market selection will always be constrained by the entrepreneur's experiences.

- The choice of market determines the likelihood of success and growth. If the 'wrong' market is chosen, then success will be limited or unachievable.

- Choosing a growing market is not a sufficient condition for successful growth. Other decisions will influence whether a business achieves success in its market.

Specifically, the study identified a number of competitive and growth strategies. These were:

- **Compete in high growth markets:** Successful companies compete in markets with higher growth rates. The mean growth rate of the successful companies' markets was approximately three times that for low growth companies .

- **Focus on market niches**. The average size of the market that the successful companies competed in was about half the size of the market that the less successful companies competed in. The smaller size of the market competed in is interpreted as an indication of a market niche strategy. However, within these niche markets, the successful companies were more likely to have a wider product range. This was unexpected because it was thought that, as part of their focus strategy, high-growth companies would be characterised by a narrow product range. A possible explanation for this is that the small size of the Irish market requires Irish companies to cover all product options in their niche.

---

[13] See Murray, J. & O'Gorman, C. (1994).

- **Compete on the uniqueness of the product:** Successful companies were more likely to have products that were differentiated from their competitors'.

- **Provide superior product quality and customer service**. Relative to competitors, successful companies were more likely to sell higher quality products and to have a higher customer service reputation.

- **Be innovative**. Innovation was measured by the percentage of a company's sales that came from new products. Relative to their competitors, successful companies had a higher percentage of new products.

- **Build on strengths**. Successful companies grew by emphasising their existing strengths and by developing into related markets.

CONCLUSION

This chapter has highlighted that there are many different ways to become an entrepreneur. However, the problems experienced by many entrepreneurs during the launch of a new business are quite similar. The success of a new business is dependent on identifying a competitive strategy and a market-entry strategy. Many new businesses fail to explicitly develop these strategies and suffer, as a consequence, from low profitability.

QUESTIONS

1. Describe the different ways of becoming an entrepreneur. Illustrate your answer with examples.

2. What problems will a business experience during the launch period? How might an entrepreneur cope with these problems?

3. What market-entry strategies are available to a small business?

5. Why do many small businesses fail to implement their competitive strategy effectively?

6. Identify the reasons for the success of a small business in your locality.

6. In a group, identify the competitive strategies and the competitive advantage of five businesses.

PROFILE: ELAINE COUGHLAN, ATLANTIC BRIDGE VENTURES[14]

Elaine Coughlan, a chartered accountant, spent eight years at Ernst & Young as a senior audit manager specialising in advising SEC-registered clients in the technology sector and handling IPO transactions. She was attracted by the excitement of knowledge-based entrepreneurial companies and decided to leave the relative security of one of the 'Big 5' accountancy firms and to become involved in guiding these young companies to successful growth.

> *I had worked and trained in a large and very traditional organisation which had start-up companies as clients. It became clear to me that the reason entrepreneurial and smaller companies can beat the 'big guys' is that, in those large companies, the decision-making process is like turning around a large ocean liner. Large companies can easily get caught in this static of slow decisions, poor focus and lack of an aggressive 'can do' approach to new markets, products, ideas.*

> *I found these start-up companies, which had deep domain technology and products, much more dynamic and at the coal face of creating 'real' businesses, with real technology. These are the kind of companies that Ireland now aspires to create more of in the knowledge economy.*

Against this background, she went on to accumulate over 13 years' operational experience in technology companies from early stage of development through to exit. She gained extensive mergers / acquisition (M&A) and exit experience having been involved in three successful technology IPOs and secondary market placements, which raised over $1.6 billion in capital for both the companies and investors (IONA Technologies plc, CBT Systems plc and Parthus Technologies plc (CEVA Inc).

> *It was incredibly rewarding to work with some of the smartest engineers creating world-beating products that succeeded on a global scale. And coming from a small country only made the success even more satisfying.*

In May 2000, Elaine played a central role in organising a successful IPO of Parthus Technologies plc. Two years later, upon completion of the $500M merger of Parthus and Israeli-based CEVA Inc., Elaine decided to find a way to apply her accumulated knowledge and experience not just on behalf of one company, but on behalf of many.

---

[14] This profile appeared in Fitzsimons & O'Gorman (2006).

While many others may have been content to rest on the laurels of their past success, Elaine Coughlan, together with Brian Long, Paul Harvey and Kevin Dillon, decided to back their own judgement further and to put together a new venture capital company, Atlantic Bridge Ventures. Elaine is a general partner and CFO of the new venture, with responsibility for finance, treasury, legal and investor relations.

Elaine explains what motivated her and the other founding partners to set up Atlantic Bridge Partners:

> *Given this experience we wanted to do it again – but instead of doing just one successful start-up, we felt that we should invest in many and use our skills and know-how in terms of founding and exiting businesses successfully.*

An integral part of the new VC focus is to add more than finance to its investment portfolio and to leverage the knowledge and experience of the founding partners and management team to deliver strategic and operational value and to adopt a transatlantic approach to building businesses to maximise shareholder value.

Even with the wealth of experience that the founders of the new VC brought to its establishment, it was not without challenges:

> *Starting from zero is both exciting and daunting. It is also a slow process to create meaningful value ... you have to be 'long term greedy'. Given that you start at zero, you have to have confidence and the belief in yourself and your team that you will succeed in the long term. It helps having a team that share the same vision and ethos to get through the tough days and celebrate the successes.*

Elaine cites the founding investors, Enterprise Ireland and her partners in the fund, as offering that very critical support through the early days. Elaine believes a positive attitude and strong resilience to be paramount:

> *It is important never to under-estimate what can be achieved; to expect to get some knock-backs along the way, but to get right back at it; and to persist, irrespective of how tough it sometimes is.*

Even given the rollercoaster ride of a start-up, Elaine Coughlan is adamant that she would do it all over again:

> *There is nothing to beat the feeling of starting a business with a long-term vision of success and having 'wins' after taking risks.*

While she would recommend entrepreneurship to others, she would do so with some caveats, emphasising the importance of getting the fundamentals right:

> *... but it's not for everyone given the risks that people have to take starting off. I think you need a well-thought-out defensible idea and business model and then you need great people ... The entrepreneur can lead, but the really successful ones lead a really great loyal team around them.*

6

THE BUSINESS PLAN

Why should an entrepreneur go to the trouble of writing a business plan? The simple answer is that starting a business is difficult and the entrepreneur must manage a wide range of different activities. The process of preparing a plan forces the entrepreneur to think through the different aspects of the new venture. Having completed the business plan, the entrepreneur should have identified the market opportunity and how it is to be exploited. Specifically, the entrepreneur must develop an entry strategy and a competitive strategy (see **Chapter 5**).

The first part of this chapter discusses why the entrepreneur should write a business plan and details where the entrepreneur should get the required information. This is followed by an outline of the format of a business plan. Each section of the business plan is discussed in detail. **Chapter 7** contains a sample business plan for a restaurant.

WHO WRITES THE BUSINESS PLAN?

The entrepreneur is the person best placed to produce a meaningful plan. By preparing a business plan, the entrepreneur ensures that there is a viable business opportunity. The business plan can reduce the financial and personal risk involved in starting a new business. The entrepreneur is taking the risk and therefore should be involved in the preparation of the business plan. The disadvantage of outsourcing the preparation of the business plan is that the entrepreneur loses out on some of the benefits of engaging in the planning process. Having a real understanding of the marketplace dynamics, the customer profile in terms of usage and buying patterns and insights into competitor market positions provides the entrepreneur with a clear sense of purpose and direction, as well as the optimal business model for market entry.

However, entrepreneurs do not always prepare their own business plan. The preparation of a business plan is a difficult and time-consuming process and many entrepreneurs seek external assistance when preparing one. The entrepreneur may get an outsider to write the complete plan, to prepare the financial information or simply to help gather market information. Where the entrepreneur sees the plan essentially as a document for raising finance or an unnecessary burden imposed by an external financing agency, it is more likely that an outsider will be used.

Some entrepreneurs will pay an outsider to prepare the business plan because they believe they lack the management skills to prepare the plan themselves. In a survey of entrepreneurs who prepared business plans, one entrepreneur explained that at an early stage he used external agents to do some planning for him, because he 'imagined' that there was some skill involved which could only be 'bought in'. However, on seeing the contribution of the external advisors, the entrepreneur prepared all his own plans in future.

FIGURE 6.1: ADVICE ON WRITING A BUSINESS PLAN

◊ Keep the plan short, simple and concise.

◊ Keep your plan focused. Don't be over ambitious at the start.

◊ Forecast sales based on accurate market information.

◊ Justify your claims and avoid unsubstantiated statements, for example, 'there are no competitors', 'this is a huge market', etc.

◊ Use simple language as readers of the business plan may not understand technical jargon. They may question your ability to sell the product if you can't communicate to them.

◊ Don't have surprises. Identify potential problems and name all investors.

WHO READS THE BUSINESS PLAN?

The plan will be read by a variety of people, each of whom may be interested in different aspects of the document. The entrepreneur may use the business plan to raise capital from private investors, financial institutions, venture capitalists and / or State agencies. The plan may be used to attract a potential business partner or key staff into the business, or to gain credibility with potential customers and suppliers. Therefore, the plan needs to be comprehensive enough to address each of their particular concerns. Some entrepreneurs prepare separate plans for themselves and for external readers of the plan. The 'internal' document might address issues that the entrepreneur believes are best kept secret from potential investors and lenders. A list of people who are likely to read the plan is outlined in **Figure 6.2**.

FIGURE 6.2: READERS & THEIR INTEREST IN THE BUSINESS PLAN

Lending institutions, State agencies and venture capitalists:
◊   Funding requirement; cash flow projections; proposed market; level of risk involved; costings and pricing; financial viability; industry structure and competition; entrepreneurs' experience.

Customers
◊   Quality; product functionality; after-sales service; warranties; product range.

Senior managers / Business partners
◊   Required equity investment; pay structure; levels of responsibilities; promotion prospects.

WHERE TO GET THE INFORMATION

When preparing a business plan, the entrepreneur must identify the critical pieces of information required to evaluate the market and plan the business. The entrepreneur should identify what information will be needed, where this information can be sourced, and how this information is to be analysed and presented in the business plan. The most difficult information to identify is the size of the potential market and the position of competitors in the market. **Figure 6.3** lists the principal information that the entrepreneur will have to collect.

FIGURE 6.3: PRINCIPAL INFORMATION REQUIREMENTS

◊　Market size, industry sector size.

◊　A demographic profile of the target market/customers.

◊　Trends in market, technology, consumers' tastes and preferences.

◊　Competitor profiling: number, size, strengths and weaknesses.

◊　Profitability in the sector.

◊　Barriers to entry.

◊　Pricing policies, promotion and advertising practices.

◊　Proposed location: size, facilities, rents and activity patterns.

◊　Appropriate channels of distribution.

The most important source of information for many entrepreneurs is their personal experience of working in the sector. Information is central to making a decision on whether there is a viable business opportunity and how best this opportunity can be exploited. The process of gathering information and evaluating a business opportunity is often unsystematic and haphazard. Most entrepreneurs will use their contacts in business to gather specific pieces of information they may need and to get advice on their proposed business

An entrepreneur may use secondary sources of data to get background information on the sector. This is common when the entrepreneur is new to the business and when the concept is new. Secondary data can be gathered from published reports, newspapers, specialist / trade magazine articles, and statistics that have been compiled by other people for a variety of purposes. These sources should be used by the entrepreneur to identify past and current trends and events in the business sector. The information obtained from secondary sources is often limited due to its broad nature. **Figure 6.4** lists the sources of secondary information.

FIGURE 6.4: SOURCES OF SECONDARY INFORMATION

◊ Local and university libraries.
◊ Government and EU agencies.
◊ Enterprise Boards – www.enterpriseboards.ie.
◊ The Companies Registration Office – www.cro.ie.
◊ Central Statistics Office – www.cso.ie – and Eurostat – epp.eurostat.ec.europa.eu.
◊ Chambers of Commerce – www.chambers.ie.
◊ Trade Associations and Journals.
◊ Websites (OECD, World Bank, *The Economist,* etc).

Once the entrepreneur has built up a picture of what is happening in the particular market, primary sources of information may be used. Primary sources of information are gathered by going out to talk to the various players in the market place, such as competitors, customers, suppliers, experts, etc. Some funding sources require entrepreneurs to undertake an in-depth market validation exercise, whereby they socialise the product / service offering with potential customers. In doing so, the entrepreneur gets a real insight into the buying behaviours of potential customers, and an understanding of competing products / services.

So how should the entrepreneur approach this task? The entrepreneur should speak directly with potential customers and, where possible, get a commitment to buy from the new business. Commitments from customers can help the entrepreneur persuade an investor to invest or lend money to the new business. The entrepreneur should visit competitors and collect material about their product / service. This may be possible by attending a trade fair and by pretending to be a potential customer. Some entrepreneurs work in the particular industry to gain valuable experience in order to fully understand the operations of a business, and then start-up their venture. Industry experts can offer some valuable overviews on the developments within specific sectors.

THE BUSINESS PLAN

FIGURE 6.5: TABLE OF CONTENTS OF A BUSINESS PLAN

1. **Executive Summary**
   1.1 Principals involved in the Venture
   1.2 The Product / Service
   1.3 Target Market
   1.4 Level of Profitability
   1.5 Funding Requirement & Return on Investment

2. **Description of the Product/Service**

3. **Industry & Competitor Analysis**
   3.1 Political, Economic, Social & Technological Trends
   3.2 Market Opportunities & Threats
   3.3 Industry Structure
   3.4 Competitor Profiles

4. **Marketing Plan**
   4.1 Market Size & Market Segments
   4.2 Customer Profile & Behaviour
   4.3 Market Research
   4.4 Marketing Strategy
      Positioning Strategy / Pricing Strategy / Distribution Strategy / Promotion & Sales Strategy / Service & Quality Strategy
   4.5 Estimated Sales

5. **Production Plan**
   5.1 Location
   5.2 Production Process & Facility Layout
   5.3 Equipment Requirements & Costs
   5.4 Sources of Raw Materials
   5.5 Cost of Production, Warehousing & Transport
   5.6 Legal Requirements

6. **Human Resources & Organisational Structure**
   6.1 CVs of Entrepreneurs & Senior Management
   6.2 Managerial Responsibilities & Reporting Structures
   6.3 Staffing & Skills Requirements
   6.4 Employment & Labour Legislation

7. **Financial Plan**
   7.1 Cash Flow Forecast
   7.2 Profit and Loss Accounts
   7.3 Balance Sheets & Funding Sources
   7.4 Break-even Analysis & Return on Investment

8. **Critical Risks**

9. **Start-Up Schedule**

10. **Appendices**

EXECUTIVE SUMMARY

This is the first section of the business plan and it should be short and concise. The executive summary outlines the opportunity for the venture, why the opportunity exists and how the entrepreneurial team intends to exploit this opportunity. It should describe the proposed business and justify how the business will achieve its sales targets. The executive summary should outline the funding requirements and the expected return on the required investment. This is crucially important, as it is the first part that a banker or investor will read. Prospective investors will read the summary quickly to determine whether the venture is of interest and may decide to read no further. Consequently, the layout, format and presentation of the executive summary are crucial. The summary is usually the last section of the business plan to be written.

DESCRIPTION OF BUSINESS

This section of the business plan should outline in detail the business that the entrepreneur proposes to start. This is important because outsiders may not have the background knowledge or be as familiar with the concept as the entrepreneur. Often entrepreneurs fail to explain their ideas in a comprehensive manner because they wrongly assume that others will quickly grasp the business idea. This description should enable the reader of the plan to ascertain the size and scope of the venture, the proposed product/service that will be offered, where the business will be located, who will purchase the product and why they choose this service in preference to alternatives. If appropriate, the entrepreneur should include a sample of the product – for example, a copy of the menu for a restaurant business.

INDUSTRY & COMPETITOR ANALYSIS

In this section, the entrepreneur analyses the factors impacting on the growth and development of the target market and the competitors currently operating in the market. The purpose of this analysis is to assess the attractiveness of the target market and to identify any constraints or pressures that may exist. The entrepreneur should understand the factors that are driving the growth and development of the market. The analysis of competitors should identify their current market position and their competitive strengths.

Having completed an industry and competitor analysis, the entrepreneur should be able to answer the following questions:

- Why does this opportunity exist?
- What threats does the new business face?
- What determines the level of profitability in the industry?

- Who are the competitors and what position have they adopted?
- The size of the market and the potential sales of the new business.

There are a number of models the entrepreneur might use to structure this analysis. These techniques include STEP analysis, SWOT analysis, Porter's Five Forces model and Competitor Profiling. In using these models, the entrepreneur must be pragmatic. The models are tools to assist the entrepreneur in answering questions about the business opportunity and the strategy the new business should pursue. The entrepreneur must not become over-involved in analysis, as this may delay decision-making. Undertaking an industry and competitor analysis can be a time-consuming process. The difficulties that an entrepreneur may face in undertaking such an analysis are outlined in **Figure 6.6**.

FIGURE 6.6: PROBLEMS IN UNDERTAKING AN INDUSTRY ANALYSIS

◊ **Defining industry boundaries incorrectly**: An entrepreneur might fail to define the firm's industry and its boundaries properly.

◊ **Poor identification of competitors**: The venture might concentrate on local competition and ignore national or international competitors.

◊ **Poor definition of invisible capabilities**: This is where the firm fails to focus on competitors' intangible resources. Some of these invisible factors may account for competitors' success in a given market.

◊ **Paralysis by analysis**: This is where a venture carries out thorough analysis, but this thoroughness and striving to gain more information to reduce the uncertainty may mean the venture does not make any decisions in relation to its own operations.

◊ **Inaccurate assumptions about competition**: The venture makes certain assumptions about competitors' operations. These assumptions may not be substantiated and may be inaccurate.

◊ **Getting information**: The entrepreneur may not have the time or resources to gather the information required to start-up the venture.

STEP Analysis

The STEP (Social, Technical, Economic, Political) model assists the entrepreneur in thinking about the broader issues that have created the new business opportunity. The output of a STEP analysis should be the key factors that have created the market opportunity and a listing of the key external factors that will impact on new business – for example:

- **Social factors**: The business plan should highlight the social factors that have created this opportunity and which explain the nature of demand in the market place. Factors such as population size, demographic structures, type of lifestyles, the culture and values of the population and the degree of segmentation in the market are of particular importance. The changing demographic profile of the Irish population is creating a number of opportunities, for example, private third level colleges and health services for the elderly.

- **Technological factors**: The entrepreneur should assess how technological developments will impact on the development of this market. These developments may create an opportunity for the entrepreneur. Additionally, the entrepreneur must identify what are the minimal technological requirements of the venture. Technological developments have created opportunities for new businesses, such as Irish businesses selling shamrocks, holidays, and electrical goods over the Internet.

- **Economic factors**: Economic factors may limit the potential of the proposed venture. Issues such as inflation rates, spending patterns, consumer confidence, strength of national currency, interest rates, sustainability of current economic activity, must be examined. Ultimately, these factors will affect how much capital the business can afford to borrow. In times of growing economic prosperity and higher incomes, there are opportunities for new luxury and high quality products.

- **Political factors**: Political and legal factors may create opportunities or difficulties for the proposed business. For example, the decision by the European Union to deregulate the airline industry created the opportunity conditions that lead to the establishment of Ryanair.

SWOT Analysis

SWOT is an acronym for Strengths, Weaknesses, Opportunities and Threats. Opportunities are the factors in the external environment that the new business will act on. These might be changes in consumer tastes and preferences that mean that consumers are demanding a new product. Threats are the external factors that may impact negatively on the new business. They could be the level of competition or changes in technology. The strengths and weaknesses refer to the new business itself. Strengths and weaknesses are internally-focused, whereas opportunities and threats are externally-focused. Strengths are things that the new venture will do well – for example, the experience of the entrepreneur, access to a prime retail location, access to an overseas supplier, etc. Weaknesses are areas in which the new venture will be at a competitive disadvantage.

Porter's Five Forces

Porter's (1985) Five Forces Model identifies the competitive nature of the industry. The factors in this model explain the level of profitability in the industry and who has the competitive strength. There are five key areas to consider when undertaking an industry analysis:

- **Competition:** This is at the heart of the model and is concerned with the nature and the level of rivalry among existing competitors, the number of competitors and the level of differentiation in the industry.

- **Suppliers:** What is the power of suppliers to the industry? Usually, if there is a smaller number of suppliers or if they have some scarce resource, they will be in a more powerful position and will be able to charge higher prices.

- **Buyers:** What is the power of buyers in the industry? Buyer power increases as they learn more about a product. An example of this is that PCs have become commodity-type purchases as people become more knowledgeable about them. When buyers are concentrated relative to suppliers, for example, supermarkets relative to many small companies, they tend to be more powerful.

- **Potential entrants:** The ease of entry into a market affects overall profitability levels in an industry. Industries that have high barriers to entry tend to be more profitable. Barriers to entry include the need for large scale (in cement manufacturing), the need to invest in building a brand image (in the drinks industry), and access to distribution (in the motor fuels industry).

- **Substitutes:** Are there substitute products for the current product or service? Substitute products are not competitive products but products that could potentially compete if prices fell or if performance increased. For example, plasma televisions are still more expensive than existing televisions, although prices are dropping fast. As the technology develops and costs reduce further, these televisions will compete directly with existing products.

As an example of Porter's model, consider the soft drinks industry. The soft drinks industry is very profitable. Strong brands place the soft drinks manufacturers in a strong position relative to retailers, as the retailer must stock a brand such as Coca-Cola in order to satisfy customers. Suppliers to the soft drinks are not important as the raw materials of water, sugar and flavouring are readily available. The large investment necessary to build up a brand image and to get access to distribution channels reduces the threat of new entrants and reduces overall competition. There are no obvious substitute products. Competition is predominately based on marketing; Pepsi and Coke avoid price competition, where possible. All of these factors help to maintain profitability for producers of branded soft drinks. However this is a dynamic situation and the introduction of Virgin Cola and 'quality' own label soft drinks by retailers such as Sainsbury's in the UK, Dunne's Stores in Ireland and other leading retailers has changed the nature of competition and the attractiveness of the business.

Competitor Profiling

This involves assessing the other competitors in the target market. The entrepreneur should profile each competitor on the following:

- Size and market share position.
- Competitive strategy.
- Strengths and weaknesses.

- Image and reputation.
- Assumptions regarding how the industry operates.
- Financial position.

An important aspect of industry and competitor analysis is an analysis of competitors' intangible resources. These resources may be essential to competitive success. Examples of intangible resources are:

- Trade marks.
- Patents.
- Copyright.
- Registered designs.
- Contracts.
- Trade secrets.
- Reputation.
- Networks.

MARKETING PLAN

Having analysed the industry and competitors, the entrepreneur must estimate the size of the market and the level of sales that the new business can expect to achieve in the first three years of business. This is the most difficult part of a business plan. The level of sales that the business achieves will determine the overall viability of the venture. The sales forecasts for the new business should be based on the understanding of the factors determining demand and the competitors in the industry. For some business opportunities, there are no existing competitors or sales. This makes the task of estimating demand even more difficult. One solution is to identify a broadly similar business and estimate their sales. The remaining sections of the business plan and the financing of the business are based on these estimated sales. Estimates of market size and potential sales should be checked by talking to potential customers.

The marketing plan should outline the overall marketing strategy of the new business. The plan should answer the following questions:

- Who will buy the product / service?
- What do they want?
- How do they decide?
- Where do they buy?
- When do they buy?
- Why do they buy?

To answer these questions, the entrepreneur will need to decide who the target market is, what benefits the product / service offers, the price of the product / service, how it will be advertised, and how the product will be distributed.

The marketing plan is regarded as a critical element to the success of the new venture. Therefore, the entrepreneur has to ensure that the overall marketing strategy can be effectively implemented.

Price

The entrepreneur has to decide what price should be charged for the product / service. A number of factors should be considered when determining the price of the product:

- The price of competing products.
- The cost of producing the product / service.
- The level of profitability needed to repay investors and to reward the entrepreneur.
- The expectations of consumers.
- The image of the product.
- The mark-up that wholesalers, distributors and retailers will take.

Product pricing is a difficult process and, in many small businesses, the entrepreneur will not know the actual costs associated with the manufacture of products. The number of units produced will determine the cost per unit and the entrepreneur will not know what level of sales will be achieved. In order to introduce the product onto the market, the entrepreneur may have to use discounts to encourage consumers and retailers to try the product. Many entrepreneurs undercharge for their products, assuming that price is the most important purchasing criterion and the only source of competitive advantage. Some small businesses have increased profitability by increasing prices. This may result in lower sales but satisfied customers may continue to support the business.

Sales Methods

The entrepreneur has to decide what sales tactics will be used. Some of the options include:

- Direct selling by the entrepreneur.
- Employing a sales team.
- Using telephone or direct mailing.
- Using an agent.

The sales method chosen will have a direct impact on the cost-base of the firm, the level of service and quality delivered to customers and the degree of market penetration that will be achieved.

Promotion

How will the venture try to gain the attention of prospective purchasers? This element of the plan should outline which promotional media the entrepreneur intends to use. The options include local / national radio, newspapers, TV, online, direct mail shots, trade shows, advertisements in trade / industry magazines and sponsorship. The choice of media will depend on the customers being targeted. The plan should outline the entrepreneur's plans to develop promotional materials. This element of the marketing plan should outline the media to be used, the costs of this promotion and a schedule for the promotion and advertising campaign.

Distribution Channels

This section of the plan outlines where the product will be sold and the number of companies or individuals who are to be used to distribute it. The entrepreneur will have to decide whether the product will be sold directly to the customer or through a channel. An important consideration is the image of the product / service. The two over-riding considerations for the entrepreneur are the level of customer convenience and the efficiency of the distribution channel.

Customer Care

The venture has to establish a procedure for generating and dealing with customer enquiries. The entrepreneur should have some system for ensuring customers are satisfied with their purchases. Often, this can be done informally by talking to customers.

In addition, the venture may provide an after-sales service to customers such as a warranty or guarantee. The entrepreneur has to consider what competitors offer in terms of warranties and after-sales service and to decide whether he / she is going to offer the same or additional warranties. The entrepreneur should also consider whether the company will charge customers a call-out fee for this service or whether the cost of the service should be included in the price of the product.

PRODUCTION PLAN

If the proposed business is going to manufacture a product, a production plan is necessary.

For service businesses, the entrepreneur should prepare a plan of how the service will be delivered to customers. For example, a service business such as a café must make decisions about location, layout, scheduling, etc.

The key decisions that must be made are as follows:

- **Location**: For service businesses, location is often one of the most important decisions. In sectors such as retailing, hotels and catering, the location of the business may determine its ultimate success. The entrepreneur is in the difficult situation that resources are scare and the rental and lease costs of prime locations may be prohibitive. However, choosing a less attractive location may result in less passing trade. The location of a manufacturing business should be decided by the geographical location of suppliers and customers. The plan should outline the size of the location and the local infrastructure facilities.

- **Production process**: The entrepreneur should describe the production process and include an illustration of the production flow. The entrepreneur should consider whether it is essential to manufacture the product or whether the production process could be subcontracted to another firm. In addition, the current capacity levels should be calculated.

- **Equipment requirements**: The entrepreneur needs to identify the capital equipment required to produce the product or deliver the service. The entrepreneur might use new or second-hand equipment and may consider leasing some equipment to reduce the capital needed at start-up. The suppliers of the necessary equipment should be identified and the cost of production and installation should be calculated.

- **Sources of raw materials**: The quality of the goods and service bought-in by the business impacts on the quality of the finished product. Effective procurement of goods and services helps to maintain quality and to control costs. The raw materials required to produce the product / service should be identified and, where possible, agreements be made with suppliers. Suppliers may be slow to offer credit terms to a new business.

- **Cost of production**: The cost of production should be calculated. These costs should be broken down into key elements such as materials, labour, and overheads. Costs should be divided into fixed costs and variable costs. Fixed costs are constant and include items such as rent and rates, heating and light, etc. Variable costs depend on the level of production and include raw materials, direct labour required to produce the product.

- **Warehousing costs**: The entrepreneur has to consider the provisions for storage of the in-bound raw materials and the finished product and their movements. Basic warehousing breaks down into four operations: receiving the goods into the warehouse; transferring the goods from point of entry to the appropriate location in the warehouse; selecting the particular combinations of goods for customer order or raw materials for the production cycles; and preparing the goods for shipment to the customer.

- **Transport costs**: Transport costs can be a significant expense and can impact on the efficiency of the logistics operation, operating costs and demand for the product / service. The selection of a carrier is more than a basic procurement decision that involves evaluating the cost structures of various transportation types. Other factors that must be considered are inventory levels due to transit times; warehouse and facility design; dependability of mode of transport; handling damage via each type; cost of tracking shipments; and impact on facilities operating costs.

- **Quality issues**: The entrepreneur must consider how quality is to be maintained. In some industries, customers will require suppliers to have some form of quality accreditation such as ISO 9000. The entrepreneur needs to set out the quality standards that are applicable at all stages of the manufacturing and selling process.

- **Legal issues**: When setting up a manufacturing operation, the venture is likely to have to meet many legal requirements. These include environmental approval, health permits, planning permission, etc.

HUMAN RESOURCES & ORGANISATIONAL STRUCTURE

This section of the business plan should identify the management and staff requirements of the new business. It should detail who will be responsible for the different areas of activity in the business. Staff costs and remuneration levels for all employees should be calculated.

The organisational plan should contain the following information:

- **Management**: This should include CVs of the people who will hold key management positions. In addition, information regarding their duties and responsibilities, level of remuneration such as profit sharing, stock options and other bonus schemes, and employment contract periods should be included.

- **Staff recruitment, selection and training**: The number of employees needed and how these will be hired. If training is necessary, the entrepreneur should have a plan for this.

- **Board of Directors**: This should include information about the size and composition of the board. The advantage of a board of directors is that it provides a relatively cheap form of expert advice to the business. Also, external directors might provide the business with useful contacts. Enterprise Ireland and the County & City Enterprise Boards (the two key State agencies supporting start-ups) have recognised the advantages that outside advisors can give a business and have set up mentor schemes for small businesses. The mentor meets with the owner-manager about eight times a year and provides advice and a 'sounding board' for ideas the entrepreneur may have.

- **Employment and labour legislation**: It is essential that the entrepreneur is aware of the legal rights of employees and the processes that must be followed when hiring and dismissing employees. No matter what type of business the venture operates, it will have to comply with certain health and safety regulations. Every organisation is obliged under law to produce a health and safety statement for the workplace.

- **Legal forms of ownership**: The entrepreneur has to decide on a legal form for the business. The entrepreneur will also have to register the name of the business with the Registry of Business Names if the entrepreneur wants to trade under a name other than their own.

FIGURE 6.7: LEGAL FORMS OF BUSINESS OWNERSHIP

Sole Trader

This is a where an individual trades on their own account and there is no separation between the business and the individual. The advantage of this form of ownership is that there are minimal set-up costs and legal requirements. The risks are that the owner is personally liable for all debts the business incurs.

Partnerships

A partnership is a formal relationship between persons carrying on business in common with a view to a profit. Different partners usually bring various elements, such as experience and finance, to the business. The Partnership Agreement should deal with such matters as management of the partnership, termination of the agreement, division of profits and the level of remuneration of different partners. The advantages of a partnership is that it is relatively cheap and easy to set up and there is limited regulation. The disadvantage is that there is unlimited joint and several liability, which means not only that the partners could be liable for the debts of the business but that each partner could be liable for the entire debts of the business. Partnerships are common among professionals such as lawyers, doctors, and accountants. They are not used in most other businesses.

Limited Liability Company

Most companies are privately owned. The cost of formation can range from about €380 for an 'off the shelf' company to about €800 for one set up for a particular business. The other type of company is a public company. The shares of some public companies can be bought and sold by the public on the Stock Exchange. Every limited company has the following:

◊ **Memorandum of Association**: This outlines the type of business the company will operate.

◊ **Articles of Association**: This governs the internal running of the company.

◊ **A Minute book**: This records the meetings of the board of directors.

◊ **A Company Seal**: This is stamped on official company documents.

◊ **A Certificate of Incorporation**: This is issued by the Registrar of Companies.

The advantage of this legal form is that the owners are not liable for the debts of the business. The business is a separate legal entity. Ownership can be transferred easily and losses can be carried forward and offset against profits in prosperous years. There are many tax advantages to having a company. The downside is that there are many formalities to comply with such as filing annual returns of accounts to the Companies Registration Office.

FINANCIAL PLAN

This is probably the most critical section of the business plan. The finance section demonstrates the financial viability of the business and the level of investment required. The finance section is a financial summary of the decisions made in all the other parts of the business plan. It is important that the figures included in the finance plan are explained and that the reader understands the assumptions that the entrepreneur has made. Many entrepreneurs may find it difficult to prepare financial accounts and may employ an accountant to help them. The finance plan provides potential investors with a way of evaluating the attractiveness of the business. It also provides the entrepreneur with a set of budgets for controlling and monitoring the performance of the business during its first few years.

In writing a business plan, the entrepreneur's objective is to persuade potential investors that the business is a good investment. In raising equity finance, the entrepreneur must demonstrate the ability of the business to grow so that the investor will make a capital gain. When trying to raise loan finance, the entrepreneur must demonstrate the ability of the business to repay the loan. When raising finance from a bank, the entrepreneur must realise that the bank will often have an 'informational' advantage from previous experience of lending to similar ventures and, therefore, will be able to check whether the financial projections are realistic.

Cash management and financial control over the operations of the new business will be critical to the success of the venture. Financial statements are used to measure the current and future health of the business. The basic statements that the entrepreneur will use are cash flow forecasts, the profit and loss account and the balance sheet. One of the objectives of these statements is to demonstrate to the principals of the business how their investment capital is being used. In addition, the venture may have to produce audited statements that have to be filed under the Companies Acts.

The finance plan should include *pro forma* or forecast cash flows, profit and loss accounts and balance sheets. Additionally, it should calculate the return on investment the investor will receive and the level of sales necessary to break even.

It is essential to outline what reporting procedures the venture will put in place and what actions will be undertaken if there are budget overruns.

The entrepreneur must deal with the issue of taxation. The new business will have obligations to collect and pay taxes. The more important taxes a business must deal with are VAT, PAYE, PRSI, and tax on profits. There is a tendency for many start-up businesses to put taxation issues on the 'long finger'. It is strongly advisable that tax affairs be in order from the outset.

The Cash Flow Statement

The cash flow statement determines the demands on cash on a monthly basis and is essentially a forecast of the best estimate of all receipts and payments. This is the most important element of the finance plan. Most new businesses fail because they run out of cash. In some cases, new businesses are more successful than forecast. This is not always a good thing, since, if the business grows faster than expected, it will need additional funds to finance stock, debtors and other items at the rate at which the business is growing. Failure to manage cash and raise additional funds may result in financial difficulties.

The statement should provide a picture of the timing and amount of cash receipts and payments. This statement is only concerned with cash flow and no allowance is made for items such as depreciation. Cash forecasting should be done monthly over a 12-month period. Budgets should be compared to actual receipts and payments on every month. Some ventures may find large discrepancies between receipts and payments and, therefore, will have to prepare weekly cash flow statements.

In preparing a cash flow statement, there are three elements: preparing receipts, preparing payments and comparing the two forecasts to discover whether there is a surplus or a deficit during each period:

- **Cash receipts**: The accuracy of this element of the statement will depend on the reliability of the sales forecast. The entrepreneur must allow for delay in receiving payment for credit sales.

- **Cash payments**: This element of the statement includes all payments such as wages, light, heat, telephone, interest, taxation and loan repayments for that period, be it a month or a week.

- **Cash surplus / deficit**: The cash receipts minus the cash payments should reveal whether the firm has a cash surplus or deficit.

The Profit & Loss Account

This is a forecast of the business's sales and expenses and the resulting profit / loss for the period. This is usually calculated on a yearly basis but the entrepreneur should prepare quarterly profit and loss statements for the first year of the new business.

The profit and loss account can be divided into five broad headings:

- **Gross and net sales for the period**: The differences between the two figures arise as a result of discounts, allowances and returns.

- **Cost of goods sold**: This figure is the cost of producing the sales. The balancing figure between net sales and cost of goods sold is the gross profit / loss for the period.

- **Selling and distribution expenses**: These are estimated and deducted.

- **Administration, general and interest costs**: These are estimated and deducted.

- **Adjustments to the final net profit / loss**: Net profit / loss is gross profit / loss less expenses. This figure may need to be adjusted for tax and dividend payments.

The Balance Sheet

This is a statement of all assets and liabilities that a business has on a particular day. This is usually calculated on a yearly basis but the entrepreneur should prepare quarterly balance sheets for the first year of the new business. The balance sheet outlines the sources of funds the business will use. This statement is like a photograph, as it shows the financial position of the business on a given day, and it reflects the past rather than the future. The items in the balance sheet will be grouped into assets, liabilities and a 'financed by' section:

- **Assets**: These are the resources that the venture currently hold and can be classified into the following categories:
  ◊ **Current / liquid assets:** These assets can be converted into cash within a 12-month period.
  ◊ **Fixed assets:** These are usually the permanent facilities of the business that are used to produce the product / service. There is a further classification into tangible fixed assets, which include land, equipment, vehicles and buildings, and intangible fixed assets, which include goodwill, patents, trademarks and copyrights. Due to the fact that the assets are being used over the period, part of the income is set aside in the accounts — this is known as depreciation. The objective of depreciation is to spread the cost of the asset over its useful life.

- **Liabilities**: These are sums of money that the venture owes to others and they are grouped into the following categories:
  ◊ **Current liabilities:** Creditors, short-term loans and bank overdrafts.
  ◊ **Long-term liabilities:** This covers all the liabilities payable in more than 12 months.
  ◊ **Contingent liabilities:** These only appear in accounts in exceptional cases, for example if the venture is involved in legal proceeds and gives some form of guarantee.

- **'Financed By'**: The principals' interest in the firm can be calculated by its net worth, that is, all assets minus all liabilities. This is usually presented in a 'Financed By' or a 'Net Worth' section of the balance sheet, comprising:
  ◊ **Issued share capital:** This is capital / funds that have been raised from the principals of the venture.
  ◊ **Reserves:** This covers the profits that have not been paid out in dividends to investors or any surpluses that have accumulated as a result of the re-valuing of assets.
  ◊ **Share premium account:** This shows the premium, if any, that has been paid by investors to purchase further equity holding in the venture in the form of shares.

Break-Even & Profitability Analysis

The entrepreneur should calculate the level of sales necessary to achieve break-even and the number of months that it will take before break-even is achieved (**Figure 6.8**). The entrepreneur should do a sensitivity analysis on all figures.

FIGURE 6.8: BREAK-EVEN ANALYSIS

$$\text{Break-even} = \frac{\text{Fixed costs}}{\text{Contribution margin}} = \frac{\text{Fixed costs}}{\text{Price less Variable cost per unit}}$$

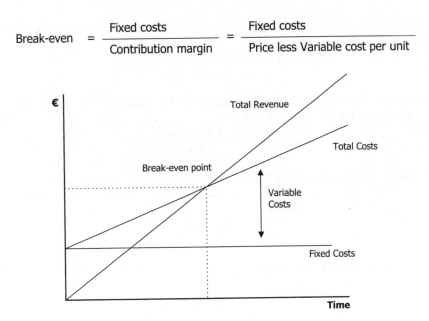

Interpretation of Financial Accounts

Another element of the financial plan should be information on the returns that have, or that will be, achieved by the business. Profitability can be calculated in a number of ways, such as return on sales and return on investment. The figures used to calculate the various profitability figures come from the balance sheet and the profit and loss statements.

Ratio analysis involves comparing one figure against another to calculate a ratio. This calculation of a ratio then is used to assess the venture's current financial strengths and weaknesses. Venture capitalists, potential investors and other stakeholders use financial ratios to assess how the business is performing. These ratios may be used to compare it over time or to other businesses in the same sector.

The broad categories of ratios are profitability, investment, short- and long-term liquidity and gearing ratios (**Figure 6.9**). Under each category, a number of ratios can be calculated.

FIGURE 6.9: RATIOS

◊ **Rate of Return of Capital Employed**: This ultimately indicates the success or failure of the business:

$$\frac{\text{Net profit before interest and tax}}{\text{Capital employed}}$$

◊ **Return on Shareholders' Investment**: This is another measure of the return on shareholders investment:

$$\frac{\text{Net profit before tax}}{\text{Share capital and reserves}}$$

◊ **Gross Profit as a Percentage of Sales**: This indicates the percentage of sales remaining after paying for the cost of goods sold. Obviously the higher the percentage/margin the better:

$$\frac{\text{Gross Profit}}{\text{Sales}} \quad X \quad 100$$

◊ **Net Profit as a Percentage of Sales**: This indicates the percentage margin of profit left after all the costs have been deducted from net sales:

$$\frac{\text{Net Profit}}{\text{Sales}} \quad X \quad 100$$

◊ **Current Ratio**: This compares the liquid (turned into cash within twelve months) assets with the liabilities due in the same period. A ratio in excess of 1 should be acceptable.

$$\frac{\text{Current Assets}}{\text{Current Liabilities}}$$

◊ **Acid Test Ratio**: This assess whether the business has sufficient liquid resources to meet its current liabilities.

$$\frac{\text{Current Assets} - \text{Stock}}{\text{Current Liabilities}}$$

◊ **Interest Cover**: This should indicate whether the venture has enough earnings to pay its interest costs after tax and interest. An interest cover of 2 times or less would be low and in excess of 3 times would be considered acceptable.

$$\frac{\text{Profit before Interest \& Tax}}{\text{Interest Charges}}$$

◊ **Turnover of Stock**: This indicates how long stock is held before it is sold. If the level of stock turnover is slowing down this may mean that stocks are piling up. Average Stock is opening stock plus closing stock divided by two.

$$\frac{\text{Cost of Sales}}{\text{Average Stock}}$$

◊ **Debtor Days**: This indicates how long it takes for debtors to pay.

$$\frac{\text{Debtors X 360}}{\text{Credit Sales}}$$

◊ **Creditor Days**: This indicates how long the business takes before paying creditors.

$$\frac{\text{Creditors x 360}}{\text{Credit Purchases}}$$

◊ **Capital Gearing**: A venture that is financed by a high level of borrowings is highly-geared. One with low levels of borrowings is lowly-geared. The level of gearing can have an impact on the amount of capital that the business can raise in the future.

$$\frac{\text{Preference shares + long term loans}}{\text{All shareholder's funds + long term loans}} \text{ X } 100$$

CRITICAL RISKS

In this section, the entrepreneur should identify and outline the key risks associated with the new business. These may be external events that the business has no control over. The entrepreneur should outline how the business might cope with these external shocks. Not to include these problems in the business plan runs the risk of losing credibility with potential investors. An investor who is aware of a potential problem or risk, and finds no mention of this in the plan, may lose confidence in the ability of the entrepreneur. An example of a potential problem is over-dependence on a small number of customers, a common situation for small food manufacturers that sell to the large retail multiples.

START-UP SCHEDULE

In this section, the entrepreneur should outline the timing of the start-up. Key events are prototype development, securing funding, locating premises, hiring staff, making the first sale, receiving the first customer cheque, etc. The entrepreneur may include a flow chart of these events. Failure to manage this schedule is a common problem for start-ups. Delays in starting can be very costly for a new business, as they usually mean increased expenditures and a longer time before revenues flow into the business.

APPENDICES

The appendices of the plan usually contain back-up material that is not necessary to the main text of the document, including items such as letters of intent from distributors, customers, suppliers and subcontractors. Documentation gathered from primary and secondary sources used to support the plans may also be included.

CONCLUSION

The preparation of a business plan by an entrepreneur involves a systematic analysis of the business idea. It should provide the reader with an easily accessible assessment of the feasibility of the business idea and a detailed account of how the business will operate.

Writing a business plan may require the entrepreneur to analyse the nature of the industry and the strengths and weaknesses of competitors. It should contain a detailed analysis of the market – explaining how the product / service will meet the needs of customers. The plan also should provide extensive operational detail on how the product / service will be produced, how the new business will promote the product / service to customers and how the business will be staffed. All these factors should feed into detailed financial projections for the new business. For each figure provided in the financial projections, there should be a clear explanation of the evidence and / or assumptions behind it (for example, quotes from suppliers, letters of commitment from customers, etc.).

The plan should be used by the entrepreneur as a guide to the company's day-to-day operations. The entrepreneur can enhance the effective implementation of the plan by putting in place monitoring and control procedures that can be used to assess progress on an ongoing basis. Key control elements that should be monitored closely are sales, costs, inventory and quality. Corrective action should be taken if there are major deviations from the plan and the budgets. The plan should be updated on regular basis as conditions change.

QUESTIONS

1. Outline the essential information that should be contained in a business plan.

2. Write a report for an entrepreneur outlining the content of the marketing section of the business plan. How does the marketing plan impact on the finance plan?

3. Identify the information required to prepare a business plan for a new business that will supply a cheese product to the retail multiples. Where would you source this information?

4. Use the STEP and Porter models to analyse one of the following industries:

    ◊ The 3G mobile telecom market in Ireland
    ◊ The hotel sector of the tourism industry
    ◊ Online recruitment industry

8. Choose a local industry and carry out a Competitor Profile of the leading competitors.

9. An investor has asked you to analyse the accounts of the Riverside Café Business Plan (**Chapter 7**). Write a report for the investor and make a recommendation on whether the Riverside Café is a good investment opportunity. (Use the ratios in **Figure 6.9**, where appropriate.)

10. Prepare a Start-up Schedule for a new service business.

11. In a group, identify a business opportunity and prepare a business plan to raise the necessary capital from a financial institution.

PROFILE: FERGAL BRODER, LOTUS AUTOMATION[15]

The best piece of business advice that Fergal Broder, founder of Lotus Automation, got was 'Why not got out on a limb? That's where all the fruit is.' (*The Irish Times*, 2006). Lotus Automation provides solutions for industrial calibration, automation and engineering services to a range of industry sectors worldwide, including pharmaceutical, medical devices, semi-conductor, oil and gas, food and beverage and waste water. Lotus Automation has grown from three employees in the start-up office in Sligo in 1989 to 300 employed globally in 2007, through a combination of organic growth and acquisitions. Some 170 are employed in Ireland. The company has grown in both its core business and laterally into related businesses, most recently the area of energy utilities construction and maintenance. This has seen sustained growth levels of 50% *per annum*. Key to the company's growth has been its partnership with leading multinationals; included among its clients are Intel, Boston Scientific, Siemens and Hewlett-Packard.

Fergal began his career as an engineering technician in Sligo and then worked in Aughinish Alumina in Askeaton, County Limerick. From this experience, he saw a niche in the automation market and returned to Sligo in 1983 where he set up Automatic Control Engineering (ACE), in partnership with a colleague. Six years later, ACE ceased operations and Lotus Automation was founded, initially offering switchgear and equipment, manufacturing, maintenance and industrial calibration services in the North West of Ireland, as Fergal (2002) describes:

> *Initially, I saw the gap in the North West market. There was nobody in the region providing those kind of services. It started off with a North West base; primarily to service the North West, and grew from there.*

By 1993, Lotus Automation had won its first major technical services contract with a US Fortune 500 company and expanded its services offerings to include operations, maintenance and technical training. Such was the growth of its business activities that, three years later, in 1996, it moved to larger premises and employed 60 people, predominately on the technical side. In that year, Lotus Automation also established a technical field services division, which laid the foundation for winning its first international technical services contract three years later. Between 1999 and 2001, the company established a presence in the UK, secured another major technical services contact with a multinational based in the US and opened an engineering office in Massachusetts, established a presence in the North American market as Lotus Automation USA. By 2003, the growing international focus of Lotus Automation lead to the establishment of a dedicated

---

[15] This profile is adapted from a case written by James Cunningham and Rachel Hilliard, J.E. Cairnes Graduate School of Business & Public Policy, NUI Galway, as part of the Ernst & Young Entrepreneur of the Year Case Series 2007.

sales division operating out of its Irish headquarters in Sligo, in addition to the establishment of a number of strategic product partnerships with international suppliers, which were offered and distributed to Lotus Automation customers.

In 2004, a major strategic move was undertaken with the setting up of Lotus AMC (Asset Management Consulting) and, in early 2005, the company made its first major international acquisition of the electrical and mechanical division of JH Kelly based in Auburn, Massachusetts. Post-acquisition, JH Kelly was renamed to KM Kelly, and now provides clients with best-dollar-value for their electrical, mechanical and instrumentation control by providing services, including power distribution, low voltage, instrumentation and control, process piping, lighting, equipment setting and calibration. In mid-2005, Lotus USA offices were opened in Washington State and Lotus Automation acquired sister companies PO&M and PII, based on the West Coast of the USA in early 2006. PII provides workplace training and performance improvement for maintenance of manufacturing utility, construction and engineering facilities. PO&M assists customers with project execution through a wide variety of services, including design and drawing review, construction management, site management, commissioning and start-up support. By mid-May 2006, Lotus Group USA was awarded a significant construction management contract for the Spiritwood Energy cold-fired Combined Heat & Power plant in North Dakota by UniField Engineering and this provided it with a bridge-head into the US power market, which is one of its key market targets. Another contract win followed in September 2006, where Mint Farm Energy LLC awarded the construction management support contract for the building of its 320MW gas-fired combined cycle power plant in Longview, Washington.

There are currently three regional businesses: Lotus Automation IRL, Lotus Automation UK and Lotus Group USA. Lotus Group USA is the umbrella for four subsidiary businesses: Lotus Automation USA, KM Kelly, PII and PO&M. Lotus Automation's business activities are divided intro three divisions, namely Services, Products and Consulting. The company is also considering expansion into the expanding Chinese market, possibly through a joint venture. Competing as a services business in the global marketplace is challenging and one of the central competitive advantages for Lotus Automation is its people, who are highly trained and flexible, supported in an informal organisation with minimal hierarchy. Such flexibility has given them a competitive edge and allowed the company to leverage its multinational partnerships globally. A sign of this flexible and adaptive culture is seen in the high ranking that the company received for the FÁS-sponsored Excellence through People awards for effective communication and people involvement, in 2005 and 2006. The business is based on technical knowledge intensity, but Lotus Automation's work is based on the knowledge and technical excellence of its people in managing other companies' technology.

7

RIVERSIDE CAFÉ
BUSINESS PLAN[16]

[16] The authors acknowledge the contribution of Geraldine Loughlin and Kevin Marmion to this chapter.

EXECUTIVE SUMMARY

I am seeking a loan of €20,000 to set up a café in Ballydermot, a provincial town where there has been major industrial development and tourism. Improvements in leisure facilities, particularly golfing, fishing and water sport, attract an increasing number of tourists to the area each year. The restaurant will be specifically targeted at these segments.

The provision of wholesome and nutritious food will give the café an advantage over its two competitors, who have been concentrating on the fast-food market, a market that is remaining static. They have failed to exploit a new market segment, where there is a potential market of approximately 600 people from the following five customer segments: management and staff of Sierra Plastics, visitors / tourists, self-employed, Gunne's cement & gravel factory and members of the Defence Forces. Potential customers have shown a positive attitude towards the provision of a new style of café, with high levels of dissatisfaction with existing facilities. Results of a survey show that 54% will use the café 'frequently' and 38% will use it 'occasionally'.

Market research suggests that customers consider 'quality of food', 'price' and 'variety' to be the most important attributes of a café. Therefore, this venture will concentrate on these factors. The café plans to capture 30% to 35% of the potential market in the first year and to grow its market share by 5% in each of the subsequent years. The venture's pricing policy is based on industry averages and customer expectations.

The management function will be carried out by the principal of the venture, Deirdre Daly. The business will employ a fully qualified chef on a part-time basis and one full-time waitress. All sourcing of raw materials will be done locally.

The financial figures attached are based on owner's capital of €10,000 and a €20,000 loan over five years at 10% interest. This money is required to purchase initial equipment and fittings and as working capital for the first year of business. The business projects a small loss in year one, moving to profit in year two, with significant profits in year three. Net cash flow for the first year is estimated at €10,820.

I am convinced that this business will be successful and profitable and that your loan will be repaid fully. I look forward to discussing this proposal with you.

Yours sincerely,
Deirdre Daly

1. DESCRIPTION OF THE BUSINESS

The café will be targeted at people working in the area, as well as visitors and tourists to the town. *Riverside Café* will be open, Monday to Saturday from 10 a.m. to 7 p.m. During the tourist season, it will open on Sunday afternoons from 2 p.m. to 7 p.m. The café will provide dinners, sandwiches, soups, salads, beverages (see **Appendix 1**), concentrating on wholesome and nutritious food. This will differentiate *Riverside Café* from its competitors, both of whom concentrate on fast-food.

2. THE BUSINESS ENVIRONMENT

The proposed location for the venture is Ballydermot, which has been chosen for a number of important reasons:

- The town has undergone significant changes and developments in the last 10 years. The development of the Bloomfield Hotel, which is set in 300 acres, including 50 acres of lakes and gardens, has attracted increased tourist trade to the area. The surrounding area is renowned for is championship golf course, fishing and boating activities on the River Gowan.

- The location of the US company, Sierra Plastics, in the town two years ago, has increased employment. Population figures have increased dramatically over the past few years and are predicted to rise further in the foreseeable future.

- The town has formed a committee aimed at improving the tourist trade in the area. Tourism figures for the region as a whole have been increasing in recent years by about 8% *per annum*. Of particular importance are weekend breaks by Irish people.

- The town is located near the border and there is significant cross-border trade.

- I have lived in the town all my life. My family are well-known and respected in the area. I have built up a number of valuable business contacts that can be used.

3. MARKET RESEARCH & ANALYSIS

MARKET RESEARCH

I conducted a survey to get the views and responses of potential customers. The questionnaire (**Appendix 2**) was targeted at a representative group of 50 people, from all sectors of employment in the area. The most obvious and striking conclusion was that the town is severely lacking this type of service. The results of the questionnaire (**Appendix 3**) show that, while 65% of people brought lunch with them to work, 54% said they would use a café in the town 'frequently'. A further 38% said they would use it 'occasionally'. The majority of potential customers considered that 'quality of food' and 'prices' would be the most important criteria when deciding when to use the proposed café.

The priorities of the café are:

- **Fresh produce and food:** This will be sourced daily from the highest quality local suppliers.
- **"Reasonable" prices:** The majority for those surveyed were prepared to pay €5 to €15 per day.
- **Variety:** The menu will offer variety in food and beverages.
- **Fast and friendly service.**

MARKET SEGMENTS

The market has been segmented based by occupation. The main groups are:

- Clerical.
- Construction workers.
- Craftspeople.
- Farmers.
- House-wives / house-husbands.
- Managers / business-owners.
- Officials.
- Operators / assistants.
- Professionals.
- Students.
- Technical.
- Unemployed.

Potential customers have been grouped into five categories:

- **Sierra Plastics:** Potential target market of 220 people. Sierra Plastics is a US company that located in the town two years ago. Additional factory space is planned over the next two years, with between 50 and 75 new jobs resulting.

- **Gunne's cement and gravel factory:** Potential target market of 125 people. This company extracts and distributes building materials all over Ireland. It has been located in the town for the last 30 years. The owner-manager is supportive of local initiative.

- **The Defence Forces and Gardaí:** Potential target market of 155 people. While these personnel are based outside the town, they do account for a significant passing trade.

- **Visitors / tourists:** Potential target market of 90 people. These will include people staying at the Bloomfield Hotel. Some of the guests spend time visiting the town and its historic sites. People coming to the town to participate in leisure activities, such as fishing, golfing and water sports, may use the café. The completion of the new canal has meant that there will be a further increase in the number of visitors to the area in future years.

- **Local businesspeople:** Potential target market of 70 people. This segment includes those working in local public houses, newsagents, local professionals and the self-employed.

MARKET SIZE

From market research undertaken, the total market size (660) is:

- Sierra Plastics – 220.
- Visitors / tourists – 90.
- Professionals and self-employed – 70.
- Gunne's – 125.
- Defence Forces and Gardaí – 155.

3.1: PROJECTED SALES VOLUMES & REVENUES 2008-2010

	Sales Customer visits*	Sales € per customer per week**	Sales € per week	Sales € per annum***
2008	533	€8.00	€4,264	€204,672
2009	560	€8.00	€4,480	€215,040
2010	548	€9.00	€4,932	€236,736

*   *These estimates are based on research undertaken with customers (**Appendix 2**). In the survey undertaken, 54% indicated they would use this service frequently and 38% indicated that they would use it occasionally during the week. Therefore it is estimated that the customers will use the restaurant on average 2 days per week. Customer visits are assumed to fall slightly in 2010, balanced by an assumed increase in spend.*

**   *The forecast is based on an average of €8.00 spend per visit. From the customer survey, 47% said they would spend between €5.00 and €7.99 per visit, while 42% said they would spend between €8.00 and €9.99.*

*** *For the purposes of planning, it is assumed that each month has 4 weeks and that there are 48 weeks in the year. This allows for some closed periods – over Christmas or for holidays.*

4. COMPETITORS

There are two direct competitors in the surrounding area. Information about them was obtained from secondary data, visiting their premises, personal experiences and hearsay.

DEC'S DINER

This family-owned business was established in 1997.

Strengths:

- It has a prime location in the town centre, with good parking facilities.
- Due to its 10 years in business, it has built up a good reputation with customers.
- Its main business is in fast-food but, in recent years, it has provided sandwiches, salads, tea / coffee, which will be direct competition with the new venture.
- From the limited evidence gathered, it appears to be financially stable and profitable.
- It has a 39% market share and is the main competition in the area.

Weaknesses:

- It concentrates on the social trade: people who visit the 'take-away' on their way home from the pubs or night-clubs.
- While a segment of its business will be in direct competition with the venture (the sandwiches and lunches), *Riverside Café* is focused on the lunch-time market.
- This outlet doesn't advertise or promote its business and has the attitude that "we don't have to attract customers, they come in of their own accord". The management knows that they have a dominant market share and believe that no other competition can or will take it from them.

FOSTERS' TAKE-AWAY

This family-owned business was established in 1975. The business focuses on the sale of fast-food to all segments of the market, with the majority of their customers being young people between the age of 18-30 years.

Strengths:

- Long-established business and the family owners are well-acquainted with the people in the area.
- Has 25% of the existing market.
- A good location in the centre, convenient to schools, pubs and night-clubs.
- Later opening hours at weekends and week-nights.
- Sponsor of the local underage GAA teams.

Weaknesses:

- The market research rated it poor on 'quality' and 'variety'. It received a 'friendly service' rating of 'fair'.
- In recent years, it has started to prepare dinners, due to its continuing loss of market share. This is at odds with its existing reputation and image of being a 'fast-food joint'.

Between them, Dec's Diner and Foster's Take-Away hold 64% of the local market. The balance is held by two local shops that offer convenience food and a pub about five miles outside town.

Riverside Café will be competing to gain market share from the two direct competitors: Dec's Diner and Foster's Take-Away. However, direct competition will be on a relatively small scale. Both of these outlets cater for the socialising and youth market and stay open until 2.00 or 3.00 a.m. on Friday and Saturday nights. Although the competition has some distinctive competencies, our market research (**Appendix 3**) found that people were dissatisfied with the level of service provided by the two competitors. Respondents rated 'quality of service' and 'price' as the most important factors in their purchasing decision. Both outlets were rated poor on 'quality' but very good on 'price'. The focus of *Riverside Café* is to attract different segments of the market that have different needs, thus avoiding direct competition.

The common belief among the competition is that they can divide the market between them. This is evident by their limited advertising and promotion. It was evident from the questionnaire that they have failed to recognise the increasing employment sector, whose needs are not being adequately satisfied. This is where the *Riverside Café* will target successfully.

5. MARKETING PLAN

MARKET STRATEGY

Riverside Café's selling proposition is to capture the hearts and minds of the customer by providing high quality food, a variety of choice, affordable prices and a friendly and efficient service. The trend in recent years is that people are becoming more concerned about their diet and health. Therefore, *Riverside Café* will exploit this trend by only serving fresh, healthy and, where possible, locally-produced foods. The name of the venture, *Riverside Café*, suggests freshness and reflects what the business is attempting to achieve. As already outlined, the venture will be targeting people working in Ballydermot and the surrounding areas and, on a smaller scale, visitors and tourists to the town. Based on the market research with these groups, it is clear that there is a need for this type of outlet and better quality food. The sector being targeted has grown steadily over the past five years and this trend is expected to continue into the future.

PRICING POLICY

Riverside Café's pricing policy will be based on the prices customers are prepared to pay. From the market research undertaken 89% of those surveyed were prepared to pay between €5.00 and €9.99 per day. An average per spend of €8.00 has been assumed for 2008 and 2009, with an assumed increase to €9.00 in 2010. These prices are in line with industry norms.

ADVERTISING, PROMOTION & PR

An extensive advertising campaign will be conducted one month before opening *Riverside Café*. Various media will be used to inform the target market about the café. A leaflet (**Appendix 4**) will be distributed to local factories, offices and shops. Advertisements will be placed in the two local newspapers, the *Ballydermot Evening News* and *Midland People*. Free meals will be provided to local radio stations, to be used as prizes in fun competitions. A local celebrity will be asked to open the restaurant. I will run a feature advertisement in the local papers to mark the opening.

Advertising will be concentrated in the first year of opening and particularly in the first few months. In subsequent years, advertising will consist mainly of promotions during festival and holiday times and the sponsorship of local events. In particular, sports events in the factories will be sponsored. The café will be offered as a location for prize-giving ceremonies.

CUSTOMER SERVICE

A happy customer is worth more than spending on advertising. Customer satisfaction will be a priority at *Riverside Café*. I will seek feedback from customers to enable me to improve our service. In order to assess customer satisfaction, the business will put comment cards on each table (**Appendix 5**). This will have a direct impact on our operations. Where customers display dissatisfaction, the policy will be to give the customer a free meal.

6. MANAGEMENT TEAM & STAFFING

MANAGEMENT

Management will be performed by Deirdre Daly, the principal of the business (**Appendix 6**). This will involve ensuring that staff are performing the duties assigned to them, ordering from suppliers, stock-taking and generally performing the daily duties involved in operating a café. I will also be preparing the accounts, as I have relevant experience in this area.

STAFFING

The venture will employ a part-time chef to work from 9 a.m. to 2 p.m. His / her duties will include preparing the food for the day and writing the menus. Total hours worked will be 30 per week.

A full-time waiter / waitress will also be employed, whose duties will be taking and preparing customer orders, cleaning tables, etc. He / she will work 48 hours per week. A part-time waiter / waitress will be employed in the second year of operations, if sales levels are achieved.

These staff are available locally, according to the local employment agencies. To achieve the planned service and quality levels, careful consideration will be given to the recruitment and selection of suitable staff. The qualities that will be required are:

- Capability to perform the tasks.
- Ability to work in a small team environment.
- Pleasant manner.
- Clean appearance.
- Commitment, motivation and honesty.

7. LOCATION & OPERATIONS PLAN

LOCATION

At present, there is a premises vacant on the main street in Ballydermot that would be suitable for *Riverside Café*. I have already had discussions with the owner. She is committed to converting the premises into a restaurant. The total area of the premises is 1,200 square feet. It was previously used as a bakery and, therefore, needs only minor alterations – for example, new seating, modernising the decor and some adjustments to the shop front and signage. I have agreed to renovate the premises and, if the business ceases trading in that location, an independent valuer will be brought in to put a price on my renovations and the owner will reimburse me. The owner is prepared to rent the premises for €25.00 per square foot per annum, payable in monthly instalments.

The layout plan for *Riverside Café* is shown in **Appendix 7**. On entering the premises, the sandwich and salad bar will be on the right to serve those wanting a take-away lunch. Down from there will be the hot food bar, where customers will serve themselves. The kitchen is perfect for use as it stands.

EQUIPMENT

The premises includes some equipment from the previous owners. The owner has agreed to sell this equipment to me. The cost of equipment will be:

Second-hand equipment:	€
Ovens	8,000
Cash register	1,600
Other equipment	1,000
	10,600
New equipment:	
Dishwasher	1,200
Fridge	2,000
Fixtures & fittings	1,800
	5,000
TOTAL	**15,600**

SUPPLIERS

The business intends to source all raw materials locally to ensure freshness and to build up credibility in the local community. The aim is to build a lasting long-term buyer / supplier relationship. It is intended to draw up a contract with each supplier before beginning business, and to negotiate all terms and conditions to ensure that both parties are satisfied with the arrangements. The suppliers have been chosen based on the following criteria: quality of ingredients; delivery times and reliability; credit terms; and cost. The raw materials will be sourced from the following businesses, which I have already contacted.

Product	Supplier
Salads, fruit & vegetables	Western Fruit Ltd
Fish, red, white & cold meats	Harte Bros.
Salad dressing, cream, milk, cheese, yoghurt & butter	Farmers Co-op
Bread & cakes	Quinn's Bakery
Other	Smith's Cash & Carry

REGULATIONS

New food hygiene legislation came into force on 1 January 2006. Hygiene rules that were previously scattered over 17 EU Directives have been replaced by five new pieces of legislation commonly referred to as the 'Hygiene Package' and enacted in the European Communities (Hygiene of Foodstuffs) Regulations 2006 (SI369 of 2006). All 'food business operators' (FBOs) must now comply with this Regulation which lays down general rules on the hygiene of foodstuffs.

8. FINANCE PLAN

See **Appendix 8** for notes to the following financial projections.

	Jan €	Feb €	Mar €	Apr €	May €	Jun €	Jul €	Aug €	Sep €	Oct €	Nov €	Dec €	Total €
Receipts													
Cash	17,056	17,056	17,056	17,056	17,056	17,056	17,056	17,056	17,056	17,056	17,056	17,056	204,672
Owner's Capital	10,000												10,000
Bank Loan	20,000												20,000
Total Receipts	47,056	17,056	17,056	17,056	17,056	17,056	17,056	17,056	17,056	17,056	17,056	17,056	234,672
Payments													
Cash Purchases	3,411	3,411	3,411	3,411	3,411	3,411	3,411	3,411	3,411	3,411	3,411	3,411	40,932
Rent & Rates	2,000	2,000	2,000	2,000	2,000	2,000	2,000	2,000	2,000	2,000	2,000	2,000	24,000
Light / Heat / Power	450	450	450	450	450	450	450	450	450	450	450	450	5,400
Repairs			500			500			500			500	2,000
Loan Repayments						2,000						2,000	4,000
Loan Interest			500			500			500			500	2,000
Insurance	2,000												2,000
Wages & Salaries	10,110	10,110	10,110	10,110	10,110	10,110	10,110	10,110	10,110	10,110	10,110	10,110	121,320
Legal & Prof. Fees		1,000											1,000
Stationery & Telephone		400		400		400		400		400		400	2,400
Advertising		1,200	700	400	200	200	100	100	100		100	100	3,200
Capital Expenditure	15,600												15,600
Total Payments	33,571	18,571	17,671	16,771	16,171	19,571	16,071	16,471	17,071	16,371	16,071	19,471	223,852
Net Cash Flow	13,485	-1,515	-615	285	885	-2,515	985	585	-15	685	985	-2,415	10,820
Opening Bank Balance	0	13,485	11,970	11,355	11,640	12,525	10,010	10,995	11,580	11,565	12,250	13,235	0
Closing Balance	13,485	11,970	11,355	11,640	12,525	10,010	10,995	11,580	11,565	12,250	13,235	10,820	10,820

8.2: PROJECTED ANNUAL CASH FLOW FOR YEARS ENDING 31 DECEMBER
2008 / 2009 / 2010

		2008	2009	2010
		€	€	€
Receipts				
Cash		204,672	215,040	236,736
Owner's Capital		10,000		
Bank Loan		20,000		
Total Receipts		**234,672**	**215,040**	**236,736**
Payments				
Cash Purchases	1	40,932	43,008	47,347
Rent & Rates	3	24,000	24,000	24,000
Light / Heat / Power	4	5,400	5,670	5,954
Repairs	5	2,000	2,100	2,205
Loan Repayments		4,000	4,000	4,000
Loan Interest		2,000	2,000	2,000
Insurance		2,000	2,100	2,205
Wages & Salaries	2	121,320	127,380	133,749
Legal & Prof. Fees		1,000	1,050	1,102
Stationery & Telephone		2,400	2,520	2,646
Advertising		3,200	3,360	3,528
Capital Expenditure		15,600		
Total Payments		**233,852**	**217,188**	**228,736**
Net Cash Flow		**10,820**	**-2,418**	**8,000**
Open Bank Balance		0	10,820	8,672
Closing Bank Balance		**10,820**	**8,672**	**16,672**

8.3: PROJECTED PROFIT & LOSS ACCOUNT FOR YEARS ENDING
31 DECEMBER 2008 / 2009 / 2010

	2008	2009	2010
	€	€	€
Sales	204,672	215,040	236,736
Less Cost of Sales	40,932	43,008	47,347
Gross Profit	**163,740**	**172,032**	**189,389**
Expenses			
Wages & Salaries	121320	127,380	133,749
Rent & Rates	24,000	24,000	24,000
Light/Heat/Power	5,400	5,670	5,954
Repairs & Maintenance	2,000	2,100	2,205
Loan Interest	2,000	2,000	2,000
Insurance	2,000	2,100	2,205
Legal & Professional Fees	1,000	1,050	1,102
Stationery & Telephone	2,400	2,520	2,646
Advertising & Promotion	3,200	3,360	3,528
Depreciation	1,560	1,404	1,264
Total Expenses	**164,880**	**171,584**	**178,653**
Net Profit	**-1,140**	**448**	**10,736**

8.4: PROJECTED BALANCE SHEET FOR YEARS ENDING 31 DECEMBER
2008 / 2009 / 2010

		2008 €	2009 €	2010 €
Fixed Assets				
Fixtures, Fittings & Equip (NBV)	**7**	14,040	12,636	11,372
Current Assets				
Cash		10,820	8,672	16,672
Total Net Assets		**24,860**	**21,308**	**28,044**
Financed By				
Owner's Capital		10,000	10,000	10,000
Long Term Borrowings		16,000	12,000	8,000
Retained Earnings		-1,140	-692	10,044
		24,860	**21,308**	**28,044**

9. START-UP SCHEDULE

Task	Timing
Prepare Business Plan (including Market Research)	September 2007
Get Bank approval for loan	October 2007
Find suitable location and premises	October 2007
Draw up contract with lessor	October 2007
Undertake renovations	November 2007
Source raw materials and all Supplies	November 2007
Interview for staff	November 2007
Advertising campaign	December 2007
Opening of *Riverside Café*	January 2008

10. CRITICAL RISKS

There are a number of potential risks facing this business. These risks are not all avoidable and, therefore, the business has to minimise its exposure to them where possible:

- The market research may be incorrect. Market research cannot eliminate the uncertainty and risks of the business.

- The competition may react to the new venture. Reaction might be price cuts and / or by providing a similar service. A new competitor may enter the market, following the success of *Riverside Café*.

- Difficulties in getting high quality raw materials.

- Failure to secure enough financing.

- The closure of a factory in the locality, or a reduction in tourism, could reduce business significantly.

11. CONSOLIDATION & RENEWAL STRATEGY

There are a number of ways the business might grow and develop, including:

- The premises where the business is located has a second level, which currently is not being used. If the business grows and develops as outlined, this could be renovated and seating capacity could be expanded.

- The opening of similar business, in another town where there is a similar opportunity.

- If the business is not successful, the premises could be used for catering training courses.

APPENDIX 1: SAMPLE MENU

Riverside Café

Salad Counter
Ham Slice
Tuna Portion
Cheese Portion
Coleslaw
Egg Mayonnaise
Salad Bowl
Fresh Sandwiches/Rolls

Hot Counter
Vegetables (Choice of 3)
Soup
Quiche
Roast Beef
Haddock
Roast Chicken
Farmhouse Grill
Rice Based Dishes

Confectionery
Scones
Riverside Buns
Jam/Sugar Doughnut
Danish Pastry
Cream Cakes
Apple Pie
Cheesecake

Beverages
Tea/Coffee
Decaffeinated Coffee
Hot Chocolate
Minerals - Small/Large
Milk - Small/Large
Mineral Water

APPENDIX 2: SURVEY QUESTIONNAIRE

I am researching the possibility of locating a restaurant in Ballydermot, to cater for the needs of those working and living in the area. I would appreciate it if you would complete this questionnaire and I assure you that your replies will be kept in the strictest of confidence.

1. Where do you normally get and have your lunch?
   A. At Home
   B. Restaurant in Town
   If at a restaurant, please rank the following factors 1-5 on how you consider them to be satisfied.

   Quality of Food   1 2 3 4 5
   Price of Food   1 2 3 4 5
   Friendly Service   1 2 3 4 5
   Fast Service   1 2 3 4 5
   Variety on Offer   1 2 3 4 5

   (1= Excellent, 2 = Very Good, 3 = Good, 4 = Fair, 5 = Poor)
   C. Bring Lunch with You
   If you bring a lunch, would you be willing to purchase fresh sandwiches if they were available? Yes_____   No_____
   D. In another town.

2. How long is your lunch break?
   30 Minutes   _____
   1 Hour   _____
   1–2 Hours   _____
   More   _____

3. If a new restaurant opened in town, how often would you be prepared to use it?
   Frequently   _____ (4–5 days a week)
   Occasionally   _____ (1–3 days a week)
   Never   _____

4. What is the maximum amount you would be prepared to spend every day on lunch?

        €3.00–€4.99   _____

        €5.00–€7.99   _____

        €8.00–€9.99   _____

        €10.00–€14.99   _____

        Over €15.00   _____

5. Rank the factors you consider to be appropriate in providing this service?

    1. Quality of food   1 2 3 4 5

    2. Price of food   1 2 3 4 5

    3. Friendly service ambience   1 2 3 4 5

    4. Fast service   1 2 3 4 5

    5. Variety on offer   1 2 3 4 5

    (1= Excellent, 2 = Very Good, 3 = Good, 4 = Fair, 5 = Poor)

Any other comments that you would like to make:

_____

_____

_____

_____

Thank you for your co-operation

APPENDIX 3: SURVEY RESULTS

1. Where do you normally get and have your lunch?
    A. At Home   8 %
    B. Restaurant in Town   17%
        The factors below were ranked as follows:

Quality of Food	Poor
Price of Food	Very Good
Friendly Service	Fair
Fast Service	Excellent
Variety on Offer	Poor

    C. Bring Lunch with You   65%
    If you bring a lunch, would you will be willing to purchase fresh sandwiches if they were available?   Yes 52%   No 48%
    D. Go to another town   10%

2. How long is your lunch break?

30 Minutes	9%
1 Hour	78%
1–2 Hours	6%
More	7%

3. If a new restaurant opened in town, would you be prepared to use it?

Frequently	54%	(4–5 days a week)
Occasionally	38%	(1–3 days a week)
Never	8%	

4. What is the maximum you would be prepared to spend every day on lunch?

€3.00–€3.99	0%
€5.00–€7.99	47%
€8.00–€9.99	42%
€10.00–€14.99	11%
Over €15.00	0%

5. Rank the factors you consider to be appropriate in providing this service?

1. Quality of food	32%
2. Price of food	29%
3. Friendly service ambience	14%
4. Fast service	10%
5. Variety on offer	15%

(1= Excellent, 2 = Very Good, 3 = Good, 4 = Fair, 5 = Poor)

APPENDIX 4: ADVERTISING & PR

Riverside Café

Fed up and bored with your lunch?
Well now you have the option with healthy options !!
I am opening my restaurant
Riverside Café
Ballydermot
on 1 January 2008

Myself and my highly competent team of staff
will guarantee you fresh food daily,
variety, keen prices, a pleasant ambience and,
of course, a friendly service to remember.

Opening Offer of a 25% Discount

Come in and see for yourself

For further details — contact **Deirdre**
Telephone 098 765 4321

APPENDIX 5: CUSTOMER COMMENT CARD

Riverside Café

Comment Card

Customer satisfaction is our priority. By completing this card with your comments and rating, you will help us to provide you with the standards you deserve.

Date:_____   Time:_____

Comments: _____
_____
_____

Please mark in accordance with the following scale:

Excellent: 9–10   Fair: 4–5
Good: 6–8   Poor : 1–3

Marks out of 10

Food: Variety
                Temperature
                Taste
Service: Efficiency
                Friendliness
Hygiene: Food Service
                Dining Area
                Staff
Premises: Comfort
                Lighting
                Atmosphere
Value for Money:

APPENDIX 6: DEIRDRE DALY – CV

Personal Details:

Name:	Deirdre Daly
Address:	The Square, Ballydermot.
Telephone:	098 123 4567
Date of Birth:	27-2-1970

Education:

College: College of Catering, Cathal Brugha Street, Dublin

Finals:	Distinction
Second Year:	Merit
First Year:	Pass
Final Year Project:	Fresh French Pastries

Secondary School: The Convent, Ballydermot.

Leaving Certificate: 3 B2s, 1 C1, 2 D2s

Intermediate Certificate: 2 A1s, 2 B2s, 2 C1s, 2 D2s

Employment Experience:

The Bullman Inn: Manager.

Responsibility for managing the Bullman Inn. This is a public house owned by a major UK brewery. Specific responsibility for accounts, staffing and stock control. During my two years here, I was awarded "pub-manager" of the year.

Bloomfield House Hotel: Assistant Chef.

This involved working long hours in a kitchen that serviced the hotel dining room. Each week-end, several large functions would be held in the hotel (up to 500 people eating at any one time).

Lobster Bar, Cape Cod, USA: Waitress, Cashier.

The Lobster Bar could seat 75 people. I started waiting tables. After several months, I was made responsible for scheduling the other waitresses and then I was made responsible for handling the cash. I held this job for a number of summers.

The Old Lounge: Waitress.

Leisure Interests:

My main leisure activity is hill-walking and rock-climbing. I have travelled to several European countries to walk and climb. I am an active member of my local climbing club. In college I was Chairperson of the Climbing & Hill walking club.

Referees:

Bill McGrath, Lecturer, Cathal Brugha St., Dublin.

Sarah Flynn, Manager, Bloomfield Hotel, Ballydermot.

APPENDIX 7: LAYOUT OF RESTAURANT

Pay Here	Hot & Cold Beverages	Self Service Meals	Trays	Kitchen Area

In

Out

Cutlery Napkins etc.

Seating Numbers

6	4	4	4	2
6	4	4	4	2
6	4	4	4	2
6	4	4	4	2
6	4	4	4	2

Sandwich/ Salad Bar

Pay Here

APPENDIX 8: NOTES TO THE FINANCIAL PROJECTIONS

1. Cost of Sales
Based on industry average of 20% of sales. Due to the perishable nature of stock, most purchases will be made daily. Terms are cash on delivery.

2. Wages & Salaries
Part-time Chef
5 hours X 6 days = 30 hours; €592 pw X 52 weeks = €30,784
Full-time Waitress
8 hours X 6 days = 48 hours; €663 pw X 52 weeks = €34,476
Manager's Wages
€828 pw X 52 weeks = €43,056
Employer's PRSI @ 12% will be charged on top of these pay rates.

3. Rent & Rates
Rent is €25 per square foot per annum. At 1,200 sq. feet, annual total is €30,000, fixed for five years.

4. Heat, Light & Power
Estimate from the ESB based on size of premises and the nature of the business.

5. Repairs
Repair and maintenance costs of €2,000 are assumed.

6. Bank Loan
Local bank offered a loan based on the following terms: Repayable over 5 years at 10% per annum (fixed). Repayment of principal is €20,000/5 years which is €4,000 per annum. Interest is €20,000 X 10%, which is €2,000 per annum.

7. Insurance
Local insurance broker made this estimate. It includes public liability insurance.

8. Depreciation

Fixed Assets	€
Ovens x 2 (second hand)	8,000
Dishwashers (new)	1,200
Cash registers (second hand)	1,600
Fixtures (new)	2,000
Fridge (new)	1,800
Other (second hand)	1,000
	15,600

Depreciation charged at 10%

	2008	2009	2010
	€	€	€
Fixed Assets	15,600	14,040	12,636
Depreciation (at 10%)	1,560	1,404	1,264
Net Book Value	14,040	12,636	11,372

9. Inflation

All costs are assumed to inflate at 5% *per annum*, unless otherwise indicated.

8

PERSPECTIVES ON

PLANNING

The previous chapters have outlined how to prepare a business plan. Do entrepreneurs plan? Why do they invest time and money in preparing plans? What are the benefits of planning? Why do some entrepreneurs not plan despite these benefits?

In this chapter, a number of entrepreneurs discuss business planning and offer their insights into the planning process in new and small businesses. Research evidence on the planning process is discussed and an alternative perspective on planning for new businesses is suggested.

ENTREPRENEURS DISCUSS PLANNING

Chris is the owner of a large manufacturing business in the Midlands. This business is well-established and the main supplier in the Irish market. Chris has recently started exporting into the European markets.

Emma is the owner of a new café in Cork city centre. The business is in its first year of operation and Emma is working 'all hours of the day' to make a success of it.

Sean is a fish-farmer in the West of Ireland. The business has grown rapidly in the last four years and now exports most of its products to the French market.

Paul and Ciaran manufacture speciality food sauces. Their products are produced from organic ingredients and are sold as premium products in delicatessens.

Elizabeth is considering starting up her own software company to write a software programme for accountants in the UK. She has recently left college and started preparing her business plan within the last few months.

WHY DO ENTREPRENEURS PREPARE PLANS?

Chris: The Koran summarises this simply: "... if you do not know where you are going, any road will take you there ...". The most basic reason why an entrepreneur should plan is that it provides a direction to his activity. Starting a business needs all your resources, skills and time. Once you have started, all your attention will be directed to solving day-to-day problems and crises. It is difficult to stay focused on your longer-term objectives in this sort of environment. When I started, we had a lot of manufacturing problems and my attention was diverted away from marketing and distribution. Customers were unhappy with the distributor and we lost a lot of goodwill with our final customers. It took us two years to recover from this experience. A more detailed business plan might have helped us avoid many of our manufacturing problems.

Paul: A major reason for planning is to raise funds. Planning allows the entrepreneur to estimate the resources that are needed. These include not only financial resources, but also the human resources, machinery and plant. Having identified the resources needed, the entrepreneur can calculate the financial requirements of the business. A business plan is essential if the entrepreneur is to raise finance from a bank or from a State agency. We could not have secured grant aid without a business plan. Our plan allowed the bank and the government agencies to assess the risk attached to our venture. As such, the business plan is the most essential tool for external communication that we had at start-up. A clear description of how an organisation proposes to develop a business allows investors to decide whether the project is a worthwhile investment and what is the risk attached to it.

Elizabeth: To test the feasibility of the idea. A business plan requires the entrepreneur to justify the market potential of the business. The greatest uncertainty facing an entrepreneur is the market potential for the business. The entrepreneur needs to answer questions such as: 'Is there a market for this product? Why will customers buy my product/service? Who are my competitors?'. Planning allows the entrepreneur to evaluate competitors and to develop a sustainable competitive advantage. Planning forces the entrepreneur to choose explicitly a strategy for entering the market. Planning is particularly important to entrepreneurs operating in uncertain environments. For example, in the software business, failure to plan may result in a lot of time and money invested in developing a product that the market does not want. It will take me two years to develop the product. It is essential that I am sure that there is a market for it.

Chris: The entrepreneur needs to establish the financial feasibility of the business idea. Having established that there is a market for the product / service, the entrepreneur must estimate the costs of providing it and establish whether this can be done at a cost that ensures that he / she is rewarded for both the risk he / she is taking and the time that he / she will be investing in the business. The entrepreneur should examine the accounts of competitors to see whether they are making money in this market. If others have failed or are losing money, the entrepreneur must seriously question the attractiveness of the market.

Sean: In some businesses, the entrepreneur will need to test the technical feasibility of the business idea. Purchasing fish cages and putting them in the Atlantic Ocean is a complex and risky business. You must know what you are doing. The entrepreneur can use the planning process to test whether he has the technical skills to operate the business and to produce the product. This may involve the production of a prototype. The entrepreneur needs to establish that the product will work, that it is possible to produce it in the volumes necessary and that raw materials are readily available.

Paul: An entrepreneur needs to plan at the start-up stage, and on an on-going basis, to maintain control of operations during and post-launch. During the launch of the business, the entrepreneur will be working very long hours to get 'up and running'. The pressures of making it all happen will mean that the entrepreneur will be continually 'fire-fighting'. A plan will help the business to stay on-course during this period of chaos. By planning, it is possible to ensure that everybody knows what their job is to be and they also know how well they must perform. This allows a certain type of control to be imposed over the business that would not be possible without a plan.

Chris: Essentially, planning is used for allocating resources, benchmarking current activities and goals against desired performance and the performance of competitors, as an aid to decision-making and as a communications device.

The main reasons entrepreneurs prepare plans are summarised in **Figure 8.1**.

FIGURE 8.1: REASONS FOR PLANNING

◊ **To give strategic direction to the business:** What is it I want to do?

◊ **To raise funds:** Who will invest in this business?

◊ **To test the feasibility of the business:** Is there a viable market for this product?

◊ **To test the financial feasibility of the business idea:** Can I make a profit?

◊ **To test the technical feasibility of the business:** Can I make the product / provide the service?

◊ **To control the business as it develops:** What performance do I expect? Am I achieving this?

◊ **To allocate resources and time:** What should I be doing? On what should I be spending money?

WHAT BENEFITS DID YOU GET FROM PLANNING?

Elizabeth: The software business is very dynamic and there is a lot of uncertainty about market demand. Planning increased my understanding of the external environment that will impact on my business.

Paul: Planning ensures that the entrepreneur's attention is focused on those factors that will determine success. In the business plan, the entrepreneur will have set targets for sales volumes, production volumes, and a timetable for development. In our business, it was essential that we secured distribution outlets that would generate sufficient volume. The result of preparing a plan was that we spent less time on product development, an activity that we enjoyed and were comfortable doing, and more time on the road trying to secure distribution agreements. Our business plan provides us with a set of targets against which we can measure our performance.

Chris: The process of planning ensures that I consider alternatives that otherwise might be ignored. Initially, I grew my business by responding to opportunities and approaches I received from overseas customers. However, I discovered that not all of these markets were as attractive and that the cost of entering an overseas market is high. Since these experiences, I now evaluate each market and have chosen different entry strategies for different markets.

Sean: The main benefit that I got from the business plan was that it helped me raise finance. The banks and the State agencies were not interested in my business idea unless I produced a business plan. At first, I was reluctant to prepare the plan. I know the business well, through my 15 years of experience. However, I found that the plan was a very useful control tool for the business.

Now, we continually check performance against planned performance. The business plan forms the agenda of our yearly business review. The process of preparing the business plan was a significant benefit. It helped me focus on allocating financial resources and my time.

FIGURE 8.2: BENEFITS OF PLANNING

◊ Planning should reduce uncertainty about the business and the market.
◊ Planning should highlight the factors that are critical to the success of the business.
◊ Planning should ensure that alternatives are developed and considered.
◊ Planning should assist in dealing with banks, State agencies and investors.

WHAT PROBLEMS & DIFFICULTIES DID YOU HAVE WHEN YOU PREPARED YOUR BUSINESS PLAN?

Paul: The main problem that we encountered was in gathering information about the business and the market. The most difficult information to get is reliable estimates of market demand. At first, we looked at Government statistics, but the information was too aggregated to allow us to estimate reliably the size of demand for speciality sauces. Then we tried to estimate the size of competitors' sales. Competitors guard figures on their turnover, making it difficult to get any reliable estimates of total market size. And we were not able to get information from the Companies Registration Office on turnover for our main competitors, as most of them were private limited companies, which don't need to file a profit and loss account; others produced so many different products that their turnover figure told us nothing about their sales of speciality sauces. If the product or service is new, the entrepreneur will quickly discover that there is no available data on potential demand. Market research can often be unreliable as people find it difficult to estimate their usage of a new product or service. Often the best strategy is to talk to potential buyers of the product and, if possible, to talk to your competitor's sales force.

Elizabeth: My biggest difficulty to date is that I am not familiar with preparing financial accounts. Most entrepreneurs have little experience of preparing financial projections. This is often the most off-putting part of the planning process. I have the technical skills to develop the product, but I do not have the necessary business skills to write a business plan. I think I lack the business, marketing and, in particular, the financial skills necessary for the preparation of a business plan.

Sean: I thought that I didn't have the time to spend planning. It has been estimated that it takes between 200 and 400 hours to produce a business plan. I was very involved in trying to get the business started. This required meeting suppliers, potential customers, Government agencies, equipment manufacturers and financial investors. Some of the time I spent preparing the business plan might have been better spent actually dealing with these people.

Emma: At first, I didn't appreciate the benefits of planning. My business is essentially a 'self-employment' type of venture. My focus was on getting the business started and not on delaying the process unnecessarily by planning.

FIGURE 8.3: DIFFICULTIES IN PLANNING

◊   Getting reliable and useful information.
◊   Lack of skills and expertise – in particular, poor financial skills.
◊   Lack of time.
◊   Lack of understanding of the benefits of the planning process.

WHY DON'T ENTREPRENEURS PLAN?

Chris: Some entrepreneurs develop the business slowly and, as a result, have no formal written business plan at the outset. The nature and scope of the new business may not be clearly defined at start-up. The nature of some products and service businesses are such that the entrepreneur learns as the business develops. Many self-employed people, such as tradespeople and professionals, understand the business and their main concern is to develop a customer-base as quickly as possible. The issues are clear and don't need to be stated in a formal plan. An entrepreneur with a skill to sell, for example, a management consultant, may want to keep his options open for as long as possible.

Emma: Some businesses are small and the entrepreneur may believe they have a good understanding of the business. Often the entrepreneur may know all potential customers personally from previous business dealings. These entrepreneurs might talk through their business propositions with potential customers and financiers. This creates a mutual understanding as to the direction and scope of the proposed business.

Elizabeth: For many entrepreneurs, planning is an unknown. They lack the experience and skills to prepare a plan so they avoid planning.

The reasons why many entrepreneurs don't prepare plans are outlined in **Figure 8.4.**

FIGURE 8.4: REASONS WHY ENTREPRENEURS DON'T PLAN

◊   The entrepreneur is very familiar with the business.

◊   The entrepreneur wants to keep options and alternatives open.
◊   The business is too small.
◊   Planning is an unknown and the entrepreneur lacks experience of planning.

IF AN ENTREPRENEUR LACKS THE SKILLS, SHOULD HE / SHE PAY A PROFESSIONAL TO WRITE THE PLAN?

Chris: My experience is that much of the benefit of planning is actually preparing the plan yourself. If an outsider prepares the plan, the entrepreneur will be less familiar with the content and the plan will have less of an impact on the running of the business. I would recommend that entrepreneurs get assistance in preparing the financial section of the plan, if they are having difficulty doing this themselves.

IN YOUR EXPERIENCE, WHAT ARE THE LIMITS OF THE PLANNING PROCESS?

Elizabeth: One of my main concerns about planning is that my plan may go out-of-date quickly. Obviously, there will be unforeseen events that will happen in the market, which could be due to technological progress, mergers and acquisitions. I see completing my initial business plan as a first step in a planning process. The business plan will be followed by continuous planning and updating of the plan as circumstances change. The uncertainty surrounding the future may have a negative impact on the plan but it may also have a favourable effect. Changing circumstances may mean new more attractive opportunities. Some entrepreneurs want to keep all their options open. My philosophy is to focus on the software opportunity that I have identified and to monitor other opportunities. I want to avoid spending my scarce resources on other opportunities and be sure to make a success of this one.

Chris: Many aspects of a business plan are dependent on the successful implementation of another part of the plan. In the early days, I found that market feedback was different from what I had anticipated in my business plan. This resulted in a change of distribution outlet and a change in my product mix. This has a series of knock-on effects – for example, the new distribution outlets needed higher quality packaging and faster delivery. Change in one area of the business will result in large sections of the initial plan becoming useless.

Emma: Entrepreneurs are opportunistic, they seize opportunities quickly. The process of preparing a plan may lead the entrepreneur to procrastinate, what is called 'paralysis by analysis'. The entrepreneur may seek increasingly detailed information about the product or market and try to produce a more refined and detailed plan. This increased analysis may be an excuse for not implementing the idea and taking the first step to creating the new business. The implementation of the plan is of far greater importance than the preparation of the plan. In my situation, I needed to secure a lease for a premises. Once I committed myself to this, everything else fell into place. In many cases, the act of planning is not correlated with the success of a business venture; similarly, the absence of planning cannot be used as the sole explanation of business failure, though it is often a major contributing factor.

Sean: Due to day-to-day pressures, the entrepreneur cannot afford the time and effort needed to examine the long-term future of the business. There is no point in worrying about the future, if the business can't survive in the short-term. However, I accept that it is important that the long-term future of the company is not forgotten.

Paul: Entrepreneurs are required to prepare written plans. In my situation, we had talked about all the major issues and had written down our objectives and plans in some areas of activities. However, we had not produced a complete and integrated written plan. The banks and State agencies required this. At the time, we felt we got little benefit from the added effort required to produce the written plan.

RESEARCH ON PLANNING

The need to write a formal business plan can be challenging for the entrepreneur. In addition, entrepreneurs can be sceptical when it comes to the value or purpose of planning. **Figure 8.5** outlines some of the limitations of planning from an entrepreneurs' perspective. Although the literature on business planning for entrepreneurs has lots of prescriptive advice for the entrepreneur, the reality is that entrepreneurs may need a business plan to look for different forms of capital and undertaking the writing of a business plan provides clarity with respect to business direction and purpose.

FIGURE 8.5: LIMITATIONS OF PLANNING

◊ Entrepreneurs are opportunistic. Planning may result in missed opportunities.
◊ Formal written plans are time-consuming and expensive to prepare.
◊ Plans may become out-dated due to changes in the business environment.
◊ Changes in one section of the plan may result in the complete plan losing its relevance.

DO ENTREPRENEURS PREPARE EFFECTIVE PLANS?

Research by the Bank of Ireland[17] suggests that entrepreneurs, in fact, do not have a good understanding of the financial viability of their business, prior to start-up. This research shows that the financial figures produced by entrepreneurs will vary significantly from the actual outcomes, once they start trading. This study compared the actual financial performance of new businesses with the business plan that was produced prior to start-up (**Figure 8.6**).

---

[17] Research carried out by the Bank of Ireland Enterprise Research Unit.

FIGURE 8.6: SALES, COSTS & PROFITABILITY: FORECASTS COMPARED TO ACTUAL

	FORECAST	ACTUAL
Sales	100%	50%
Gross profits as a % of sales	45%	34%
Overheads as a % of sales	51%	129%
Net profits as a % of sales	4%	− 75%
Debtor Days	80	170
Stock Days	87	193
Credit Days	30	195

Causes of Business Failure

Internationally, research suggests two main causes of failure: the first is the inability of new businesses to control costs when sales are significantly less than forecast; the second is the much higher indebtedness of these businesses and their over-reliance on borrowings, rather than on equity investment. However well-prepared plans may be, they are no guarantee of success. A new business that has prepared a good business plan and has received adequate financial investment may fail due to external market changes or competitive moves that were not possible to forecast in advance.

Do Entrepreneurs Prepare Plans?

The banking sector and the academic literature espouse the importance of preparing a business plan to entrepreneurs. Research suggests that many entrepreneurs don't prepare plans and, more importantly, many successful entrepreneurs do not prepare a formal business plan.

Research on the fastest-growing US companies suggests that most companies had no formal plans (Bhide, 1986). Research on fast-growth firms in Ireland suggests that many high growth businesses have no formal plan (**Figure 8.7**) (Kinsella, 1994). The absence of a formal written plan in many successful start-ups might suggest that the preparation of a formal written plan is unnecessary. In fact, some might argue that it is a waste of the entrepreneur's time to engage in the preparation of a business plan if it does not affect the success and growth of the business.

FIGURE 8.7: PLANNING IN THE FASTEST-GROWING US COMPANIES

	USA	IRISH
No plan	41%	47%
Basic plan	26%	—
Financial projections for investors	5%	—
Full business plans	28%	53%

LESSONS ON PLANNING: A STUDY OF ENTREPRENEURS IN THE IRISH SOFTWARE INDUSTRY[18]

This study interviewed both entrepreneurs and bank lending officers. These groups are often critical of each other. Typical complaints from entrepreneurs are that the banks don't understand their business, and that they are too bureaucratic and slow in making decisions. Entrepreneurs in the Irish software industry were interviewed, because it was believed that they would engage in planning. The researcher also interviewed the lending offices for new business from the main banks. The research conclusion was that entrepreneurs often did not understand the requirements of the bank. Similarly, the banks often did not appreciate what was involved in setting up a business and undervalued the entrepreneur's commitment to planning.

The entrepreneurs claimed that they made their own plans aside from the requirements of the banks. Some entrepreneurs develop two sets of plans: those they submit to the bank and those against which their business operates. They use planning as a tool to monitor the environment and to watch for changes. Entrepreneurs claim that they develop their 'real plans' separately and do not share them with the bank. Their real plans are their own genuine expectations for the business. One entrepreneur explained that his business was doing very well and was surpassing many of his own expectations. However, in order to satisfy the bank, he had to tone down considerably his 'real' projections for the period in order that the bank would accept them as feasible proposals. Despite this toning down, his own plans were closer to the mark.

---

[18] This research was carried out by Kevin Dowdall, Masters of Business Studies student, in his thesis, *Have Banks & Entrepreneurs a Mutual Understanding of the Planning Process?*, University College Dublin, 1996.

LESSONS ON PLANNING FOR THE ENTREPRENEUR

The key things that an entrepreneur must watch for when planning include:

- **Managing finances**: The first lesson for entrepreneurs is that managing money is a very small part of the business of the bank. The banks' main business is managing information. In this regard, banks need information about the proposed business venture on paper, where it can be referenced again and again. When the bank is ready to forward a loan, the information provided will be used as part of the loan terms and agreements. This means that the entrepreneur needs to be fully familiar with the plan at all stages of the application process.

- **Over-optimistic projections**: The second lesson is not to be over ambitious in projections for sales, lead times and so on. If an entrepreneur makes an unrealistic-looking presentation to a bank, it will not be entertained for very long.

- **Ability to repay and a market opportunity**: Banks are interested in how much money an entrepreneur wants to borrow, what they want it for, how they intend to pay it back and how quickly they will pay it back. The bank also wants proof that the market exists and is big enough to carry the business. The bank has only a passing interest in the product or how it works – repayment and profitability are its key interests. Entrepreneurs are considered to be a serious risk by the banks and lending institutions in general.

- **Communicating the business plan**: The business plan is used to communicate the objectives and for the control of resources. It is very important that the bank understands what the entrepreneur's proposals are. The clearer and easier a plan is to follow, the more likely it is to be well-received by a bank representative. Brevity is the key to good communication – say it once and say it well. With regard to control, the plan should explain how the entrepreneur proposes to manage the venture and the level of experience the entrepreneur has in the area.

- **Building the relationship with the bank**: Banks have an experience advantage over small business, as they have seen many small businesses both succeed and fail. They know when plans are viable and when they are not. They know when an individual will drive a business and when he / she will chase it. Entrepreneurs should get to know the bank representative, take advantage of his / her experience and use him / her as a consultant, rather than as a burden. Most importantly, at all times, the bank representative must be kept informed of the organisation's position with regard to finance and markets.

- **Banks' 'gut feeling'**: The seventh lesson is that bank representatives will use the 'gut feeling' rule when processing an application. It is in the entrepreneur's best interests, therefore, to gain the confidence of the bank representative and, at the same time, to promote the business venture.

- **Personal credibility**: Finally, when an entrepreneur has found the bank and bank representative that is the best for their needs, remember that the bank's loan pivots on the entrepreneur's personal credibility. The entrepreneur must establish a rapport with the bank representative if there is any hope of the relationship flourishing.

LESSONS ON PLANNING FOR THE BANKER

Bankers should be aware of the following when considering business plans:

- **Patience and understanding**: Banks must understand that entrepreneurs presenting plans have a different way of thinking about business and planning. Entrepreneurs do not like to be constrained by the formal planning process; however, this does not mean that they are poor planners. That said, entrepreneurs often spend so much of their time developing a product to sell that they lose sight of the cost of producing it. Patience is required on the side of the banks. Even if it seems that a product is going nowhere and that nobody would ever want to buy it, it is still important that the bank should insist that the entrepreneur presents some hard financial data about the proposal before making a decision.

- **Informational resources**: Banks should tell the entrepreneur the information they will need to assess the proposal and the process that is involved in the bank's examination of the proposal. This should help prevent the entrepreneur missing out on the bank's informational needs. Rather than attending several information-gathering meetings, if the entrepreneur knew from the outset that he / she needed to provide a certain kinds of information then that could be arranged immediately.

- **Entrepreneurs' limited resources**: Banks need to remember that small businesses have limited resources. They are always short on experience and time. Written plans are not always available and it is unlikely that entrepreneurs will present very detailed interim proposals.

- **Rigorous analysis of plans**: Banks need to be very cautious that entrepreneurs are not simply telling them what they want to hear. This may involve them moving away from the hard financial data to look behind the entrepreneur. Whatever the bank chooses to do, simple financial analysis may soon become less important.

PLANNING IN NEW & SMALL BUSINESSES

COMPARED TO LARGE BUSINESSES

Experts suggest that entrepreneurs need to prepare a formal written business plan. This approach to planning is based on models of planning in large companies. The research discussed above shows that many entrepreneurs don't prepare written business plans and, of those that do, many are quite poor at it. There are many factors that make planning different in the small business context and make the formal planning model suggested by experts inappropriate for new and small businesses.

The Relative Availability of Resources

Big business can afford to allocate resources to dedicated accounting, planning and production departments as deemed necessary and to buy-in external advice when needed. New and small businesses generally do not have the resources to purchase the same services. The result is that the entrepreneur or small business owner is compelled to do his own consultancy work, becoming responsible for the different functional areas.

The Impact of Environmental Changes

New and small businesses are very susceptible to small environmental changes. For example, the loss of one customer may cause a new business to fail. Big and established businesses normally have sufficient resources to allow them survive minor environmental disturbances.

The Impact of Competition

Many new and small businesses operate in industries with low barriers to entry. The implication of this tends to be a very competitive marketplace and severe price competition. In an effort to generate sales, many new businesses will sell below cost. Unless the new competitor can develop a sustainable competitive advantage, it too will be the victim of the entry of more low-priced competitors. Large competitors will often have developed a more sustainable competitive advantage, for example by branding their products, by achieving economies of scale, etc.

Breadth of Experience

In planning in a large organisation, a complete set of skills and experiences will exist. Entrepreneurs and small business owners may not always have the same breadth of functional experience. Even where small business owners do have industry experience, they may not have the necessary level of experience for managing a whole organisation from book-keeping and finances through to recruitment and selection.

Role of the CEO

In large organisations, one of the key roles of the CEO is to make strategic decisions concerning the growth of the organisation. In comparison, the entrepreneur and small business manager has responsibility for the functional management of the business. Normally, the entrepreneur will be involved in providing the service to the customer.

Time Focus

The entrepreneur tends to be concerned with the present and does not have the time to be strategising about the future. The small businessperson has so many duties to carry out that he cannot possibly devote a lot of time to consciously working through where the organisation is going to be in, say, five year's time. His main concern is in how the organisation is going to call in its debts and pay its bills by the end of the coming month. Small businesses tend to have a shorter scale, and more functional, emphasis to planning.

AN ALTERNATIVE TO THE FORMAL PLANNING MODEL

Process *versus* Planning

The absence of a formal written plan does not mean that there is no planning process. There is a mistaken assumption that planning is about the production of a business plan. In many new and small businesses, the entrepreneur plans the development of his business but he may not take the trouble to put this plan to paper. In a general sense, planning is a reflective activity that precedes the making of a decision. In some situations, this period of analysis might be written up in a formal process but, for many decisions, it is more sensible to implement the decision immediately and proceed to consider other decisions and problems.

Some new businesses start-up on an incremental or part-time basis. As a result, they may not have a formal written business plan at the outset. Instead, the entrepreneur will probably have talked through his business proposal with stakeholders (for example, customers, suppliers, bankers, staff) and will have reached a mutual understanding with these stakeholders as to how the business should operate.

Partial Solutions *versus* Complete Plan

Planning is a problem-solving tool for entrepreneurs. At start-up, the entrepreneur must solve a series of problems of a varied nature. Some problems relate to immediate issues while others will have longer-term implications. Entrepreneurs do not have the time to fully evaluate every option or to consider all issues at once. The preparation of a business plan assumes that all issues are known and can be addressed in advance. The reality of start-up is that many issues and problems emerge during the start-up period and it is difficult to anticipate all of these in advance.

Soft *versus* Hard Information

Another mistaken assumption about the preparation of a business plan is that it is based on hard and detailed facts. However, this sort of detailed information is rarely available. In particular, when entrepreneurs are estimating the market potential of the business opportunity, they will seldom have access to the necessary market information. Entrepreneurs rely on 'soft' forms of information. These include gossip, hearsay, and various other intangible scraps of information that the entrepreneur might get from individual customers, suppliers, competitors and friends. Often the quality of this information is superior to 'hard data' of a more general nature. Entrepreneurs need not have complete and perfect information to prepare a plan and make decisions. The future of a business may be built on some information received from a small number of potential customers rather than a grand market survey. Often, it can be difficult to prepare a written business plan based on this 'soft' information.

Short-term *versus* Long-term

The nature of start-up is that the entrepreneur will focus attention on immediate issues and problems. Many of these decisions have long-term implications – for example, the choice of premises for a retail business. The entrepreneur must be conscious of the long-term strategic implications of short-term operational issues. The entrepreneur should ensure his daily activities lead towards the attainment of his long-term objectives.

THE ROLE OF DEFINING EPISODES

Defining episodes for an SME can have an impact on the manner in which the entrepreneur views the value of planning for the future. It is through defining episodes that enterprises are able to create the opportunity for reflexive strategic practice and change. A study of the strategy management practices in the Irish independent television production sector (Quinn *et al.*, 2006) highlighted that the business start-up phase is typically characterised by quasi-strategic activity, creativity-driven management and an emphasis on production, as opposed to formal business process and activities. Defining episodes bring home the realisation to owners their weaknesses in planning, financial control and lack of direction due to commissioning traps. The response to these defining episodes of the companies within the study was to embrace formal strategy development processes; others embraced a more incremental approach. However, the onset of the defining episode resulted in the emergence of a more cautious outlook and a desire to safeguard the business with a more strategic perspective. In the context of this study, defining episodes focused on three main issues: financial crisis, luck and change in management and, in all cases, the episode signified a significant break from the past (see **Figure 8.8**).

The theme that emerges is that defining episodes serve as a catalyst for a change in behaviour and a significant break from the past approaches to planning, as well as a catalyst for a more rational strategy development process. To prevent the re-occurrence of crisis, measures such as planning and control procedures became important to the study companies as was their desire to have greater control over external events. The defining episodes forced some founders to remove themselves from the everyday operational routine and to engage in some strategy activities and to initiate change, by using a combination of outsider influence and the adoption of more formal strategy development processes.

THE ROLE OF OUTSIDERS IN PLANNING

In a small business context, the responsibility of planning often rests with the entrepreneur, who has direct contact with the marketplace and whose experience is influential. Outsiders to the SME also can have an influence on the how the entrepreneur crafts a business strategy and the formation of planning activities within the business. The study of the independent TV production sector in Ireland (Quinn *et al.*, 2006) found the main sources of outsider influences were management consultants, non-executive board members and government agencies (see **Figure 8.9**).

FIGURE 8.8: DEFINING EPISODES – TRIGGERS & TIMELINES

Company	Trigger	Episode	Timing
Alpha	**Continued growth. crisis in leadership & development**	Lucky meeting at US TV market resulting in merger with larger global company: *'I suppose it was a stroke of luck that I had decided to go to another TV market in the States ... A change in direction in a single meeting by chance ... the elevator pitch still works in this business and I happened to bump into a major decision-maker and was able to pitch them an idea which was never on our plan ... it ended up being a conversation about who owned Alpha ... merger talks went on for a year and we merged last year'.*	4 years
Beta	**Crisis in leadership / direction (period of flux between creativity and direction)**	Change in leadership: Company restructured; new MD appointed; company objectives changed. *'I mean the only big thought we had was that we needed to create a reasonably strong, albeit micro, business ... although we work in a small domestic market, we need to create some renewability and some reliability and reasonable cash flow, because otherwise we couldn't underwrite any other developments in other markets'.*	15 months
Gamma	**Crisis in leadership amongst two founders**	Change in leadership: Roles appointed to founders. *'He is just going to focus on business development, he was just getting distracted, getting pulled left right and centre. Now he is not involved in the overall running of the business day-to-day in the office ... we have an accounts person now and a production manager and, between them, they look after the office'.*	6 years
Delta	**Complacent (over-reliance on domestic market, weak position)**	Lucky break with successful entertainment production took management focus so new management appointed – then long-running series cancelled.	7 and 10 years
Lamda	**Market constraints in TV production**	Leadership: Capture value along the chain, diversified into post-production, so never reliant on TV. *'I think you have to have some structure and environment to think about what you are doing and to set objectives'.*	2 years
Sigma	**Crisis in leadership (inexperienced founder)**	Change in leadership: New MD appointed; transformed 'hippie company'. *'I would admit we had a 'hippie' company ... that's great, but hippie companies generally don't survive or grow too much ... the task was to turn it from a hippie company into a real company, and that's a challenge.'*	1-2 years

FIGURE 8.9: THE ROLE OF OUTSIDERS: THE IRISH INDEPENDENT TV PRODUCTION SECTOR

Management Consultants

Alpha participated in a number strategic planning workshops held by Screen Producers Ireland (a representative organisation for independent film and TV producers) and followed up these workshops by working with the consultant on a one-to-one basis. The use of the consultant provided a fresh approach and unbiased thinking and was outside day-to-day operational demands, as Alan outlines: '[she is] able to look at what we are at, completely clean of any baggage we have got here and has hit the nail on the head with regards some of the issues that we are trying to address here'. Consequently, Alan now champions the formal strategy development processes. He doesn't believe growing the business to a degree and scale can happen by accident, it has to be planned for, and not planning beyond commissions is planning for failure. The plan provides alternatives, so there isn't a reliance on one decision which they have little control over – as he notes: 'If you don't plan for success, it won't happen'.

Non-executive Board Members

Board members often play an active role in crafting strategy. The cases of Beta and Sigma are interesting as the 'outsider influence' made the transition from board member, and consultant respectively, to managing director. As **Figure 7.8** showed, their objectives were to turnaround the business from a 'hippie' company of the creative founder to a 'real business' (Sigma), bringing their financial and commercial sensibilities to the fore, and advocating more 'renewability and reliability' (Beta).

Government Agencies

A number of government agencies have specific responsibility for developing and promoting the sector. Agency departments are concerned with developing international markets for companies, providing grants, staff training and development and ensuring growth. Beta benefited from the support of a government agency, getting a feasibility grant to look at the external market to try to establish what its unique offering was – as Carl explains: '[By understanding] why people in other territories would buy programming from us or ideas from us, we have created a pretty tight focus on what kind of genres of programming we want to make and where we think we have something unique to bring to the market.'

Source: Quinn, O'Reilly & Cunningham (2006).

CONCLUSION

In this chapter, we discussed the reality of preparing a business plan. There are many advantages to preparing a business plan both in terms of the final document and also the process of preparing the plan. However, research shows that many entrepreneurs don't prepare plans and that, of those that do, many are poor at planning. The biggest difficulty is preparing accurate and meaningful financial projections. The chapter suggests that real-life business planning is different from the 'textbook' model and also looked at the role that defining episodes and the role of outsiders can have in terms of planning in an SME context. Entrepreneurs plan for the short term, focus on immediate issues and concerns and are motivated to solve problems.

QUESTIONS

1. Why should an entrepreneur write a business plan?

2. Research suggests that entrepreneurs are poor at planning. What are the difficulties that entrepreneurs encounter when writing a business plan?

3. How is planning in a small business different from planning in a large business?

4. Write the content of a speech that you would present to a group of bank managers that explains planning from the perspective of the entrepreneur.

5. Does the format of the business plan outlined in **Chapters 6** and **7** reflect the reality of planning in new businesses?

6. What impact do defining episodes and outsiders have on planning within SMEs?

7. Talk to an entrepreneur or small businessperson about their planning process.

PROFILE: BRODY SWEENEY, O'BRIEN'S SANDWICH BARS[19]

O'Brien's Sandwich Bars (O'Brien's) is one of Ireland's best-known brands and a leader in the gourmet coffee and sandwiches sector. Founded in the tough economic climate of the 1980s by entrepreneur Brody Sweeney, O'Brien's has been developed from a small start-up into an international brand, through the franchising model, and now has a global footprint in the UK, Europe and Asia. Half of O'Brien's outlets are in the UK, where it has a market share of approximately 20%.

Early January 2006 marked the beginning of another chapter in the O'Brien's story, with the appointment of Fiacra Nagle (MD of O'Brien's Ireland since 2002, having joined the organisation in 2000) as Group CEO. This move was accompanied by Brody Sweeney, founder of O'Brien's, taking up the position of Executive Chairman in order to allow him time to pursue political ambitions.

O'Brien's began business in 1988, when Brody opened his first store in Dublin's South Great Georges Street. Opening a made-to-order sandwich shop in the tough Irish economic climate of the late 1980s was considered by some observers as foolhardy. O'Brien's were before their time, as not everyone was ready to appreciate (and pay a premium for) made-to-order sandwiches.

It was 1994 before O'Brien's had their first franchisee, when Brody sold one of the existing stores – in the St. Stephens Green Shopping Centre – to Tom Cunningham, an accountant. The store had a newsagent attached, which, at the time, was the more valuable part of the business. As a 'sweetener' on the deal, Brody agreed not to charge his new franchisee royalties until a further three franchises were sold. Within a short period, three more franchises had been opened and Tom began paying royalties as agreed. In fact, Tom became O'Brien's first multiple-franchisee, when he purchased a second store and, subsequently, opened three others. Brody, himself, admits that the turning point in the business was the second sale:

> 'It's possible to win a trophy once or make a sale through a fluke or through good salesmanship. Being able to do so more than once takes the strength and depth that only a great team has'.

The name O'Brien's came about as Brody felt that he needed a catchy title, something that would distinguish his company, but that would also bring out the 'Irishness' of the business. He found, from the phonebook, that O'Brien was one of the most popular names and he settled on this. Indeed, the 'Irishness' of the

---

[19] This profile is adapted from a case written by Chris O'Riordan, James Cunningham & Denis Harrington, which was published in Henry & McGowan (2007).

business has come more to the fore in recent years, as O'Brien's has expanded internationally – the quality association appeals to customers, many of whom have never even been to Ireland. Today, O'Brien's have found that the 'Irish' angle is of much less significance in Ireland and the UK, to the point that it has renamed itself 'O'Brien's Sandwich Bars' in these countries.

O'Brien's keeps a tight control on its franchise operators in all markets, but supports each franchise operation, through new product development, the careful selection of appropriate sites and the focus on customer service as Brody himself commented in his recent book (Sweeney, 2005):

> *'I still get a great sense of excitement and achievement from seeing a full car park outside an O'Brien's store or standing behind a till, slightly incredulous that people are happy to hand over their hard-earned cash for the privilege of eating and drinking in one of our stores.'*

The success of rolling out the franchise model internationally has been mixed. Entering the Spanish market had some initial difficulties. O'Brien's first store was set up in Marbella, an ideal location because of the volumes of Irish and UK tourists in the summer and ex-pats all year round. The local trade has also flourished and the franchisee has noticed that the traditional custom of tapas and long lunches is changing – people want quick and convenient food. However, the second store in Fuengirola – in a shopping centre – started quite slowly. The franchisee observed that, while traffic was high, customers were coming in and leaving again. The root of the problem was that they did not know what they were supposed to do (Smyth, 2005):

> *'We have a 'made-to-order' concept and they are looking at the menus, confused as to what they should do next. Rather than ask, we have found that many will just leave'.*

To overcome this problem, the company launched a promotional campaign whereby leaflets (in Spanish) are given to customers when they arrive, outlining how to order, from selecting the bread type and fillings to what drink they would like. This has proven successful and was a case of adapting the O'Brien's concept to local culture.

One of O'Brien's biggest disappointments in its 18-year existence has been its failure in the United States. Established only a few years earlier, 'Brody's Sandwich Bars' closed in 2004 – according to O'Brien's financial statements, the US operation lost $400,000 in the year ending 31 December 2003 and owed €747,000 to the Irish business.

9

FINANCING THE ENTERPRISE

One of the most important financial decisions at start-up is the raising and management of financial resources. The entrepreneur must put financial figures on the business idea. This will require an estimate of potential sales revenues and costs and of the amount of funding needed to start and operate the business. Funding is needed for purchasing fixed assets and for the working capital requirements of the business. Once the entrepreneur has identified the financial requirements of the new business, it is necessary to raise the capital through debt, equity or both. The entrepreneur must then manage the capital and cash flow in the business. Poor cash flow management results in otherwise good ideas failing as businesses. This chapter examines the factors to consider when raising finance, the types of finance used by small businesses and sources of this finance.

RAISING FINANCE

DEBT & EQUITY FINANCE

An entrepreneur may use a combination of debt and equity finance. Debt finance is money that the entrepreneur borrows. Equity finance is money invested in the business in return for a share in the ownership of the business. It is important that the entrepreneur balances the use of debt and equity.

The advantage of debt finance is that the entrepreneur retains control of the business. However, there is a risk attached to borrowing money, as the lender will usually have sought security for the loan. Failure to repay a loan may result in the new business failing. An over-reliance on debt finance is particularly risky for new businesses, because of the lack of established cash flows. A further risk of debt finance is that increases in interest rates may require higher monthly loan repayments.

The advantage of equity finance is that there is no monthly cash outflow from the business. Equity investors are paid dividends from profits, only when the business can afford them. Equity investors in new businesses usually expect their ownership stake to increase in value because of the success of the business. This profit is realised when the equity investor sells the stake in the business. Many entrepreneurs find it difficult to attract outside equity investors and only have limited equity of their own to invest in their new business. Some entrepreneurs are slow to attract outside equity investors because they feel they may lose some control of their business.

FACTORS TO CONSIDER WHEN RAISING FINANCE

Nature of the Business

Not all businesses have the same capital requirements. A restaurant business will usually not need funding to test the feasibility of the idea. In contrast, a new bio-technology business may need funding to research and develop a prototype. A new manufacturing business may need funds to purchase machinery and stocks. In contrast, a new software company may not need much capital to purchase equipment, but it will need extensive capital to fund the entrepreneur's time during the product development stage. Businesses that generate large cash flows will usually need less financing.

Stage of Business Development

The stage of development of the new business influences the level of risk of the investment. At an early stage, the new business needs capital that does not have to be repaid. An entrepreneur who needs to research a market and test the feasibility of a business idea does not want to borrow money to fund this expenditure. At this stage, the business has no revenues and will be unable to repay a loan. A business with a trading history will be more attractive to an investor because it has demonstrated that there is a market for the product / service.

Control & Ownership

Is the entrepreneur prepared to sell an equity stake in the business? This will mean that the entrepreneur is accountable to the investor. It may mean sharing managerial control. Most entrepreneurs find it difficult to offer equity to outside investors. The entrepreneur often delays selling equity in the belief that, as the business grows and develops, the price that will be received for the equity will increase. However, the lack of finance in the interim may impede the growth and development of the business.

Time

What will the finance be used for? If the finance is to fund long-term needs such as fixed assets or working capital, it is essential that long-term sources of finance are used. Many new and small businesses find it difficult to raise medium and long-term finance, because of the high risk attached to the investments.

Exit Strategy

In raising finance, it is essential that the entrepreneur develops a way for the investors to 'exit' from the investment. How will the investor get the capital and any profit out of the business? Most investors will want to 'cash-in' their investment after a period of time. One of the easiest methods is to bring the venture to the stock market. This provides the initial investors with the choice of holding onto their investment for further capital gains or of selling their shares on the stock market.

PROBLEMS WHEN RAISING FINANCE

The entrepreneur faces a number of problems when trying to raise finance. These include:

- **Lack of collateral**: The new venture has no assets or trading history against which an investor can evaluate the risk of the investment. Banks still may seek personal guarantees from entrepreneurs for loans.

- **Lack of accounting expertise**: The entrepreneur may be inexperienced in preparing loan applications and *pro forma* accounts. The cost of an accountant and their professional advice might seem quite high for the new business.

- **Identifying sources**: The entrepreneur may be inexperienced in raising finance and may be unsure of where to seek it. There are a large number of agencies and bodies that assist new start-ups but the entrepreneur may find it difficult to identify the most appropriate source.

- **Interest charges**: From the perspective of the bank, applications for small loans are relatively expensive to process. The same time and effort are needed to assess a €20,000 loan application as a €200,000 application loan, yet the profitability of the latter should be significantly higher. Banks charge a premium rate to entrepreneurs to compensate for the higher costs of processing loan applications and to cover the higher risk attached to a loan to a new business.

For Irish SMEs, the single biggest problem they encounter in raising finance is the risk of the venture, followed by the lack of collateral requirements (Forfás, 2006). In particular, for business at a start-up phase the high risk associated is a significant factor in not being able to access finance (see **Figures 9.1** and **9.2**). The study revealed that the top three effects on finance / equity were:

- Working capital and cash flow constraints (65% of respondents).

- The inability to invest in marketing and advertising (59% of respondents).

- The inability to hire new employees and finance R&D (51% of respondents).

FIGURE 9.1: PROBLEMS ENCOUNTERED IN RAISING FINANCE / EQUITY IN THE PAST THREE YEARS

	Responses	% Companies
Lack of collateral requirements	17	30
Considered high risk	31	55
Unclear business plan	7	13
Lack of track record	14	25
Amount of finance / equity not attractive to investors	16	29
Total number of companies	**56**	

Source: *Forfás (2006)*.

FIGURE 9.2: PROBLEMS ENCOUNTERED IN RAISING FINANCE / EQUITY BY DEVELOPMENT STAGE IN THE PAST THREE YEARS

	Start-up	Development phase	Steadily growing	Considering expansion
Lack of collateral requirements	18%	25%	43%	50%
Considered high risk	73%	54%	50%	50%
Unclear business plan	27%	13%	0%	0%
Lack of track record	36%	33%	7%	17%
Amount of finance/ equity not attractive to investors	27%	25%	29%	50%
Total number of companies	**11**	**24**	**14**	**6**

Source: Forfás, *SME Finance Equity* (2006).

APPROACHING AN INVESTOR

The decision to seek external capital is a difficult choice for an entrepreneur. As noted earlier, entrepreneurs tend to exhibit a strong desire for control and, consequently, they tend to be slow at involving 'outsiders' in an ownership role. The reality is that, for many entrepreneurs, there is a need for outside capital. Entrepreneurs who are prepared to risk involving outsiders in an ownership role are often those that get the capital that grows the business.

The process of raising external capital can be time- and resource-consuming. The entrepreneur will have to prepare a business plan and presentation for the venture capitalist or other potential investors. In some instances, entrepreneurs will develop an 'elevator pitch', which begins with a brief overview of the business and the capital requirement (see **Figure 9.3**). This is distributed to potential investors and, based on interest, then followed up with a business plan, presentations and face-to-face meetings. During this process, entrepreneurs usually ask potential investors to sign non-disclosure agreements (NDAs).

There are a number of different factors that affect the decision of an investor to invest in a new or growing business. The most important are:

- **People**: The investor is investing in the management potential of the entrepreneur, which is essential to the growth of the new venture. This can be more important than the business idea. The investor will examine the management record of the entrepreneur and the breadth of functional managerial skills required to run the business. The investor may insist that the entrepreneur hires marketing and finance professionals to enhance the management team's capabilities. Many investors have a preference for an entrepreneurial team rather than an individual entrepreneur. In the US, it is considered reasonable to have started and failed a number of times before finally becoming successful. At the seed stage, the venture capitalist must make a decision based on the entrepreneur. Even if the idea has good potential, it cannot be realised without an entrepreneur with the appropriate skills.

- **Product / service idea.** The investor has to make a judgment on the future demand for the product / service. Where possible, the entrepreneur needs to demonstrate the product in operation. Investors are particularly pleased to see an existing customer base that have purchased and, where appropriate, re-purchased the product / service. If the business is at an early stage of development, the entrepreneur should have a working prototype of the product.

- **Magnitude of the investment.** The investor will consider the fit between the proposal for funding and their own existing investment commitments. Many investors choose to specialise in certain sectors or in a certain stage of funding. Other investors may seek a spread of investments and may reject a proposal because they believe they are over-extended in a particular sector. Rejection from an investor does not mean that the proposal is flawed. Entrepreneurs often have to 'knock on the doors' of many venture capitalists before they raise the finance they require.

FIGURE 9.3: TYPICAL STRUCTURE OF AN 'ELEVATOR PITCH'

◊ The company.
◊ Key attributes.
◊ Stage of development.
◊ Funding.
◊ The proposition.
◊ The market.
◊ The product / services.
◊ Product / service benefits.
◊ Pricing.
◊ Intellectual property.
◊ Management team.
◊ Financial summary.

THE 'VALLEY OF DEATH'

The financing requirements of a new venture often do not peak at the start-up phase, as losses, slow sales and high costs inevitably create the need for more finance. Studies of the cumulative cash flow position of new businesses suggest that these cash deficits peak within two to three years of start-up. This cash requirement has been referred to as the 'valley of death', also referred to as the 'J-Curve' effect (**Figure 9.4**). It is during this time that most new businesses fail.

FIGURE 9.4: THE 'J-CURVE' - THE 'VALLEY OF DEATH'

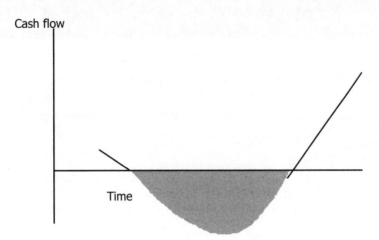

There are a number of ways that the entrepreneur can seek to reduce this cash flow deficit:

- **Plan more accurately:** The most difficult figure to estimate is sales. Entrepreneurs are often unsure of potential sales revenues and the timing of these revenues. Sales revenues, costs and capital requirements all need to be estimated more accurately. The ability to plan more accurately is increased with the entrepreneur's knowledge of the sector and previous experience of starting up a business.

- **Balance the use of equity and loan capital:** Too much reliance on loan capital increases the risk of failure. Loans must be repaid and incur a monthly interest charge. Equity investors expect to make their profit through capital gains and do not expect monthly repayments.

- **Reduce the capital expenditure requirement of the business:** This can be achieved by renting premises rather than buying them and by leasing equipment rather than purchasing it. There is a tendency of Irish companies to invest in premises and land rather than in more productive assets.

- **Cash management:** Efficient cash management can increase a new business's chances of survival. Cash management involves ensuring that money owed is collected on time. This often does not happen because the entrepreneur is 'busy' running the business. Some entrepreneurs are slow to pressurise customers for payment because they fear they might lose future sales. Cash management also ensures that expenditures are controlled and that the business takes advantage of discounts that are available.

TYPES OF FINANCE

There are three types of finance that a new venture may need:

- Seed capital.
- Venture capital.
- Development capital.

Seed capital and venture capital are referred to as 'early' stage financing, while development capital is referred to as 'later' stage funding. To confuse matters further, sometimes all three types may be referred to as 'venture' capital.

SEED CAPITAL

Seed capital is used to test the feasibility of a new business. It is usually required in manufacturing and high technology new ventures, when there is a technological uncertainty concerning the product or process, and investors must be satisfied about the technical feasibility of the business opportunity. Seed capital may be used to fund the entrepreneur's time to develop a new product / process. In situations where there is a technical breakthrough, the entrepreneur may use some of the seed capital to file for patent protection.

Seed capital is the highest risk of all capital for new businesses. Therefore, it is inappropriate to borrow this type of finance. Seed capital is usually raised from family and friends, and sometimes from private investors. The State agencies in Ireland award feasibility grants to some new businesses.

In making a seed capital investment, the investor must be aware of the high level of risk. The majority of seed capital is lost. The investor should investigate the entrepreneur and the process for developing and commercialising the new product / service. Sometimes, the inventor / developer is more interested in the technical performance of the product and will continue to improve the product rather than bring it to the market. Also, if the inventor / developer is having difficulty, the investor should avoid being pulled into a cycle of investing more on the promise that this is the last amount needed to complete the feasibility testing.

VENTURE CAPITAL

Venture capital is capital that is required to start-up the business. At this stage, there are more sources of finance available. This type of capital is used to purchase the assets of the business and to cover the initial operational losses that will be incurred. Working capital and operational losses are costs that many entrepreneurs fail to include when they are calculating their capital requirements. For some new ventures, start-up / venture capital will be required for up to the first five years of operation. There is a high risk attached to this capital, as the failure rate for new businesses in the first five years of operation is up to 60%.

A Forfás study on *SME Finance Equity* (2006) revealed that state grants and bank loans are significant sources of finance used by SMEs (see **Figure 9.5**). This study also found that 70% of companies with less than 10 employees had difficulties in raising finance and that the highest need for finance for businesses were at the start-up and development phases. BES funding has grown as a key source of funding in comparison to the 2002 study, where 14% of respondents used it as a source of raising finance compared to 21.7% in 2005, the latest year for which figures are available. In particular, over half the businesses in the development phase relied on BES (53%) and the Seed Capital Scheme (55%).

FIGURE 9.5: SOURCES OF FINANCE / EQUITY 2003 - 2005

	Responses	Percentage
Business Expansion Scheme (BES)	55	21.7
Seed Capital Scheme	22	8.7
Family and Friends	24	9.4
Other Private Investors	97	38.2
Leasing/Hire Purchase	46	18.1
State Grants	108	42.5
Bank loan/mortgage/overdraft	122	48.0
Other	22	8.7
Total number of companies that raised finance / equity and indicated a source in the survey	**254**	

Source: Forfás, *SME Finance Equity* (2006).

DEVELOPMENT CAPITAL

Development capital is used to finance the growth and expansion of the business. This capital is lower risk than either seed or venture capital, because the business now has a trading record. Investors of development capital are particularly concerned with having an exit for their investment. The exit method that they prefer is the floating of the company on the stock exchange.

Also included in 'later' stage financing is replacement capital. This is money that is used to buy out the entrepreneur from the business and to fund management buy-outs.

SOURCES OF FINANCE

Raising finance can be a time-consuming and frustrating process for the entrepreneur. There are many sources of finance. The more important sources are listed below, however there are other sources that are available to particular businesses and in particular geographical areas.

When raising finance, the entrepreneur may need to offer investors benefits beyond a straight cash return, for example one Irish hotel in financial difficulties offered an American customer of the hotel a free two-week holiday for the remainder of his life as part of an investment deal.

Sources of finance include:

- **Family and friends**: This is a very common source of finance for small start-ups. It is a particularly good source of high risk capital. Problems may arise if there is not a formal legal contract between family members, however.

- **Bank loans**: This is the most common source of finance for most small businesses. The advantage for the small business is that the entrepreneur can retain control and ownership of the business. Over-reliance on debt finance may increase the financial risk of the business. Too much debt at the start-up stage may create a large cash outflow of interest repayments. Historically, it has been difficult for small businesses to raise long-term debt finance from banks. The banks prefer to lend for asset-backed loans and are slower to lend money for the working capital requirements of a business.

- **Government agencies**: The most important of these agencies is Enterprise Ireland, which supports manufacturing and internationally traded services, for example financial services. Grants that are available include feasibility studies grants, employment grants, capital equipment grants, R&D grants, and grants for market development.

- **County & City Enterprise Boards**: County & City Enterprise Boards give grants for feasibility studies and for start-up. They tend to invest small amounts of money, as little as €1,270 for feasibility studies, with the average grants being about €13,000. The Enterprise Boards have fewer restrictions but will only invest in businesses with less than 10 employees and where the financing need is less than €130,000. CEBs will not invest in start-ups that duplicate other existing businesses or are against public policy. Also they operate at a local level and part of their brief is to encourage entrepreneurship.

- **Retained earnings**: This is an important source of finance for many small businesses. Retained earnings are the profits of the business that are re-invested back into the business. The advantage of reinvesting profits is that the equity investment of the business increases without diluting the entrepreneur's control. Also tax is payable on dividends.

- **Venture capitalists**: They usually take an equity participation in a business. Most venture capital in Ireland is targeted at businesses at the development or growth stage. Increasingly, venture capital has become available for new start-ups, particularly in high technology sectors such as software. The venture capitalist will usually take an active involvement in the business in areas of financial management and strategic planning.

- **Private investors**: These may be individuals who have made their own money in a different business and are interested in financing other entrepreneurs. This money is usually raised through personal contacts or through accountants.

- **Business Innovation Centres**: These have been set up with the assistance of the EU. The six in Ireland provide a wide range of services to people wanting to start their own business. They also provide information and access to sources of seed capital. They usually take an equity holding in the new venture.

- **European Union**: The Structural Funds that Ireland receives each year are disseminated through various operational programmes. Programmes that may be of interest to small businesses are LEADER+, and INTER-REG,

- **Seed Capital Scheme**: This scheme allows entrepreneurs to claim six years' of tax back if they start a business. Little use has been made of this scheme, due to its complicated structure and the fact that it is not well-known.

- **Irish Enterprise Exchange (IEX)**: There has been increased use of the stock market as a source of finance for small companies. The IEX was launched in April 2005 with eight listed companies – by mid-2007, 29 companies were listed, with market capitalisation of over €3 billion. IEX companies include Boundary Capital, Zamano, Origin Enterprises and First Derivatives. The equivalent market in the UK is AIM (Alternative Investment Market).

APPROACHING VENTURE CAPITALISTS

The process involved in raising venture capital finance has a number of clear stages (**Figure 9.6**). First, the entrepreneur should establish that the venture capital is appropriate for the new venture. The entrepreneur needs to establish that the venture capitalist will consider investing in the particular industry and that the new business is at a stage of development that is appropriate to the venture capitalist. Having identified a number of potential sources of venture capital, the entrepreneur should submit a business plan.

FIGURE 9.6: STAGES OF VENTURE CAPITAL SCREENING

Stage 1: Screening of Proposals

The venture capitalist will read the business proposal. Up to 80% of proposals will be screened out at this stage.

Stage 2: In-depth Examination

The remaining proposals will be examined in-depth. This will involve an analysis of the accounts, the product / service, and the market. The venture capitalist will have discussions with suppliers and customers of the proposed venture.

Stage 3: Meeting the Entrepreneur

If the venture capitalist is still interested, the entrepreneur and the management team will be invited to make a presentation of their proposal. A site visit to the business may follow.

Stage 4: Due Diligence

If the venture capitalist makes a decision to invest, it will carry out a 'due diligence' report, which is a complete audit of the business. The due diligence will check that the financial accounts are a true reflection of the state of the business. The venture capitalist will want to ensure that there are no hidden liabilities, such as outstanding actions against the company and that the company has full title to its assets. This may take between six to 12 weeks.

A venture capitalist will read the proposal and either accept or reject it, based on:

- Whether the area of investment is of interest .
- The calibre of people involved.
- Whether the financial projections make sense and the business is a solid investment.

In return for its investment, the venture capital firm will seek between 25% and 40% of the equity of the business. The venture capitalist will rarely invest in over 50% of the equity, as it wants the management team to have a stake in ensuring the continued success of the business. The venture capitalist will seek a number of places on the board of the company to protect its investment. Venture capitalists will also seek a commitment from the entrepreneur that there is an exit mechanism. This will usually mean a commitment to bringing the company to the stock market within approximately five years of the initial investment.

Venture capitalists seek a high capital appreciation on their investments. This is necessary because only a few of their investments are successful. The portfolio of a typical venture capitalist will have more businesses that fail to reward the venture capitalist for the risk (**Figure 9.7**) than those that are successful. Research carried out by the Centre for Entrepreneurial Studies at University College Dublin showed that Irish venture capitalists invested €1 billion between 1994 and 2004, with 86% of this investment in high-technology firms. Furthermore, the study found that expenditure on R&D by Irish venture capital-backed high-technology companies represented approximately 28% of the total Irish business expenditure on research and development (BERD). The study also found that non-monetary benefits of venture capital investment included improved corporate governance, increased focus on shareholder value, enhanced credibility for the company and improved access to business networks.

FIGURE 9.7: A VENTURE CAPITALIST'S PORTFOLIO

20%	Companies successfully floated on the stock market.
40%	Companies merged into larger companies.
20%	'Living Dead' – companies that survive but do not meet investors' expectations.
20%	Companies fail.

CONCLUSION

Cash is the lifeblood of new and small businesses. This chapter identified the crucial issues that an entrepreneur should consider when financing a new business idea. The challenge facing most entrepreneurs is to raise enough finance and to ensure that the appropriate type of finance is raised. Sources of finance for new and small businesses were outlined. Investors will use the finance plan to evaluate the business proposal.

QUESTIONS

1. What factors should an entrepreneur consider when raising finance?

2. What factors should an investor consider when investing in a new business idea?

3. It is often said that 'cash is the lifeblood of a new business'. How can an entrepreneur maximise the cash flow of the business?

4. A friend from college is considering starting a software business. Where might she get finance to fund the development of her new product idea?

5. Find out the criteria that a funding agency or investor in your area uses when investing in new or small businesses.

6. From reading the profile of John Concannon, JFC Manufacturing (see next page), develop an elevator pitch for JFC Manufacturing using **Figure 9.3** as a guide.

PROFILE: JOHN CONCANNON, JFC MANUFACTURING[20]

John Concannon was educated in St Jarlath's College, Tuam and, on leaving school, worked in transport and helped out on the family farm for nearly 10 years. However, he wanted to educate himself further and do something different with his life. He took night courses in marketing and psychology, and read about business and business people who had set up their own businesses.

His first real business venture was selling smoke alarms door-to-door based on a bank loan of IR£1,000. He only sold one smoke alarm, but he learnt a key lesson – the need for effective sales and marketing techniques. Such techniques have become key ingredients in the growth of JFC. He then went on a professional selling course, while working on the family farm, which provided the inspiration for his first product idea – a plastic-based feeding system for cattle – which essentially combined three feeding buckets:

> *I was feeding calves one day and thought the job could get done more quickly if I fixed three buckets together ... Other farmers saw the idea and wanted something similar, so I refined the design and got a plastics manufacturer to make the bucket.*

He twice attempted to raise funding from IDA Ireland at the time; he was refused but received a grant of IR£1,800 from the Galway Enterprise Board, which allowed him to buy some tools to finish off the plastic products that Rom Plastics had manufactured for him. Selling his feeding system was tough in the Galway region, so he decided to base himself in Listowel, Co. Kerry, where he set himself a target of 20 units per day selling to farmers. This proved successful, but he had yet to break into the co-op market. Driving back from Kerry, he stopped at the Mitchelstown Co-op in Garryspillane, Co. Limerick, where he gave a sales presentation that overcame the co-op bureaucracy.

JFC's first premises were in the Dunmore Industrial Estate in Tuam, where Concannon installed the first rotational moulding machine. As activity increased, Concannon purchased machinery from Crolly Dolls in Donegal for IR£4,000, which was one-tenth of their original value. Two years later, the business moved to Weir Road, JFC's current location, as it had bought more machines in Scotland and needed additional space to store them. JFC began to recruit some of the engineers who had worked in the Tuam sugar factory to assist with the configuration of the machines and with new product development.

Concannon's sales and marketing skills came to the fore as JFC attended various agricultural shows and other trade events, which offered opportunities,

---

[20] This profile is adapted from a case study written by James Cunningham, J.E. Cairnes Graduate School of Business & Public Policy, NUI Galway, as part of the Ernst & Young Entrepreneur of the Year Case Studies Series 2006.

not only to sell products, but also to keep up with trends and happenings in the industry. These shows also allowed John to scout for talent in his quest for international expansion in the UK, mainland Europe and Poland.

Product Development & Innovations

By 2005, the company turnover had reached €30 million, based on sales of a range of products to markets that included transport, equestrian, hospitality, materials handling, medical, agriculture, environment, road-building and the construction industry. This proliferation of product ranges was possible because the company had invested heavily in R&D:

> *R&D has delivered products and processes that have given us the advantage over the competition … For a small company to have 10 people in R&D is expensive, but JFC is getting the return on its investment.*

International Expansion

JFC now exports to over 30 countries, including America, Japan, Korea and Australia, and continues to attend national and international trade shows with these exports accounting for over 60% of the company's total sales.

Expansions in both Holland and Poland have come through personal contacts, developed through attendance at international trade fairs, with initial operations being run out of apartments. In 2004, JFC opened a manufacturing plant in Poland, about 20 kilometres from Warsaw, which represented a €4 million investment. As Concannon explains:

> *We had to create a new product range that would be suitable for the Polish market and culture. We also had a language and distance barrier to overcome, but so far the results have been fantastic and our Polish plant is operating well ahead of targets.*

By 2006, the Polish plant employed 10 people, had two moulding machines in operation, and runs at one-fifth of the cost of its Irish counterpart.

New product development continues apace. Successful international expansion in the UK and Poland has tested the management team. The JFC culture, as well as changes in the legislative environment, has provided some new market opportunities. The rise in fuel prices and the bulky nature of some of the products provide ongoing challenges for JFC. In meeting these challenges, Concannon knows that he needs to focus on nurturing and developing managerial talent in order to bring JFC through the next phases of international expansion. Like any other business in this situation, the issue of succession comes to mind. The future offers opportunities to diversify into new product areas and for further acquisitions. The future challenge for JFC, as Concannon notes, is:

> *… continuously hammering home the difference.*

10

GROWTH STRATEGIES[21]

Why do the majority of new start-ups stay very small or self-employment businesses, what are referred to as 'micro-businesses'? Research evidence from the UK (Storey, 2006) suggests that most new businesses do not achieve significant growth. This UK research showed that for every 100 new start-ups, only four will grow rapidly. In fact, 10 years after start-up, these fastest-growing four businesses will account for half of all employment in those businesses that have survived. This chapter explores why only a small number of start-ups achieve growth. It outlines a model of the growth process and details the problems that the entrepreneur must 'solve' at each stage.

FIGURE 10.1: THE IRISH GRAPHIC DISPLAY INDUSTRY

The Irish graphic display industry is highly fragmented, so much so that it is difficult to find agreement among participants on its boundaries. There is a multitude of competitors, nearly all of which are small, owner-managed businesses, serving a highly-varied market. Products are used by advertising agencies in corporate exhibitions, trade shows, in-store displays, visitor attractions, museums and heritage centres. Product 'lines' are diverse, as each product will be tailored to suit customer needs. Competition has become more intense as the industry growth rate has slowed and businesses have had to work harder to capture the business that does exist.

The Irish industry is primarily Dublin-based. Marketing is primarily business-to-business and, in a small city like Dublin, personal contacts can be the key to attracting customers. Size is generally not an advantage when dealing with suppliers and buyers. In many cases, the small size of many of the businesses in the industry allows them to serve customers more effectively, with a high level of flexibility, quick reaction times and a highly personalised service. The industry has a heavy creative content. Firms must first visualise their customers' needs and then turn them into something tangible. To do this, a personal service must be offered, as there will be a high degree of user-producer interface as the design and production process progresses.

---

[21] The authors acknowledge the assistance of Aileen O'Toole in the preparation of this chapter, based on her thesis, *The Growth Problems of Small Firms in the Irish Graphic Display Industry*, Masters of Business Studies, 1996, University College Dublin.

Question 1: Is the ability and motivation of the owner-manager central to the success or failure of small businesses in this industry?

The entrepreneurs managed to avoid many of the mistakes made by small business owner-managers that are potential growth barriers – for example, lack of managerial ability, unwillingness to delegate, a narrow product-market base. The entrepreneurs demonstrated high levels of motivation, coupled with an element of realism about their shortcomings. This allowed them to seek help in areas where their skills were deficient. All have had little difficulty with delegation. Their ability to overcome the problems their businesses faced, and to develop innovative solutions to problems, appears to be one of the most important elements in their businesses' success.

Question 2: Is lack of finance a growth problem for small businesses in this industry?

No evidence was found to suggest that the availability of finance was a problem for the small businesses studied. The prevailing opinion amongst the entrepreneurs was that funding is usually available, providing the idea is good and it is presented effectively to the lender. Surprisingly, there was relatively little reliance on grants from State agencies and, after their respective start-up periods, no grants were obtained.

Question 3: Are 'labour legislation' and 'red tape' barriers to growth for small businesses in this industry?

The costs of the benefits that must be provided to employees were criticised. However, they have not discouraged any of the entrepreneurs from hiring additional staff. Labour legislation was considered 'inconvenient', rather than problematic. The legislative area that the entrepreneurs saw as providing the most significant problems for small businesses attempting to grow was taxation. The entrepreneurs claimed that punitive taxation prevents the re-investment of profits within the business and decreases the methods by which they can motivate their employees financially. The level of 'red tape' was considered to be more of an inconvenience than a problem.

Conclusions

◊   By far, the biggest growth problem for small businesses in the Irish graphic display industry is the fragmented structure and limited markets of the industry itself. This may have forced the entrepreneurs of the businesses in the study to deviate from their core market niche into ancillary niches or sidelines in order to grow their businesses.

◊   The fact that lack of finance is no longer the serious growth problem it was once thought to be is something that public policy-makers have begun to recognise. Government should now turn its attention towards alleviating the tax burden on small businesses in an effort to promote further growth amongst small businesses within this industry.

◊   The findings emphasise the centrality of the entrepreneur to success in a small business. The dynamism and commitment of the entrepreneurs was obvious and their substantial abilities, coupled with their realism, accounted for their success.

◊   A significant growth problem that emerged in the cases (possibly related in some way to the level of 'red tape' encountered) was the lack of time that entrepreneurs had to develop their businesses. This problem was especially severe before the first management layer was introduced, but it was still an ongoing problem for the entrepreneurs.

WHY DO SMALL BUSINESSES STAY SMALL?

EXTERNAL BARRIERS TO SMALL BUSINESS GROWTH

These include:

- **Market size**: Market size can be a serious barrier to growth for many small Irish companies. The size of the domestic market is limited by Ireland's small population. This means that small businesses must begin to export or operate in overseas markets when they are still quite small. Transport costs required to export may make a product / service uncompetitive.

- **Market structure**: The structure of the market in which a small business operates may have an effect on its ability to grow. In markets characterised by a standardised product, the new business will be at a disadvantage relative to larger businesses; while in markets with many different customer requirements, the business may be able to grow within a niche.

- **Labour costs and labour legislation**: High labour costs can act as a deterrent for growth in small businesses. The cost of labour increases with size, as more non-manual workers are recruited who demand higher wages. In addition, the larger the business gets, the greater the non-wage costs per employee, as employee facilities must be of a higher quality and benefits must also be increased. Complying with labour legislation can create additional costs that unfairly burden small businesses. Many of the smallest businesses are exempt from such legislation, but growth in employee numbers may mean that the legislation is applicable. This may act as a de-motivating influence for entrepreneurs contemplating growth.

- **'Red Tape'**: The level of paperwork required to operate even the smallest of businesses places a heavy burden on the entrepreneur. The Small Firms Association argues that a small business faces an excessive burden of legal and regulatory issues in the areas of tax (VAT, PAYE, PRSI) and industrial relations. Research on fast-growth businesses in Ireland found that the major problem experienced by Irish small businesses attempting to grow was the time constraints on management. These entrepreneurs also reported that government bureaucracy, the volume of paperwork and the time it took to 'get things done' was problematic. The Business Regulation Forum Report (2007) quantified that Irish business could potentially save €500 million each year, through the easing of regulatory burdens. The Forum recommended that a regulatory reduction programme should focus on the areas of tax, health and safety, environmental regulation, requests for statistical information and employment and company law.

INTERNAL BARRIERS TO SMALL BUSINESS GROWTH

These include:

- **Finance**: The ability to raise finance is a problem for new and growing businesses. Small businesses face a number of difficulties in raising finance, including:
  - ◊ **Low profitability:** Many small businesses have low profitability and find it difficult to generate internally the level of capital they require.
  - ◊ **Level of funding:** The level of funding required for expansion can be very high, when compared to the existing capital base of the business. This increases the bank's level of risk and, consequently, banks seek a higher return on investment.
  - ◊ **Timing of funds:** The small business will require funds in lump sums, rather than in small incremental amounts. For example, a food manufacturer wishing to increase capacity may have to acquire new premises, purchase new machinery and invest in the development of its market. These expenditures will be required before the benefits of the increased size will be experienced.
  - ◊ **Competitive market structure:** Typically, small businesses are found in highly-fragmented industries such as wholesaling, retailing, services and job-shop manufacturing. These industries have low barriers to entry, making it easy for new competitors to enter the industry, increasing overall competition and lowering profitability. Competitors in these industries will often decrease prices to increase turnover but, in the process, they reduce overall profitability.

- **Narrow product base**: Most small businesses have a very narrow product range. The business may have been successful based on the entrepreneur's initial product / service. However, most entrepreneurs are slow to invest in product or market development.

- **Innovation**: The small business may not have the skills or resources to invest in product / service development and improvement. The initial business idea may have been innovative but, since start-up, the entrepreneur may have had to direct resources into managing the business on a day-to-day basis.

- **Poor planning**: Most entrepreneurs are opportunistic when developing their businesses. Growth may require a more structured and formalised approach to market analysis. Most entrepreneurs do no strategic planning.

- **Quality of staff**: The quality of the workforce in small businesses may also inhibit growth. Small businesses tend to start from a lower quality base in terms of employees. This may be due to the fact that the company may not be able to afford high quality staff, or because high quality staff may not be attracted to working in a small business with limited opportunities for advancement. In addition, the lack of resources available to train the existing work force, and thus increase its quality, may act as a barrier.

THE ENTREPRENEUR AS A BARRIER TO GROWTH

The centrality of the entrepreneur in the small business is a powerful determinant of the future direction of the business. The very characteristics that are required to start a small business successfully can work against the entrepreneur when the decision to grow the business is taken. The term 'founder's disease' describes the failure of the founding entrepreneur to either adapt to the needs of a growing business or to leave the business.

The entrepreneur may retard the growth of the business for a number of reasons:

- **Desire to retain control**. Entrepreneurs seek to control the business. They may resist sharing control with others, preventing the entrepreneur hiring outside professionals or encouraging staff development and progression. The desire to maintain control may also reduce the capacity of the business to raise funds. Often, entrepreneurs are unwilling to sell an equity stake in the business.

- **Poor managerial ability**. Most entrepreneurs and small businesses have very limited managerial skills. Often entrepreneurs have become successful because of their ability to create the product / service. Entrepreneurs frequently resent the increased formalisation that is associated with growth. A period of growth may highlight the entrepreneur's difficulties and weaknesses.

- **No exit strategy**. There may be barriers to the entrepreneur exiting from the business. A family business may lack an 'heir apparent'. Even if there is a suitable candidate within the family, many entrepreneurs are reluctant to pass on control. The business may not survive without the entrepreneur. It may be difficult to sell the business at a price that the entrepreneur considers acceptable.

In order to be successful, the owner-manager must not only have the will to grow but also, and perhaps more importantly, the skills necessary to manage the business. Changes in the attitude of the entrepreneur and the acquisition of new skills are almost always necessary if a business is to grow successfully. Some entrepreneurs cannot make the transition from being at the centre of a small business to being a manager of a large business.

A MODEL OF THE GROWTH PROCESS

Organisations do not grow of their own accord. Growth is the result of managerial decisions and actions. The growth of a small business can be described in terms of a number of common and identifiable stages (**Figure 10.2**). The transitions that occur as young, small and simple businesses become older, larger and more complex are similar in most small businesses. Most businesses appear to face similar problems at each of these stages. By understanding these stages, the entrepreneur should be able to anticipate the problems that he/she will have to deal with in the future. A business may fail at any stage or may get 'trapped' at a particular stage and progress no further.

FIGURE 10.2: A MODEL OF THE GROWTH PROCESS

Start-Up   Launch   Through   Survival   Growth
Decision   the Knothole

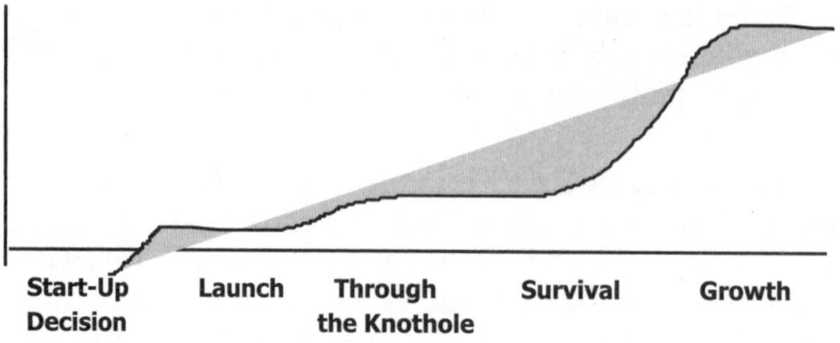

START-UP DECISION

The most important decision the entrepreneur takes is to start the new business. It is normally an unconscious decision that happens over a long period of time. Experiences of family or friends in self-employment might sensitise the entrepreneur to the idea of starting a business. One of the most common characteristics among entrepreneurs is that a family member was involved in starting a business.

The personal creativity of the entrepreneur may be important. It may allow the entrepreneur to perceive opportunities where others see problems. The perception of a market opportunity may encourage the entrepreneur to start a business. This is referred to as being 'pulled' into entrepreneurship. However, any entrepreneurs are 'pushed' into entrepreneurship. Circumstances such as losing a job, failing to get a promotion or frustration with the development of a business may 'push' an entrepreneur to start-up.

Crucial to the creation of a new business are the ambitions and personal characteristics of the entrepreneur. Support of family, spouses and friends may have an input into the decision.

The start-up decision stage may involve the development of a concept and the testing of its feasibility. The entrepreneur may develop a prototype of the product. The entrepreneur may begin to plan for start-up and may prepare a formal written business plan. In many businesses, the entrepreneur may have spent many years thinking about the product / service opportunity or on developing the product / service idea.

LAUNCH

The most important activity during the launch stage is the acquisition of the resources necessary to get the business up and running. The entrepreneur will need resources such as premises, finance, and staff. Before the business is launched, the entrepreneur may need to sell the new idea to potential customers and investors. The business faces very high levels of uncertainty during this phase, for example, whether customers will buy the product, how often and at what price. During the launch phase, the entrepreneur is very dependent on outsiders. This is why personal contacts and experience in business are very important for entrepreneurs. The entrepreneur should focus on short-term activities that build the confidence of outsiders.

Initially, the business may be selling to 'soft' customers. These are customers who buy the product / service because of a personal connection with the entrepreneur – for example, a former employer or customers of a former employer. However, these customers may not continue to use the business as it develops, due to higher costs or lower quality relative to competitors.

This stage is characterised by an informal atmosphere. Staff will feel a strong sense of loyalty and mission, everybody will get involved in getting the business going.

THROUGH THE KNOTHOLE

Having survived the initial launch period, the new business must establish itself as a viable business concern. This period may be chaotic and stressful. The entrepreneur will have two main concerns at this stage:

- To establish a production process capable of producing the product / service in the quantities required.
- To develop the customer base of the business from the initial 'soft' customers.

There will be a lot of learning by the entrepreneur during this phase, about the business and what it will take to make it successful. The entrepreneurial activity that occurs during this period will play an important part in shaping the early development of the business. A strong sense of loyalty and mission will still exist among staff. Communications within the business will be very informal and will be free-flowing. A significant number of businesses fail during this stage.

SURVIVAL

Surviving the stressful 'through the knothole' stage means that the business has established itself in the market-place. The focus of the entrepreneur's attention should now shift to the efficiency and profitability of the business. This may involve a review of costs, of the products produced and an assessment of the overall efficiency of the business. During this stage, the owner-manager will begin to formalise the organisation. Rules, systems and procedures may be introduced. The organisation and management style will become more conservative. The owner-manager may hire additional managerial or supervisory staff – for example, a production manager. There will be a change in the attitudes of employees. They no longer will have the same sense of loyalty as was evident during the start-up and through the knothole stages. New staff will have been hired who were not part of the initial start-up. Increasing pressure for formalisation may lead to a decline in innovativeness. It is now necessary to protect the business that has been created. The majority of new businesses never progress beyond this stage. These businesses remain self-employment businesses for the entrepreneur.

GROWTH

This period of growth may only happen if the owner-manager chooses it (**Figure 10.3**).

The business has now established its distinctive competencies and has some product-market successes. To grow the business beyond the limitations of the existing niche will require acquiring resources in an attempt to realise the advantages that would result from larger scale. This may require the entrepreneur taking a risk that may be 'larger' than the initial start-up risk, perhaps even 'betting the whole business'. It is essential that the entrepreneur has a good understanding of the future of the business.

This stage of growth is very management-intensive. The entrepreneur will probably play a less direct role in the day-to-day management of the business. New structures and procedures may be introduced. Internal informal 'social' control may no longer be appropriate. Professional managers may have to be hired in all functional areas of the business. Finance is crucial, if the business is to grow significantly. The entrepreneur will probably need to use the accumulated cash and the borrowing power that the company has established. It may be necessary for the entrepreneur to lose some control of the business by selling equity.

Businesses may continue to grow indefinitely or they may reach a plateau. Those that become medium-sized businesses are often referred to as 'lifestyle' companies. They provide the owner-manager with the opportunity to withdraw from the day-to-day running of the business and to pursue other interests. Other businesses may be bought out and, therefore, may cease to grow as independent businesses. This is common in high-technology businesses – for example, small biotechnology companies get bought out by larger competitors, if they are successful.

FIGURE 10.3: WHAT MOTIVATES AN ENTREPRENEUR TO GROW A BUSINESS?

Growth may be sought for a number of reasons:

◊ **Survival and stability**: Larger businesses have a lower failure rate. This may be due to their larger resources and their ability to influence the market they operate in. These larger resources allow the businesses to weather downturns in demand, short-term financial problems or mistakes by management. The same problems may bankrupt a smaller business.

◊ **'Status'**: The size of the business confers status on the entrepreneur. Size may be the benchmark used by external evaluators to judge the success of the business.

◊ **Scale**: Larger turnover allows the business to achieve lower costs and higher profits. Achieving economies of scale can result in significant savings in a small business.

◊ **Salaries**: Business growth may be pursued in order to obtain an increase in management salaries.

◊ **Adventure and risk**: Why do entrepreneurs who have attained as much personal wealth as they desire continue to be aggressive in the marketplace? Entrepreneurs may grow their businesses because they like to take risks.

MANAGING A GROWTH BUSINESS

The model below can be used to highlight the problems that the entrepreneur will have to address and 'solve', if the business is to grow (**Figure 10.4**). The major strength of the model is that it is useful in gaining an understanding of the rather complex phenomenon of business growth and organisational development. However, different businesses will experience the stages and problems at different times. The problems and stages are a function of the age of the business, the size of the business and the business sector. Increases in the age and size of a business tend to be associated with increased organisational formality and conservatism. The sector in which the business operates will affect the business size required to support turnover, for example some businesses need complex organisation structures despite small numbers of staff while others may have large numbers of unskilled workers and relatively unsophisticated organisational structure.

FIGURE 10.4: PROBLEMS AT EACH STAGE OF THE GROWTH MODEL

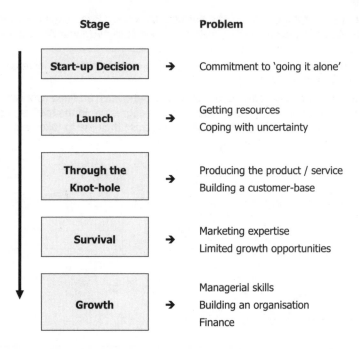

Stage	Problem
Start-up Decision	→ Commitment to 'going it alone'
Launch	→ Getting resources / Coping with uncertainty
Through the Knot-hole	→ Producing the product / service / Building a customer-base
Survival	→ Marketing expertise / Limited growth opportunities
Growth	→ Managerial skills / Building an organisation / Finance

The problems and issues of each stage must be 'solved', if the business is to grow. However, the factors that make a business successful at one stage of growth may not be applicable to the next stage and, indeed, may cause the business to fail, if a new set of skills is not learnt. This creates an enormous pressure for the entrepreneur.

In the early stages of growth, the business depends on the entrepreneur's ability to make and sell the product. The operational abilities of the entrepreneur are most important at this time. The entrepreneur's ability to build and manage an organisation is not central to success – for example, the entrepreneur's ability to delegate is irrelevant, as there are few, if any, employees to delegate to. As the business grows, the entrepreneur may have to develop new skills. The entrepreneur must spend less time 'doing' and more time 'managing'. The organisation must become more sophisticated and complex in dealing with external changes – for example, better internal and external information may be required, or better decision-making styles may be needed. And, as a business grows, the administration challenge increases.

A survey of entrepreneurs of high-growth businesses in Ireland suggests that some entrepreneurs are better at managing the growth process (**Figure 10.5**) (Kinsella & Mulvenna, 1993). 'Fast-growth firms' (FGF) were identified in terms of growth in profitability. Each FGF was compared to a similar or 'matched' business. The matched businesses were in the same industry sector but had not experienced growth. Overall, the FGFs employed more than three times as many as the matched businesses.

FIGURE 10.5: FAST-GROWTH FIRMS IN IRELAND

The study reached the following conclusions:
◊ FGFs were more aware of their marketplace, had a better understanding of their competitors, and kept in closer contact with their customers.
◊ FGFs access a wider range of sources of finance at start-up and during growth than do the matched businesses. Grants are more important to FGFs.
◊ FGFs believed that exporting would be very important to their future development. The matched businesses did not.
◊ A higher proportion of FGFs were actively selling in export markets, making them less dependent on the domestic market.
◊ FGFs had a larger share of the domestic market than did the matched businesses.

Managing rapid growth is about managing the transition from a personalised to an impersonalised leadership style and from a simple and informal organisation structure to a more formal organisation structure. A company experiencing rapid growth will face the following challenges (Hambrick & Crozier, 1985):

- **Instant size**: This can create problems of disaffection, inadequate skills and inadequate systems.

- **A sense of infallibility**: This may result from the success of the strategies and plans employed by the organisation in order to bring about growth. Such organisations can become complacent in monitoring the environment for changes and new competitors.

- **Internal turmoil**: This is created by the strain of growth. An influx of new people results in a staff, who are not familiar with each other or with the company, jockeying for position. Turf battles abound, decision-making suffers and people burnout or leave.

- **Extraordinary resource needs**: Often, quickly-growing businesses are cash-starved.

How can the entrepreneur best deal with these challenges? The key to dealing successfully with rapid growth is the ability to anticipate growth before it happens. An entrepreneur must ensure that the business has the resources and skills to handle growth, in advance of actually needing them. Successful businesses avoid being lulled into a false sense of infallibility by using all available sources of information, even those that are unlikely to offer good news. They also develop processes for giving controversial data a fair airing. Successful businesses endeavour to halt a breakdown in decision-making that may result from the internal turmoil that the business is experiencing. This may be achieved by decentralising and using cross-functional decision-making teams. This also helps to assimilate new people and to speed up the decision-making process. Extraordinary resource needs may be coped with through the use of deferred compensation and stock options for workers and performance-related pay rather than fixed salaries.

CONCLUSION

Small businesses have common stages of growth and development. Achieving growth in a small business is a difficult challenge for the entrepreneur. Most small businesses remain small. This may be due to external market factors, to internal organisational weaknesses or due to the motivation and skills of the entrepreneur. Entrepreneurs who choose to grow their business must solve a number of difficult problems at each stage of growth. Essential to this growth process is the transformation of the business and the entrepreneur's ability to manage the business.

QUESTIONS

1. Discuss the internal and external barriers to small business growth.

2. In order for 'a business to grow, the founder must go'. Discuss.

3. Describe and discuss a model of the growth process. How might this model be useful to an entrepreneur?

4. What organisational challenges must an entrepreneur manage if a business is to achieve rapid growth?

5. Identify a business that has achieved rapid growth. Describe the growth and development of this business.

6. 'Is growth good for business?' Discuss.

7. Using the profile of Jan Berg (see next page), map out the stages of growth for his company, Marine Management.

PROFILE: JAN BERG, MARINE MANAGEMENT[22]

A fascination with maritime matters influenced Jan Berg's choices from an early age. Coming from Norway, a country with a long and well-established maritime tradition, this was not so unusual. Graduating with a Masters of Science from the Faculty of Marine Technology at the Norwegian University of Science & Technology, Jan's immediate thoughts were not related to starting a new business but rather to getting as wide a range of experience as he could within his chosen industry.

With this in mind, he travelled to the Middle East to join the world's largest ship repair yard, Dubai dry docks. It was in Dubai that he met an Irish girl, who was to become his wife. The couple choose initially to live in Norway, so that Jan could further deepen his knowledge and experience. There, he held executive positions in shipping and offshore exploration companies. Eventually, Jan and his wife decided to return to Ireland. This explains how a Norwegian, with extensive experience of international shipping, found himself in Ireland – a country with an underdeveloped maritime industry, but, as Jan says, with plenty of potential.

As part of his MBA thesis, *'The Irish Shipping Industry in an Industrial Cluster Perspective',* for the Smurfit Business School in UCD, Jan investigated this potential and became convinced that Ireland was an excellent choice for significant shipping company activity, given its geographical location, and the fact that it was an English-speaking, neutral country with a vibrant economy and a productive and highly flexible workforce. Moreover, the approval in December 2002 by the European Commission of new tax incentives[23], introduced by the Irish government to attract the international shipping sector to Irish shores, was perfectly timed to coincide with the launch of a new marine services company. It was against this background that Maritime Management was established.

The new business, the first of its kind in Ireland, seeks to capitalize on the competitive advantages that Ireland has as an international base for shipping company activity and on the economic efficiencies provided by the tonnage tax. These advantages can be gained by operating ships in international trade from a base in Ireland.

The company offers ship management, maritime consultancy and marine surveying and associated maritime services to the international and local maritime and shipping industry. It has a particular focus on companies that are looking to Ireland as a base for their maritime operations. For the local maritime, fishing and offshore industry, special marine services and naval architects, which in the past were only available abroad, are now on their doorstep.

---

[22] This profile appeared in Fitzsimons & O'Gorman (2006).

[23] The tonnage tax.

Jan Berg is not someone who always wanted to be an entrepreneur – quite the reverse. He describes himself as *'very much a company man'*. When he saw the potential that existed in Ireland to develop not just a company but a whole industry, however, he could not resist the challenge.

Jan points particularly to the support he has received from the NovaUCD Campus Company Development Programme as being a key component in the turning of an aspiration into a reality. Still housed in NovaUCD, the continuing involvement of the university as a shareholder in the business brings an added dimension, Jan believes, that is very important to the new venture.

I found the start up support in Ireland great: entrepreneurship is much more valued here than it is in Norway. If I were still in Norway, I would never have developed the determination to become an entrepreneur.

While full of praise for the support that he has received in Ireland, Jan is very critical of the high costs that start-up companies must face, particularly in terms of professional fees and insurance cover:

... compared to Ireland the cost of these services in Norway is marginal.

Jan believes that these high costs kill off many start-ups before they ever get off the ground.

He also finds that the environment in Ireland is *'family-hostile'*, compared to Norway, where better childcare facilities and a greater equality in the roles of men and women, with regard to family and professional responsibilities, provide more opportunity for women to develop careers outside the home and a better family-work balance for the men.

Jan does not regret his decision to move with his family to Ireland and is very excited by the prospect of being part of the development of a new industry, virtually from scratch. He sees the maritime industry in Ireland as being at a similar stage of development that the IT and pharmaceutical industries were in the early 1980s and he believes that its potential is equally impressive.

11

INTERNATIONALISATION

The small size of the Irish market means that many Irish companies must internationalise, to achieve growth through exporting. Also, in many technology and specialised businesses, the market in Ireland may be so small that the entrepreneur has to start exporting almost as soon as they start-up.

In respect to internationalisation of a business, the entrepreneur must make two key decisions:

- First, what are the appropriate international markets?
- Second, how best to generate sales in these markets, and how best to support customers?

The basic choice is to sell directly to customers or to use an intermediate distributor or agent. There are many problems and difficulties for the new and small business that is trying to sell into overseas markets. This chapter examines these issues.

CHOOSING AN INTERNATIONAL MARKET STRATEGY

For a new business to succeed in either domestic or export markets, its product / service has to have some unique competitive advantage. A clear understanding of the target market and where the business' own product / service fits into the market is fundamental to success. Market knowledge is about understanding the market needs and translating these into products and services. The business should know how to approach the potential buyer, how often they purchase the product / service, what price they are prepared to pay, and what level of service they require. Sources of market information are to subscribe to trade magazines and e-mail discussion lists; to attend seminars and exhibitions; and to join professional organisations in the industry.

FIGURE 11.1: LARGO FOODS GOES INTERNATIONAL

Largo Foods manufactures over 60 different crisp product lines (*Perri, Hunky Dorys* and own brand labels) and was founded in 1983. In 1996, it secured cabinet space in 280 supermarkets across Britain for its additive-free *Potato Cuisine* brand. It has developed a good relationship with the UK multiples. Over 40% of Largo's sales are produced for foreign markets, such as the US, Lebanon, Singapore, Iceland, Dubai, Russia and Malta, where *Perri* is the brand leader. Largo also produces and supplies organic crisps to EuroDisney.

Raymond Coyle, CEO of Largo, has a reputation for working the trade fairs, particularly the ISM in Cologne, which has enabled him to build an impressive contact-base. He works closely with the retail sector and is very responsive to their ideas. The motivation driving Largo's exports is the realisation that *Tayto* is the dominant player in the Irish market, with about 50% market-share — to survive, Largo had to export. Competition on the home market has intensified as Walker Crisps have made significant market share gains, with their market entry to the Irish market backed up by a high profile advertising campaign endorsed by Roy Keane.

In 2007, Largo employs over 400 staff in plants in Ashbourne, Donegal and the Czech Republic and has four distribution centres in Dublin, Cork, Carlow and Belfast. Recent product innovation has focus on broadening its range of crisps, savoury and sweet popcorn and corn snacks. The most significant product innovations have include *Hunky Dorys Kezzils* launched in 2001, which have a shelf life of six months and have 35% less fat than other product ranges. Further product innovations have come in Largo's light, low fat and low calorie crisp ranges.

To position a product / service effectively in an export market, there are three critical and interrelated questions that the entrepreneur must answer:

- **What niche will the business' product / service target and what margins are achievable?** Businesses must research new export markets before market entry. For a small business, the costs of new market entry are very high and failure in an overseas market may 'bring down' the business. Research prior to market entry will ultimately save the business money. New and small businesses should focus financial and management resources into a niche market that is large enough to be profitable for the business but not large enough to attract the interest of larger competitors. Ideally, it should have worldwide potential. If a business attempts to sell to a broad target market, their message may not be heard by potential buyers. The difficulty for the entrepreneur is how best to define the niche market? Some businesses state that they are targeting a niche market, when, in fact, their focus is too broad. The benefits of finding a niche export market are:

◊ **Market penetration:** The business should be able to identify potential buyers that match the target market criteria.

◊ **Low levels of competition:** This should make it easier to get established in the market and to gain market share.

◊ **Premium prices:** It should be possible to charge customers a premium price.

◊ **Competitive advantage:** The business should be able to build a sustainable competitive advantage based on the market knowledge that it develops.

The market research should not just be surveying or gathering of statistics. It should lead to a greater understanding of the market, of the buyers' expectations of the product/service, and of the structure of the distribution channels. A percentage of the product development budget should be set aside to investigate the market acceptability of the product/service.

- **What are the sales process and buying cycles in the target export market?** Once the new business has accurately defined its niche, the entrepreneur needs to research the buying processes operating in the target export market. This research should outline the stages involved from the initial inquiry to actual purchase. The business should seek ways of reducing the number of steps in the buying cycle, in order to maximise their profit margin, since a long buying cycle would have a strong negative impact on cash flow. For example, the buying cycle in the software industry is:

  ◊ Price of the software.
  ◊ Product functionality.
  ◊ Product technology.
  ◊ Product development.
  ◊ Upgrades.
  ◊ Technical support.
  ◊ Training and implementation.

- **Who are the main competitors and what are their weaknesses?** The entrepreneur needs to identify the main competitors, their size, product range, financial capabilities, pricing policy, product functionality, customer support and use of distribution channels. A business with a strong focus strategy may appear to have no competitors in their niche; however, other businesses may be covering the same market in a different way.

BUILDING THE CUSTOMER-BASE

HOW MUCH DOES IT ALL COST?

The general rule is that developing and exporting to foreign markets is expensive. It can be difficult for the business to secure sufficient funding, when attempting to enter the overseas market. Existing overseas experience and existing overseas customers can help the business secure funding for new export markets. A comprehensive business plan can help raise funds. If the business seeks the financial support of third parties, it has to realise that this is a time-consuming process. The lead-in time for this could be as long as eight months.

FIGURE 11.2: COSTS OF OPERATING IN FOREIGN MARKETS

◊ Travel and subsistence.
◊ Meetings and seminars.
◊ Telephone, fax & e-mail.
◊ Sales promotional material costs.
◊ Field saleperson(s).
◊ Office facilities.
◊ Discretionary expenses (for example, meals and presents).

DIRECT OR INDIRECT CHANNELS OF MARKET DELIVERY?

Given Ireland's geographical location, building a customer-base in a foreign market can be a difficult and expensive task. The issues of market access will have fundamental implications on how the business will develop. Clearly, the existing elements of the classic marketing mix are important — product, price and promotion — but it is place that has added significance, given the fact the business is exporting a product / service.

The business needs to consider:

- How will it generate sales in foreign markets?

- Will third parties be involved in generating sales leads and business development?

- Does the business need to establish a presence in the target foreign markets?

- What customer support arrangements will the business make for its export customers?

- Should the company have offices and a presence in key markets?

- Can the business avail of, or enter, joint marketing and co-operation arrangements with other companies in the same industry when exporting products / services?

The business might choose to develop its customer-base directly by setting up operations in export markets. Alternatively, the business might use third parties to represent itself in export markets. The entrepreneur will need to consider a number of factors in making this decision. Of particular importance is the type of customer support required, the pace of development the business is seeking and the resources of the business.

FIGURE 11.3: FACTORS INFLUENCING THE CHOICE OF DIRECT OR INDIRECT EXPORTING IN THE SOFTWARE INDUSTRY

In case of the software industry, it is price and the value of a deal that governs the choice of distribution channels. The software business has limited raw materials and other inputs, therefore a trade-off has to be made between higher revenue from direct selling and a lower cost base from choosing the indirect route.

Influencing Factors	Choose Direct Channels	Choose Indirect Channels
Price	High	Low
Volume	Low	High
Software complexity	High	Low
Buying cycle	Long	Short
Support requirements	High	Low
Other service elements	High	Low

DIRECT CHANNELS

A direct channel means that the business sells directly to customers in the export market. The business retains responsibility for every aspect of the sale, from generating the initial sale to customer support. This is one of the main benefits of using direct channels but it means that the business has to have a good sales team.

If the business goes the direct route, a presence in the foreign target markets may be necessary for generating sales and for delivering customer support. A physical presence in a market is important for a number of reasons:

- Prospective clients want to see a tangible commitment and presence in the market.

- Prospective clients can deal directly with the business.

- Developing a new customer base can be done more easily in the target market.

There are other alternatives to setting up an office in a foreign market that give potential customers a point of contact. The most important factors for any business considering the options outlined below is that, the easier it is for potential customers to contact the business, the greater the response rate is likely to be. Alternatives to setting up offices in export markets include:

- **Remote call forwarding**: A potential customer dials a local number, which is automatically routed through to the business's Irish office.

- **Virtual offices**: This is where the business has an arrangement that provides it with an address and telephone answering service in the export market.

- **Serviced offices**: This is a similar set-up to the previous arrangement but includes shared secretarial support and some office space.

- **Staffed field office**: This involves some key personnel of the business establishing the field office in the export market and running the office in the initial stages. This is the most expensive option.

Generating Sales Leads Directly

The key decision for the business is to choose a method of sales generation that will deliver the greatest level of 'lead' generation for the minimum capital outlay. Some of the methods that can be used include:

- **Direct mail**: Direct mail is personal advertising sent directly to the potential customer. Direct mail should deliver pertinent information to a carefully-selected group of individuals. If it fails to do this, it can be described as 'junk' mail. Studies show that, on average, 80% of direct mail is opened and 63% is read. There are three critical elements that can enhance the direct mail process:
   ◊ **Use of a good 'source list' of addresses:** When a business is choosing which external list to use, it has to consider the following: the origin of the names and the information, when the list was last updated and how often the list has been used by other companies.
   ◊ **A good 'offer':** The business should emphasis the uniqueness of its product / service.
   ◊ **Follow up on the lead:** The objective of the follow-up may be to set up a meeting with the interested parties or to get feedback on the product / service.

- **Advertising**: Advertising in an export market should generate sales leads and should build the business's profile in the market. The objective is to generate sufficient interest that a potential customer will contact the business for further information about the product / service. If the business plans to advertise, its advertisements should:
   ◊ Gain the attention of the target market and, particularly, the individuals who make the purchasing decisions.

◊ Generate interest in the product / service.

◊ Create the desire in the target market to buy the product / service.

◊ Provide a way for the potential buyer to respond to the advert.

- **Trade exhibitions and showcases:** By participating in a trade exhibition, the business should meet with customers directly. Additionally, trade exhibitions should allow the business to assess competitors and to learn about future trends in the market. Sales generated at these types of events may be low, unless the business has promoted its attendance heavily before the actual event, through mailing, trade publications and magazines. The layout of the stand, product / service demonstrations, quality of the sales materials, the conduct and level of competence displayed by the business's representatives should constantly reinforce the unique selling point of the business. Trade exhibitions can be a relatively low cost way of meeting with buyers. For JFC Manufacturing (**Chapter 9**), participating in tradeshows is an important means of generating sales, contacts and maintaining real-time market information.

- **Promotion and publicity**: In most markets, there are usually trade magazines dedicated to particular products / services. These publications are receptive to press releases, which can sell the benefits of the product but must contain some hard news as well. Other ways of promoting the product / service include speaking at trade conferences and writing articles in trade magazines.

INDIRECT CHANNELS

Using indirect channels to enter, or operate in, an export market involves using the services of a third party, which can lower costs and speed up market entry. However, using a third party means a loss in control and less direct feedback from customers. The third party may not be as committed to selling the business's product / service as the business would be itself.

Alternative ways of generating sales and supporting customers indirectly include:

- **Agents**: These are businesses that sell the product / service on commission. Depending on the product / service, it may be difficult to find a suitable agent with the expertise and knowledge of the product and target market. In addition, there can be difficulty in getting an agent with the right mix of market contacts and entrepreneurial flair. Arrangements with agents usually take one of the following two forms:

  ◊ **Introducer:** In this case, the agent merely provides the initial sales lead and possible introductions to prospective buyers.

  ◊ **Sales agent:** This is where the agent takes on the responsibility of identifying leads, demonstrating the product / service, dealing with further inquires and closing the deal. Consequently, the commission that the agent receives under such an agreement is much higher.

- **Distributors**: A distributor doesn't make sales, but just takes orders. It is up to the business in the target market to generate demand for the product. In most cases, the business will come to some form of arrangement with the distributor on joint co-operation with promotions and, where possible, may include the product in the distributor's catalogue.

- **Original equipment manufacturer (OEM)**: Depending on the nature of the product / service, the business could enter an agreement with an OEM manufacturer. This may mean bundling the product with the OEM's product. The margins in this type of arrangement tend to be low. The benefit is that there is minimal sales cost and the OEM can generate volumes of business that are far beyond what the business could achieve on its own.

CUSTOMER SUPPORT

Customer expectations for customer support have increased significantly in most industries. The business must establish a level of customer support that satisfies or exceeds customer requirements. The key for any business is to exploit the potential of the customer relationship effectively, while, at the same time, minimising the cost of customer relationships.

If the business takes the direct channel route and directly supports customers, the decision has to be made whether to do it from an Irish base or from the target market base. Supporting customers from an Irish base may be seen as a disadvantage by foreign customers. However, if the business can demonstrate that it successfully supports other foreign buyers from Ireland, this may become less of an issue.

Customer support can be a significant cost, if it is not carefully managed. Where indirect channels are used, it is essential that a decision is made about who will provide customer support. If the business uses indirect channels, the business becomes removed from its customers and may lose out on customer feedback. Maintaining effective customer support is advantageous, because it provides feedback. Customers can be used to test new ideas, to provide feedback on product performance, and to learn about competitors. Additionally, it may be possible to earn revenue by charging customers for service contracts or maintenance contracts.

CHOOSING A PARTNER

No matter what type of partnership the business enters into with a third party, it is essential that the business gets it right from the start. Entering an export market is an expensive process and will consume a lot of management time. Many companies get only one chance at entering a new market. The process that is involved in identifying and evaluating potential partners is as follows:

- Decide on what type of partnership is most suitable for the business.
- List all potential partner candidates.
- Evaluate the potential partners on the following criteria: customer-base; resources; market knowledge; sales and marketing skills; geographic scope; commitment.
- Meet with the short-listed partners to discuss possible arrangements and verify that some form of 'chemistry' exists.
- Enter an arrangement for a trial period in order to sort out any problems that may arise.
- After the trial period, enter a legal agreement.

Most small Irish businesses are not in a strong negotiating position to 'lay down the law' when negotiating a partnership arrangement. However, the deal should include the following points:

- Level of commission.
- Target sales volume.
- Staffing levels.
- Promotional activities.
- Penalties for non-achievement.
- Opt-out clauses.
- Exclusivity.

The management of the distributor / agent is key to the success or failure of a business in an export market. The involvement of each party can be developed by:

- Allocating responsibilities and developing joint marketing activities.
- Communicating regularly, to keep abreast of latest developments.
- Swapping market intelligence in relation to new developments in the market.
- Putting in place a formal process of meetings, reviews and targets.
- Appointing persons in both businesses to be responsible for managing the partnership relationship.

INTERNATIONALISATION: EXPORT PROBLEMS

EXTERNAL BARRIERS

External barriers include:

- **Financial problems**: These problems include currency devaluations and the high cost of capital in foreign markets.

- **Government export policy**: Government policy towards exporters and exporting is a crucial determinant of success, either easing a business's exporting problems or creating additional problems due to high travel costs or poor infrastructure. Importantly for small businesses, governments may provide advice on how to enter foreign markets.

- **Overseas competition**: The business may experience strong competition from competitors established in the foreign market. Many exporting businesses cite 'competition' as a major obstacle to exporting.

- **Bureaucracy**: The preparation of documentation such as shipping documents, export licenses, bills of lading can be a very time-consuming process. This problem is more significant in small businesses, due to a lack of management and financial resources.

- **'Red tape' in importing countries**: Governments may block imports in a number of ways, such as imposing tariffs and increasing custom inspections. Procedural barriers may arise due to cultural differences and differences in local regulations and requirements.

- **Delays in payments**: There can be significant delays in the length of time taken to make payments for products / services supplied to overseas markets, due to poor documentation or slow payment by the purchaser. This impacts on an exporter's cash flow and financial position.

- **Export documentation**: In theory, the advent of GATT and various EU agreements should have reduced the amount of paper that accompanies shipments. However, several empirical studies have concluded that delays in preparing complex export documentation still pose significant problems to exporters.

- **Logistical constraints**: The problems of physically getting the product to an overseas market can add significantly to the cost of the product. Some governments have imposed restrictions on the use and type of heavy goods vehicles that can be used on their national routes at certain times of the week. This, therefore, can impact on the business's ability to deliver the product within certain time commitments.

INTERNAL BARRIERS

These include:

- **Inability to finance exports**: For some businesses, lending institutions perceive the risk of exporting as being too high, given the size of the actual business, the high cost of exporting, and the insufficient level of capital in the business. New businesses tend to underestimate the cost of exporting and the level of price competition in export markets.

- **Product / service considerations**: The product / service may require significant adaptation before it can be sold into a foreign market. These problems can relate to packaging and labelling, quality and safety standards, and the establishment of a suitable design and image for the overseas markets.

- **Lack of international marketing expertise**: For an exporting drive to succeed, it is necessary to have top management commitment. Some problems may occur due to inefficient marketing strategies and low managerial commitment to the whole exporting process.

- **Difficulties in sourcing reputable distributors**: A business may have difficulty in finding a reliable and capable distributor. In addition, this process can be compounded by the fact that the legal system may be 'pro' distributor, making it extremely difficult to terminate the services of a distributor. To help overcome this difficulty, the business should use trade missions or personal visits to the target overseas market to gain the necessary information and contacts.

- **Lack of information and market research**: Before a business considers entering a foreign market, it has to gather good quality information. However, sourcing this information often can be a problem, due to the location of the market, a lack of expertise in collecting and collating market intelligence, and linguistic barriers.

- **Poor communication with foreign customers**: Customer habits, languages and other cultural nuances have an impact on the way relationships with foreign customers are forged and maintained. Foreign cultures can be difficult to understand. Translating product attributes into foreign languages can present problems.

- **Lack of promotion in foreign markets**: Overseas promotion can be problematic. The tendency among exporters is to standardise promotional practices rather than adapt them to local conditions. Empirical studies have shown that small businesses have greater problem in this regard, because they have fewer resources to overcome communication problems.

CONCLUSION

This chapter has outlined the various steps that a business has to go through, in order to minimise its own risks and to maximise its rewards in foreign markets. It is important to note that there are significant risks and uncertainties attached to exporting a product or service. A business has to plan its export strategies to reduce these risks and overcome the potential problems that were outlined in the chapter. Due to the limited size of the Irish market, it is imperative that firms look further afield to develop their customer-base.

QUESTIONS

1. What factors should an entrepreneur consider when choosing an export market?

2. Discuss the implications of directly generating sales in export markets?

3. What are the indirect channels of building a customer-base?

4. What criteria should an entrepreneur consider when seeking a partner in an export market?

5. What internal and external problems might a small business experience when exporting?

6. Develop an export strategy for a food product.

7. From your reading of the Web Reservations International case (see next page), identify international barriers for service companies headquartered in Ireland.

PROFILE: RAY NOLAN, WEB RESERVATIONS INTERNATIONAL[24]

'Never in our wildest dreams could we have expected this kind of growth, for two guys in Ireland to own a whole sector.'

Tom Kennedy owned the Avalon House Hostel in Dublin, Ireland. In the mid-1990s, in an effort to make the business more efficient, he contracted Ray Nolan, a self-taught computer programmer and owner of Raven Computing, to develop a software programme that would allow his hostel to manage the check-in and out process. Following the successful installation of the software at Avalon House Hostel, Nolan resold the reservations management system as *Backpack* to a number of other hostels.

In 1999, Ray Nolan and Tom Kennedy founded Web Reservations International (WRI) and created an online reservation site for hostel bookings – www.hostelworld.com. The company is now the biggest global provider of confirmed online reservations for the budget accommodation sector. The *Backpack* software was modified to enable hostels to be seamlessly integrated with the online booking system at www.hostelworld.com. Only 10 copies of *Backpack* were sold in 1999, but this figure reached 100 by 2001. Nolan and Kennedy both decided to leave their respective jobs and WRI now employs 75 people. The company's revenue grew by 1,436% from 2000 to 2002, compared to the industry average of 269% for the top 50 technology companies in Ireland. In 2007, WRI delivers online reservations to over 50,000 properties in 165 countries, through a network of owned sites and affiliate partners, processing 70,000 bed-nights per day and handling over €300 million in bookings annually. In the year ending December 2006, WRI generated EBITDA of €19m.

The budget / youth / independent traveller (BYIT) market comprises students, youths, backpackers and independent travellers. Typically, they are web-savvy, value-conscious and tend to take extended vacations and set the travel trends for the business travellers of the future. Nolan (2002) describes this market

'... as the most web-friendly segment of the market. Web Reservations International is already the leader in technology and booking revenue in this market and we intend to grow even faster in the future.'

Changes in the BYIT market, coupled with the successful redevelopment of the *Backpack* software and the hostelworld.com and other related websites, afforded

---

[24] This profile is adapted from a case study written by James Cunningham and William Golden, J.E. Cairnes Graduate School of Business & Public Policy, NUI Galway, which won the Irish Case Writing Competition 2004 and which was first published in Cooney (2004).

WRI a dominant position in this market. WRI runs over 500 websites targeted and runs OEMs sites for selected global companies in this sector. The purpose of having 500-plus individual sites is to ensure that anybody searching for a hostel will ultimately land on a WRI-owned or managed site.

In pursing its dominance of the BYIT market, WRI licences its reservation technology to a wide range of affiliate travel websites. WRI targeted the travel agent market, overlooked by many industry players in the dot.com rush. WRI's Travel Agent Extranet System means that travel agents do not have to contract individual rates, invoice the providers and they have direct access to worldwide budget accommodation. As Kennedy describes:

> 'We have developed the software to benefit travel agents and affiliates such as Rough Guide and Time Out, which can offer a worldwide reach to accommodation and share in the commission we can generate.'

The business model is simple and effective as Nolan describes:

> 'WRI's model is simple: it handles hostel bookings through a huge network of websites, and makes its money by holding onto the deposit paid for the accommodation'.

International coverage means that WRI has never a slow season. Growth of the business has been bolstered with key acquisitions, such as hostels.com (2003) and Hostels of Europe (2004).

In 2007 a significant acquisition of domain name was made. Boo.com provides a traveller with a different means for searching, as Nolan explains

> 'Travel is about great experiences, and that should start with the planning and selection process. We've collected all of the key components required to make the right choice and put them together in one site. The traveller is our primary concern. If they're not satisfied, then neither are we.'

Only time will tell if this becomes the dominant means for travel searches and bookings.

12

ENCOURAGING & SUPPORTING ENTREPRENEURS

Ireland is a nation of small businesses, according to the Small Business Forum (2006). Of all the businesses in Ireland, 97% employ less than 50 staff; the vast majority employ less than 10 staff. There are approximately 250,000 small businesses in Ireland. Collectively, they employ about 770,000 people, which is 39% of the workforce or more than half of the total private sector, excluding agricultural employment.

This chapter explores the factors that determine the level of entrepreneurship in a society or a region. Each of these factors is discussed in detail. This is followed by a review of the State agencies that support new and small businesses. The findings of the Task Force on Small Business (1994), of the Culliton Report (1992), and of the Small Business Forum (2006), which provide the backdrop to the development of entrepreneurship in Irish society, are presented.

FACTORS THAT INFLUENCE ENTREPRENEURSHIP

During the last four decades, countries have produced very different rates of economic growth and prosperity. The extent and type of entrepreneurial activity in an economy is an important determinant of overall national wealth. How can entrepreneurial activity be encouraged? There are a number of factors that determine the level of entrepreneurial activity in an economy (**Figure 12.1**).

There are two basic explanations for the level of enterprise in an economic region:

- The first explanation is that economic conditions determine the level of enterprise. A lack of economically-viable opportunities discourages people from starting businesses. The implicit assumption of this explanation is that, as opportunities appear, people will act to exploit them. This is referred to as the 'demand' side argument. Many of Margaret Thatcher's economic and social policies were based on this argument. Her belief was that people would start businesses and work harder, if the right economic incentives existed.

- The contrasting explanation is that the 'supply' of entrepreneurs is determined by cultural and social factors. The assumption underlying this explanation is that entrepreneurs have certain psychological characteristics, which are developed in individuals by the social and cultural conditions that they live in. These characteristics take time to develop and, therefore, the 'supply' of entrepreneurs is considered to be 'fixed' in the short run.

FIGURE 12.1: THE DETERMINANTS OF ENTREPRENEURSHIP

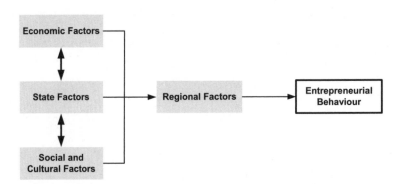

ECONOMIC FACTORS INFLUENCING ENTREPRENEURSHIP

Entrepreneurial behaviour is influenced by the number and type of market opportunities. If there are few business opportunities, there will be little enterprise. However, even if there are lots of opportunities, entrepreneurs will only exploit them, if they are perceived to be profitable. The profit potential of an opportunity is dependent on both the cost of supplying the market and the size and nature of the market.

The Profit Potential of an Entrepreneurial Opportunity: Costs

The significant costs in a new business are the cost of capital and of labour. Other important costs are raw materials, transport, telecommunications and land. An entrepreneur will calculate the cost of these factors implicitly before starting a business. The cost of these factors is determined by their availability and, in some cases, by Government actions. The cost of doing business is higher in most European countries than it is in the US – for example, in Europe, the cost of labour is high due to Government regulations and taxes; the cost of capital has traditionally been high due to poor budgetary management; and the costs of telecommunications and transport have been high due to regulation and inefficient State-owned monopolies.

In considering a specific market opportunity, an entrepreneur will need to consider the barriers to entry. Barriers to entry include large capital requirements, product differentiation, and access to distribution channels. These barriers can make it more difficult and expensive to enter a market. Often, entrepreneurs don't identify the barriers to entry – for example, in the food sector, many 'product-driven' entrepreneurs fail, because they don't identify access to distribution channels and the capital needed to build a brand as barriers to entry.

The Profit Potential of an Entrepreneurial Opportunity: Revenues

The size and nature of market demand influences the decision to start a business. Economies that are characterised by many market opportunities will encourage entrepreneurs to start-up new businesses. Deregulation can create new market opportunities. Companies such as Ryanair, O2 and FM104 have been created in response to industry deregulation. The State can increase or decrease the number of opportunities by changing the level of regulation that is required to start-up and operate a business.

SOCIAL & CULTURAL FACTORS INFLUENCING ENTREPRENEURSHIP[25]

The level and type of entrepreneurial activity in an economy is influenced by social and cultural factors. These factors may foster and encourage the traits necessary for entrepreneurship. Such traits include initiative, energy, independence, boldness, self-reliance and willingness to take risks. If enterprise is encouraged as an overall approach to life, it will become a part of the norms and values held by the society. An enterprise culture is one in which the acquisition of these qualities is both highly valued and extensively practiced.

These social and cultural factors influence entrepreneurial behaviour:

- **Legitimacy of entrepreneurship**: Legitimacy refers to the degree to which certain modes of behaviour are accepted by a society. A society with a high degree of legitimacy of entrepreneurship encourages people to learn about enterprise and to exploit this knowledge by engaging in entrepreneurship. The level of legitimacy of entrepreneurship varies between societies. The US is a society that actively encourages entrepreneurial activity. The degree of legitimacy accorded to entrepreneurship determines who engages in it. Where there is high legitimacy, entrepreneurship will be dominated by the people from 'mainstream' society. The lower the legitimacy, the more likely it is that entrepreneurs will come from socially-marginal groups.

- **Social marginality**: In many societies, it is those in marginal groups that act most entrepreneurially. Many marginal groups are more entrepreneurial, because they are restricted from traditional career paths and social routes. Marginality may be in terms of religion or ethnic background. However, not all marginal groups act entrepreneurially. For members of a marginal group to choose entrepreneurship as a career, it is necessary that there is a high level of legitimacy for entrepreneurship within the group.

- **Social mobility**: Social mobility is the degree of mobility within the social structure. Social mobility is high, if people within a society can change social roles and occupations. Mobility is low, if people find it difficult to change careers and to change social status. Blocks to mobility may be social or geographical. There are several different views as to how social mobility impacts on the emergence of entrepreneurship. First, there is an argument that high mobility encourages entrepreneurship. As it gets easier to move up and down the social structure, more people will choose entrepreneurship as a career path. The 'American Dream' is an articulation of an aspiration for a society with high social mobility. Second, there is an argument that low mobility encourages individuals to act entrepreneurially. People choose entrepreneurship because traditional career paths are blocked to them. This is often referred to as 'social blockage'. Overall, it may be the case that it is

---

[25] The authors acknowledge the contribution of Joseph Gannon, Business Research Programme, Michael Smurfit Graduate School of Business, University College Dublin, to this section.

necessary to have some combination of both flexibility and rigidity in social mobility.

State Factors Influencing Entrepreneurship

Government influences the level of entrepreneurship in a number of ways by:

- Determining the nature of market conditions and the cost of exploiting market opportunities.
- Influencing social and cultural factors.
- Acting entrepreneurially itself. The nature of the system of governance itself also has an effect on the level of entrepreneurial activity.

The most important factor is the relationship between central and local government, in particular, the autonomy of local government. Ireland is one of the most centralised democracies in Western Europe. Central Government dominates and there is virtually no autonomy at local level. Greater local autonomy should result in regions and individuals taking responsibility for their own economic welfare.

State's Impact on Economic Factors

The State influences the attractiveness of business opportunities in a number of ways:

- **As a purchaser of capital**: The State increases the cost of capital to competing users, such as entrepreneurs and industry, by purchasing capital. The State needs to purchase capital to fund State expenditure and to pay-off national debts. In Ireland, the State raises capital in many ways – for example, through the sale of Government Bonds and An Post saving schemes.
- **By setting interest rates**: The Government may use interest rates as a means of controlling inflation. Lower interest rates mean that it is cheaper to raise capital and to start a business. The single-figure interest rates of recent years have made many business opportunities more attractive. In Ireland, following monetary union, the Government has a decreasing influence on interest rate policy, since interest rates are now determined by the European Central Bank.
- **The tax system**: The tax system has a significant impact on the ability of people to save and accumulate resources. These savings may become the seed capital for a future business. Also the tax system can determine the potential return people will earn, which in turn affects investment decisions. In Ireland, Government policy initiatives such as offering tax breaks for owners of city centre car parks and apartments resulted in an increase in economic activity in these sectors.

- **Competition policy**: The enforcement of a tough competition policy in the marketplace by the Government can ensure that there are more opportunities for business. Recent deregulation in many industries has created new business opportunities.

- **As a purchaser of goods and services**: The Government, as a significant purchaser of goods, can create significant opportunities for small businesses. This requires the buyers in Government departments to consider purchasing from smaller companies. Under EU law, the Government cannot discriminate in favour of Irish businesses when purchasing goods and services.

- **Grants and financial assistance**: The State has a direct impact on the cost and availability for capital for many entrepreneurs through the provision of grants and 'soft loans'. A grant is a form of free capital. The objective of these incentives is to make it more attractive and profitable to start a business. Financial assistance may be in the form of grants, subsidised loans, equity investments, and tax relief. This financial assistance may be given for a specific purpose, such as R&D, marketing, or feasibility studies. In many cases, the rules and regulations governing State assistance makes it unattractive to potential entrepreneurs.

- **Laws and regulations**: The Government has control over many of the laws and regulations that impact on business. Amendments to these could make it simpler to do business in Ireland – for example, the tax system could be simplified.

- **'Prompt payment' legislation**: Slow payment by debtors increases the working capital requirement of small businesses. In Ireland, the State is now attempting to reduce the dependency of many small businesses on bank borrowings by enacting 'Prompt Payment' legislation. This requires businesses to pay their creditors on time. Failure to do so means the invoice attracts an immediate interest charge. Prompt Payment legislation exists in many other countries.

The State's Impact on Social & Cultural Factors

The role of the Government in encouraging enterprise is crucial. Government ideology has a significant impact on the choices the Government will make in terms of taxation and spending policies. The most visible difference between political parties is in their attitude towards the role of the State and the extent to which it intervenes in public life. The attitudes of Government towards entrepreneurial activity can increase the overall legitimacy of entrepreneurship.

The Government also controls the education system, which is often an under-used policy instrument. The education system has a significant impact on people's career choices. In Ireland, the education system could be more proactive in suggesting self-employment as a legitimate career option, although, in recent years, the Irish Government has begun to introduce enterprise into the secondary school curriculum.

The State's Impact as an Entrepreneur

Historically, the State in Ireland has acted entrepreneurially by creating many State and semi-State companies – for example, companies such as Bord na Mona, Irish Sugar (now Greencore), Irish Shipping (now Irish Ferries), ACC Bank (now part of Rabobank), and ICC Bank (now part of Bank of Scotland), and Telecom Éireann (now eircom) were all created by the State. It is a Government policy that the semi-States should develop their commercial mandate. Currently, the Government is looking to privatise many of the remaining semi-State companies.

REGIONAL FACTORS

Role Models

Role models influence entrepreneurs both directly and indirectly. A successful entrepreneurial role model in a region or locality may encourage and justify entrepreneurial activity in general. Role models can also directly impact on the level of entrepreneurship by providing encouragement, advice and finance to prospective entrepreneurs. There are some well-known role models in Ireland – for example, Noel C. Duggan, Fergal Quinn of Superquinn, and Gillian Bowler, the founder of Budget Travel. Unfortunately, until recent times, in many rural areas in Ireland, the successful role model is often the person who emigrated and succeeded in the US or the UK.

Local Infrastructure & Support Services

The presence of a basic local infrastructure is essential, if entrepreneurial activity is to occur. Research in the UK has suggested that an increase in the availability of low-cost, small premises results in increased entrepreneurial activity. In many regions in Ireland, including some cities, it can be difficult to get low-cost premises when starting up. The lack of availability of skilled and trained staff may also prevent the development of a business.

The Government may provide business advice directly, through a mentoring scheme or by grant-aiding the purchase of such advice and expertise. The main areas in which start-ups and small businesses require assistance are marketing, financial management and strategic management. A mentoring scheme encourages experienced businesspeople to support entrepreneurs and small businesspeople by offering advice.

Established Firms

Entrepreneurs will normally have gained a significant amount of work experience before they start their new businesses. The presence of suitable businesses in a locality will impact on the business experiences of entrepreneurs. The type of business that this experience is gained in is important. There are a number of factors that influence whether an employee will leave a business and start-up on their own:

- **Size of the business:** Research evidence has shown that entrepreneurs tend to have work experience in small rather than large businesses. The reason for this maybe that managers in small businesses are exposed to more functional areas. There is much more specialisation in large companies and it is common for staff to work in only one functional area.

- **Business sector:** Some sectors have a higher 'spin-off' rate than others. Sectors with high barriers to entry have lower spin-off rates, for example the drinks sector. Sectors with lower barriers to entry, for example the software sector, tend to have a high 'spin-off' rate.

STATE SUPPORT FOR ENTERPRISE

GOVERNMENT POLICY ON ENTERPRISE

A number of reports have influenced the Government's thinking and policies on entrepreneurship.

The Culliton Report

The Industrial Policy Review Group, chaired by Jim Culliton, issued its report in 1992. In this, Culliton argued that it is:

'... time to accept that the solutions to our problems lie in our hands. We need to foster a spirit of self-reliance and determination to take charge of our future'.

Recommendations from the Culliton Report included:

- **Taxation**: The Report recommended that the tax system should be reviewed fundamentally on a phased, but continual, basis. It recommended that the tax base be broadened by abolishing many tax reliefs, exemptions and deductions. Specifically, the group recommended that the standard tax rate be extended, resulting in fewer people paying tax at the higher rate. It suggested the taxation system be reformed to ensure that there were fewer distortions between the numerous savings options.

- **Infrastructure**: The Report argued that, without the proper infrastructure, it would be difficult for business to operate. The three most important aspects of infrastructure are transport, communications and energy costs. The Report argued that it is important that State-protected monopolies be induced to operate efficiently, as the cost of their inefficiency is passed on to industry. Furthermore, it suggested that there is a need for Irish ports to be made more competitive and for energy costs to be minimised. Specifically, the Report recommended that the Irish Government be more proactive in developing Ireland's environmental policies and should build on its green image, rather than reacting to developments.

- **Education, enterprise and technology**: The Report recognised that education and training are a critical element of Government policy that affect not only industry but also our overall economic welfare. The Report argued that the education system has become increasingly academic in nature and that the system needs to de-emphasis this bias towards the liberal arts and the traditional professions. It suggested that, within the education system, a high priority should be attached to the transfer of usable and marketable skills. The Report recommended that a high quality and respected stream of technical and vocational education be developed. This stream would operate with close ties to industry. The Report recommended that grants be given for general training schemes for the existing workforce. It suggested that the State training agency, FÁS, needed to separate its 'training for industry' function from its 'support for the unemployed' function.

- **Direct support for industry**: The Report recognised that the activities of the numerous State agencies involved in supporting industry are now less important then they used to be. Specifically, the Report recommended that the budgets for grants for attracting overseas companies should be reduced. Grants for indigenous industry should be replaced with equity investments by the State, where possible. The Report suggested that grants should be focused on supporting clusters of related industries. The report concluded that the commercial State enterprises need access to more capital for investment.

- **Institutional strengthening**: The Report recommended that the Department of Industry & Commerce (now Enterprise, Trade & Employment) should redefine its role. Its new role should be to develop and implement policy for industrial development and the creation of a business-related legal and regulatory environment. In redefining its role, the Department would need to reduce some of its existing activities and to place greater emphasis on employing people with industrial experience. The Report recommended that, within the Industrial Development Authority, the role of supporting indigenous industry and that of attracting overseas investment should be separated (this lead to the creation of Enterprise Ireland to support indigenous industry, and IDA Ireland to attract inwards investment).

- **Food industry**: The Report specifically examined the food industry, because of its importance to the Irish economy. The Report recommended that the food sector needs to achieve the lowest cost of production possible, consistent with a high quality; that the problem of seasonal milk production needs to be addressed; and that the 'green' image of Irish food needs to be developed.

Many of these recommendations have now been implemented.

The Task Force on Small Business

The Task Force on Small Business issued its report in 1994. Its key recommendations included:

- **Raising money**: The Task Force recognised that sourcing funds can be difficult for many small businesses. Many small business people argue that there is a shortage of funds available. Many small businesses are not financially attractive to lending institutions, because of the high level of risk and high relative administrative costs for the bank. The sources of finance used by most new and small businesses are personal savings. When most small businesses try to expand, they rely on internally-generated profits. However, the tax system constrains the ability of individuals to save and, therefore, to reinvest in their business. The Irish taxation system encourages people to choose high-return, low-risk projects. As a result, a small business-owner might achieve a higher capital gain on their personal home than on the increase in the value of their business. The Task Force's recommendations were:

◊ The establishment of a loan fund that would lend specifically to small business. A number of these loan funds have been created, for example the ICC €126 million Small Business Expansion Loan Scheme. These funds provide long-term loans to small business.

◊ Tax relief should be given for investments made prior to start-up. Since 1997, entrepreneurs can claim expenses made prior to start-up as taxable expenses.

◊ Money from the County & City Enterprise Boards should only be given with the appointment of a mentor to the business.

- **Prompt Payment:** The ability to get paid affects the capital requirements of a small business. The Task Force showed that the average number of days required for payment in Ireland is 79 days, nearly two-and-a-half months. Since this is only an average, there are many customers who are even slower than this. The Task Force recommended that 'prompt payment' legislation be enacted for the public sector in Ireland. Seven of the EU member States have mandatory rules governing payment times and terms for Government purchases. The Task Force believed similar legislation for the private sector would be too difficult to enforce.

- **Rewarding risk:** The Task Force recommended that the Government address the relationship between risk and return for small business-owners. The level of failure in new and small business is high. In addition to investing their own capital, most small business owners work more than 55 hours a week. The financial return they receive for this work, for investing their capital, and for taking a risk, is low. The Task Force recommended that the tax on profits be reduced, that the rate of capital gains tax on the disposal of a business should be reduced, and that small businesses should receive tax breaks for increasing employment.

- **Reducing burdens:** The Task Force recommended that the State reduce the regulatory burdens on small business. It costs a small business more than a large business to comply with the regulatory requirements of the State. The time the entrepreneur spends complying with the paperwork required by the State could be better spent trying to develop the business. Many small business owners are reluctant, or are unable, to delegate this activity. The Task Force suggested that small firms find it difficult to comply with many labour regulations, many of which are designed from a large company perspective. The Task Force recommended that the burdens on small business be reduced in a number of ways:

◊ A reduction in number of forms to be completed by consolidating existing forms.

◊ The simplification of forms.

◊ The removal of the requirement for small firms to produce audited accounts.

◊ A simplified company registration and incorporation procedure for new small companies.

- **Providing help**: The Task Force recommended that there should be a single point of contact for all advice and assistance for small businesses. This contact point should also provide basic information about what is required to start-up and manage a small business. The Task Force recommended that greater attention should be provided to developing the management skills of owner-mangers, since this is the biggest problem facing most small businesses. To date, the help received by small businesses has focused on providing finance. The Task Force showed that Irish companies lost market-share to importers during the previous decade. The Task Force identified a number of market opportunities for small businesses: Government departments and agencies; sub-supply linkages with larger companies; and sales direct to end-users.

- **A 'new deal' for small business**: The Task Force recommended that there should be greater attention focused on small business. In particular, it recommended that legislators should be obliged to consider the impact on the small business sector of every new piece of legislation. It suggested that key Government departments should have 'user groups', comprising entrepreneurs and managers of small businesses. The Task Force also suggested that there be a Small Business Act that would give effect to many of the recommendations in its Report.

The Small Business Forum

The Small Business Forum reported in 2006. The report identified that 'action' is required in each of the following areas. For each area, the Forum outlined specific actions and recommendations:

- Issues that particularly face growing businesses:
    ◊ Difficulty in accessing finance.
    ◊ Weak management capability.
    ◊ Lack of innovation, both technological and non-technological.
    ◊ Under-exploitation of information and communications technology.

- Issues that face all small businesses:
    ◊ Burdensome and costly administrative regulations.
    ◊ Rising local authority charges.
    ◊ Poor access to information and advice.
    ◊ Inadequate infrastructure.

- Issues that face start-ups:
    ◊ Lack of a systematic approach to entrepreneurship.

Forfás

In addition, Forfás has played an important role in contributing to the development of a knowledge-based economy, by producing seminal publications, such as *Broadband Investment in Ireland* (1998), *Telecommunications: A Key Contributor in Competitiveness & Electronic Commerce* (1998) and the *Report on E-Commerce: The Policy Requirement* (1999).

The recommendations of these publications impact all Irish businesses. For example, the recommendation of the *Report on E-Commerce* included:

- Assist Irish-owned firms to move up the value chain from bespoke software to world class niches and other products (Enterprise Ireland and Shannon Development).

- Promote Ireland as the premier EU location from which to distribute content products digitally.

- Encourage major music, media and information publishers to centralise digital distribution in Ireland and to undertake value added activities, such as media asset management and royalty collection and remittance (IDA Ireland).

- Encourage Irish-owned electronics SMEs to develop e-commerce capabilities in their supplier chains using Internet solutions (Enterprise Ireland and Shannon Development).

- Encourage universities and institutions from other countries to locate their distance learning centres in Ireland (IDA Ireland).

GOVERNMENT & OTHER AGENCIES SUPPORTING ENTERPRISE

There are a large number of State agencies that support new and small businesses in Ireland. Most of these agencies provide financial support in the form of grants or cheap loans. Increasingly, agencies are emphasising non-financial advice, such as mentoring support, access to networks, and business planning advice.

In addition to these, there are many smaller, specialist and locally-based State and private sector agencies. For a comprehensive listing of agencies, see the 'Assistance' section of **www.startingabusinessinireland.com**. The key agencies include:

- **Enterprise Ireland:** Enterprise Ireland provides significant supports for Irish-owned businesses (employing between 10 and 250 people) involved in manufacturing and internationally-traded services. It also supports start-ups and micro-businesses (less than 10 employees) in the same sector, provided they have the potential to achieve rapid growth and international expansion – these businesses are referred to as High Potential Start-Ups (HPSUs), of which about 200 now receive Enterprise Ireland support each year.

- **County & City Enterprise Boards (CEBs):** There are 35 County & City Enterprise Boards. These provide supports to start-ups and micro-businesses in their locality. Increasingly, the CEBs target their support towards start-ups and micro-businesses in the manufacturing and internationally-traded services sectors, though they are flexible in responding to local needs. Supports include financial supports (loans and grants) and what are called 'soft' supports, such as access to mentors and advice.

- **Business Innovation Centres** (BICs): BICs provide supports to innovative and technology-focussed start-ups and micro-businesses. There is a BIC in each of Cork, Dublin, Galway, Limerick and Waterford.

- **FÁS:** FÁS provides a range of services as the State's training and employment body. They provide potential entrepreneurs with *Start Your Own Business* courses.

- **LEADER+:** LEADER+ is an EU initiative aimed at supporting rural development. Among the activities of the 38 LEADER companies in Ireland are supports to new businesses.

CONCLUSION

The economic, social, cultural, state and regional factors that influence the level of entrepreneurship in an economy were discussed in this chapter. These factors are all important in determining the level and type of entrepreneurship. It is apparent that economic factors are important in accounting for the overall level of entrepreneurial activity in an economy. However, accounting for the level of entrepreneurship will not explain the level of economic growth achieved. Social and culture factors explain the type of person that chooses to act entrepreneurially. Reports on industrial policy have suggested ways in which an enterprise culture could be developed in Ireland and how the State can best support and encourage entrepreneurship.

QUESTIONS

1. Outline a model of the factors that influence entrepreneurial activity. Apply this model to Ireland.

2. How do economic factors influence the level of entrepreneurship?

3. Discuss how the State influences the level of enterprise in an economy?

4. Discuss whether Ireland has an 'enterprise culture'. What factors may have mitigated against the emergence of entrepreneurship in Ireland?

5. Chose one State agency involved in supporting new or small businesses. Write a report on the supports it offers.

6. Write a report for the Government outlining the policies you believe should be implemented to increase the level of enterprise in Ireland.

PROFILE: SEAN CRONIN, SELATRA[26]

Sean Cronin had always wanted to be an entrepreneur and, during the time he spent in the early years after university, working for blue chip US multinationals, Sean was learning valuable lessons with regard to how multinationals think and operate, at the same time as being well-positioned to spot opportunities that could form the basis of a new venture.

It was when Sean was development centre manager for Logica in Cork, that a series of coincidences formed themselves into the opportunity he had been waiting for. Working with Microsoft on Mobile PC solutions and presenting Logica's products to operators, Sean became aware that what operators wanted was revenue-earning services that the new phone technology enabled. Logica, however, was not interested in developing services and the procedure was to recommend partners to supply services after the hardware and management platform had been sold to the customer.

This was in 2001/2 and colour phones were just starting to emerge. At the same time, the Java standard had just been ratified by phone vendors. This enabled an application to be written once and then played on many different handsets. This had not been the case previously, as applications up to that point had to be written for each handset, based on its individual operating system. Sean saw the potential that this situation offered. Initially, he approached his employer proposing that Logica should develop value-added applications that could be sold after the platform was enabled but this suggestion fell on deaf ears. Sean was not about to let this opportunity pass by. If his employer could not see its potential, he certainly could and decided to go after it.

> *'So I proposed to some friends and colleagues that this would be a good opportunity as colour handsets would become affordable within a year and they would be ideal for Java games and other entertainment. They would become affordable in time.'*

The difficulty was that Sean could not afford the salaries his target people wanted. This situation was to change within a few months. Logica decided to re-size and move some development work to Eastern Europe in a cost-cutting exercise. Cork, being the youngest development centre, was earmarked to close and move its 106 jobs to Prague and India. Staff suddenly became affordable and, an added bonus, they had some investment funds by way of redundancy money. So, out of this potentially difficult situation, the means to create Selatra were put in place.

Sean, and his friends and former colleagues, were convinced that they could develop a Java download platform and sell a managed service rather than a

---

[26] This profile appeared in Fitzsimons & O'Gorman (2006).

product. The key to managing within their means was to keep the investment to a bare minimum and to deliver a platform with a fully-stocked games catalogue that other games developers had spent time and money creating. The affordability of colour handsets, they were convinced, would create a market within months among the pre-paid subscriber base, which was their target market (15-35 year olds). They wanted to be in a position to avail of that opportunity as it presented itself.

> *'So we set up and invested our own money (five founders) with enough funding to run for 12 months. We expected to be revenue-generating within nine months but we did it in four and, as revenues rose month on month, we became self-sustaining with EI matching funds.'*

The availability of matching equity funds from EI, together with feasibility funding, was a key support in those early months and allowed the new company to get off the ground without having to draw in VCs or other outside equity at that early stage. During the start-up phase, Sean attended the Genesis Enterprise Programme, which provided a kick start to honing the multiple skills needed to survive in today's start-up land.

The company grew rapidly from the start and the founders considered that it was important to maximise their early mover advantage. Growth is expensive, however, and must be financed. Having managed to bootstrap the business initially with their own investment and with matching equity funds from EI, more was needed.

> *'As we grew and wanted to ramp up faster than our organic growth in revenues permitted, we took a strategic decision to raise VC money in 2004.'*

While a decision is relatively easily made, having made the decision to seek VC funding, the founders of Selatra did not fully appreciate at the outset how long that process would take and how much time would be involved.

> *'The amount of time dedicated to pitching and answering queries was far more than we had expected. We eventually found funds in July 2005, nine months from the first pitch. The term sheet negotiations and legal issues were very distracting and had to be dealt with at the same time as dealing with changing expectations from staff and partners. The cultural change that external VC partners brought into the mix was also difficult.'*

Looking back over the last few years, Sean comments that he has no regrets in having become an entrepreneur, but that he would be more aware next time of the amount of time that can be tied up securing sufficient finance to allow the company to develop and grow. Sean would caution other entrepreneurs:

> *'Don't underestimate the difficulty in fundraising for high-tech, non-asset-backed ventures in today's property-preoccupied Ireland!'*

13

TECHNOLOGY TRANSFER:
EXPLORING & EXPLOITING
RESEARCH[27]

*Ireland's economy has performed exceptionally well over the past decade and
we have built a world class reputation across a range of technologies. The
challenge now is to maintain and grow this performance.
Our future depends on how well we manage the transition to a world where
knowledge and ideas are more important than bricks and mortar.
Every economic region is trying to capitalise on new technologies
and new markets. If we are to succeed, we have to do the same, but we must
be more creative and flexible than our competitors.*
(Mary Harney, Tánaiste, July 2004)[28]

Increasingly, it is acknowledged that third-level institutions and their research
activities may form the perfect catalyst in propelling countries along the trajectory
towards becoming knowledge-based economies. Nations with strong research
systems and the capacity to leverage the commercial opportunities of their
research through effective technology transfer activities – particularly, from third-
level institutions to industry – will be best placed to prosper both economically
and socially. Third-level institutions are powerful motors for the technological and
economical development of industrial branches and regions. Significant
investment has been made by the Government into strengthening the research
capacity of Irish third-level institutions. Bodies such as Science Foundation Ireland
(SFI), IRCSET (Irish Research Council for Science Engineering & Technology) and
the Higher Education Authority (HEA) have been involved in building research

---

[27] This chapter is based on edited passages of Cunningham & Harney (2006).

[28] Mary Harney at the launch of the findings of the Enterprise Strategy Group, source: *Irish
Independent, Digital Ireland* supplement, 9 July 2004.

capacity in science, engineering and technology. In addition, the Government has made further significant commitments to increase this research capacity, which is underpinned by the major policy document, *Strategy for Science Technology & Innovation* (2006). This investment comes at a time when Ireland is not longer internationally considered a low cost country for manufacturing purposes. Therefore, our national ability to transfer technology from third-level institutions to industry is seen as a vital element in sustaining economic momentum. This chapter examines the various mechanisms for technology transfer and the barriers and stimulants to technology transfer in this context.

THEORETICAL DEBATES

The theme of research commercialisation and technology transfer has been the attention of much literature focus. In a comprehensive review, Harmon (1995) classified the literature into two groups: a rational decision-making perspective and a relationship perspective regarding technology transfer and commercialisation.

The Rational Decision-making Perspective

This perspective views technology transfer as a process that can, and indeed should, be planned, where inventors and future users of the technology function independently, without co-ordinating their efforts until the first negotiations regarding a specific technology, when the two parties find one another through a formal search process that is usually mediated by a transfer agent. The majority of these studies focus on the process of technology transfer from the research centre to industry and the major focus of these studies is to identify the most efficient methods of administering and facilitating the technology transfer process and organisational forms that facilitate this transfer. This linear model of the innovation process is based on factors such as basic research, applied research, prototype development, market research, product development, marketing and selling. It is this model that has had the greatest influence on public policy in most countries. Interventions are made at different and specific stages by strengthening public infrastructure, and improving incentives to the private sector, which was then expected to transform technology, patents and systems into new products and processes.

The Relationship Perspective

The second major group of studies reviewed and categorised by Harmon (1995) takes a different perspective on the technology transfer process, emphasising its relationship aspect. This group of studies is primarily made up of non-linear models that emphasise multi-directional linkages, interdependency between hard technology and softer issues of people management and information flows (for example, see Mitra & Formica, 1997).

A number of perspectives are found in this group of studies.

- **Communications:** A successful transfer depends on the effectiveness of information flows between a set of individuals or organisations within a complex network of communication paths.

- **Innovation:** The communication perspective errs in viewing technology transfer as a communication process rather than an innovation process – instead, policy-makers should not be as concerned with processes for transferring technology after it has been developed but rather should focus on developing transferable technologies.

- **Alliance:** Barriers can be reduced by alliance-building between inventor(s) and lead user(s), thus facilitating the identification of need from the marketplace – in this way, the alliance then develops into a relationship with the lead user, thus facilitating the technology transfer at a later stage.

- **Co-operation:** This approach studies the processes of co-operation between the parties involved that make the transfer easier. Among the facilitating processes identified in these studies are open communication, mutual interdependence, respect, trust and a willingness to compromise.

Modern views of research commercialisation and technology transfer tend to be grouped within the last perspective: co-operation. Increasingly, there is awareness of the multitude of factors that can impact on the technology process or failure of research to progress on this route.

TECHNOLOGY TRANSFER

Technology transfer refers to the process, whereby invention or intellectual property from academic research is licensed or conveyed through use rights to a for-profit entity and eventually commercialised (Friedman & Silberman, 2003). According to the Association of University Technology Managers (AUTM), the phrase 'technology transfer' can be used very broadly to define the movement of ideas, tools, and people among institutions of higher learning, the commercial sector and the public sector. Friedman & Silberman (2003) captures the process of technology transfer as outlined in **Figure 13.1**.

FIGURE 13.1: THE PROCESS OF UNIVERSITY TECHNOLOGY TRANSFER

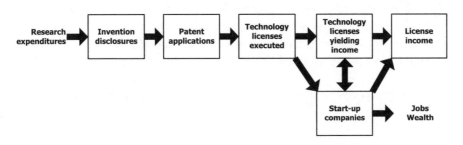

Source: *Friedman & Silberman (2003).*

THE TECHNOLOGY TRANSFER PROCESS

Typically, technology transfer begins with university and individual interaction. The sequencing of events in terms of university technology transfer is usually that a scientific discovery is made. The scientist then files an invention disclosure form with the university's technology transfer office (TTO). Once formally disclosed, the TTO must simultaneously evaluate the technical merit and commercial potential of the technology and decide whether to patent the invention, as well as deciding the geographical extent of the patent protection and its potential fields of use. This decision often poses a dilemma for many TTOs, because they have limited resources for filing patents. If the patent is awarded, the TTO will often attempt to market the technology. Inventors are frequently involved in the marketing phase, because they are often in a good position to identify potential licensees and because their technical expertise often makes them a neutral partner for companies that wish to commercialise the technology. The final stage involves the negotiation of a licensing agreement. These agreements can include benefits to the university, such as royalties, 'follow on' sponsored research agreements, or an equity stake in a new venture based on a licensed technology. Involvement does not necessarily end with a licensing agreement, rather it is quite common for TTOs to devote substantial resources to the maintenance and recognition of licensing agreements

The technology transfer process therefore typically includes a set of components, starting with investment in R&D; the actual R&D performance; the decision how to handle intellectual property; building a prototype to demonstrate the technology; the further development needed for commercialisation; and, finally, the successful introduction of a product or service on the market. This depiction in **Figure 13.2** is based on an ideal sequencing of technology development.

FIGURE 13.2: TECHNOLOGY TRANSFER: STAGE ACTIVITY OUTCOME

◊ Basic research patent.
◊ Proof of concept / invention (functional).
◊ Early-stage technology development business validation.
◊ Product development innovation: new firm or programme.
◊ Production / marketing viable business.

Source: *Adapted from National Institute of Standards & Technology (2002a).*

MORE COMPLEX TECHNOLOGY TRANSFER

Often the process is more complex than depicted in **Figure 13.2**. Evaluation of the invention disclosure, for example, can involve multiple actors, including state bodies, individual companies and the inventors themselves. Overall, technology transfer activities are manifested as eliciting and processing invention disclosures, licensing university-created knowledge, seeking additional sponsorship of R&D projects or a combination of these three. Crucially, the extent of, and mechanisms for, technology transfer will be shaped by the resources, reporting relationships and incentives of technology transfer offices.

MECHANISMS FOR TECHNOLOGY TRANSFER

In order for a university to undertake technology transfer activities, it must have developed intellectual property (IP), the legal form of protection for inventions, brands, designs and creative works. The four main types of IP rights are patents, copyright, designs and trademarks. Most technology transfer from universities involves patents – consequently, most universities have specific IP policies, for academic staff, students, researchers and research centres. Universities use IP protection to provide the legal fabric of property ownership that makes technology transfer through licensing possible.

PATENTS

The patent system provides a means for inventors to protect original work. In a university context, the process of filing of patent begins with the inventor filing an invention disclosure form with the university's TTO. The probability of patenting a technology is greater when:

- It is clearly patentable.
- It has favourable cost-benefit considerations (good commercial prospects or a potential buyer already interested in the technology).
- A potential buyer offers to patent collaboratively.
- The TTO is approached, and even persuaded, by an inventor of the technical and commercial case for commercialising the technology.

Increasingly, patents are used to demonstrate university expertise – for many universities, the patterns of publications cited in patents have been used by authors as a proxy indicator of university-industry links. The extent of patenting activities, however, is a function of the number of invention disclosures submitted to the TTO.

An OECD survey shows that European universities tend to file most of their patents in their home country, while fewer academic patents are filed at European level or overseas (OECD, 2003). This reflects the importance of filing a patent within home jurisdictions first, but there are concerns that subsequent patenting at the EU level could be deterred by the cost of an EPC patent. In the US, the introduction of the Bayh-Dole Act 1980 allowed universities and other research institutions the freedom to patent their own inventions. According to Henderson *et al.*, (1998), since then, the number of patents assigned to HEIs per research dollar spent at HEIs has more than tripled. In terms of the distribution of patents in the US, data from AUTM shows that the University of California dominates the field, followed closely by six other big universities, each with a portfolio of over 80 patents.

Nonetheless, Yale University reviewed its 850 invention disclosures from 1982 through 1996 and learned that:

- 1% (10 of 850) of total disclosures led to 70% of the $20.4 million total licensing income received.

- 4% (33 of 850) of disclosures accounted for 90% of the total income.

- 88% (748 of 850) of disclosures generated less than $10,000 each, the approximate cost of processing just one invention disclosure.

LICENSING

Licenses are permissions granted by the owner of a piece of intellectual property to another party for the use of the invention or work. Licenses can be granted on an exclusive basis to a single licensee, thus guaranteeing a strong degree of market exclusivity. But licenses can also be granted non-exclusively, to many parties, as is frequently the case for software or limited by other means – for example, for a limited time period, in a particular geographical territory or market or technological field. Companies tend to try and to negotiate exclusive licenses when the future depends on the promise of a limited number of technologies. Notably, the OECD survey found that: 'the extent to which universities grant exclusive rather than non-exclusive licenses varies widely from country to country', such that: 'no best practice appears to have emerged about how to construct licensing agreements or how to balance the public good of broad diffusion of innovations with private desires for exclusive rights' (OECD, 2003).

When university research leads to technical innovations, one route to commercialisation is to license the technology to other firms, rather than to try to exploit the technology directly. On average, TTOs negotiate few licenses (less then 10) a year. It is not necessarily the stronger patents that are the object of licenses but more usually early-stage technologies, know-how or materials (OECD, 2003) (see **Figure 13.3**). Licenses can be granted for the use of patented technologies, for technologies with a patent pending, for unpatented technologies (for example, biological materials or know-how) for which no formal form of protection has been or will be sought, for innovations covered by a *sui generis* form of protection (for example, plant varieties) or for creative works covered by copyright (OECD, 2003).

For revenue income from licensing IP, there are enormous variations nationally and within countries. In absolute terms, US universities generated the largest amount of income from licenses, over $1.2 billion per institution, followed by Germany at €6.6 billion, although income per institution can range from thousands to millions of euros.

FIGURE **13.3:** TOTAL NUMBER OF LICENSES *PER ANNUM*

Country	Total No of Licenses	Average per University	No of Responding Universities
Australia	234	7.1	33
Italy	27	1.4	20
Korea	44	8.8	5
Netherlands	250	14.7	17
Switzerland	200	9.5	21
United States	4,049	24.1	168

Source: *Adapted from OECD (2003).*

When negotiating license agreements universities generally try to rigidly cohere to three guiding principles, which are included as clauses in most agreements. These clauses are to:

- Encourage the use of publicly funded technologies.
- Ensure the broad diffusion of the research results.
- Maximise their future IP revenue streams.

Generally, when conducting agreements, universities need to be satisfied that the respective company will act in good faith in its efforts to commercialise the research. Often clauses to this effect are included in contracts negotiated, to ensure that the TTO's mission of exploiting research for the public good is fulfilled.

FIGURE 13.4: TECHNOLOGY LICENSING: USA

Of the 3,600 universities in the United States, some 500 are research universities. Of the total, one in 12 have technology licensing offices (TLOs), with 4,800 patent applications (1998) and 350 spin-off companies per year. Revenues from technology licensing are about 2% of university revenues.

In the area of technology licensing, universities have:

◊ Transparent and extensive policies.

◊ Extensive and effective contractual procedures.

◊ TLOs varying in size and competence and having professional staff.

It is a requirement for researchers to disclose inventions that may be commercialised through the office for technology licensing. An example on a scale relevant in the Irish context is the Georgia Institute of Technology. Typically, the researchers receive 30%-50% of royalties, while the TTO receives 15% and, in addition, takes equity in new spin-offs based on university technology.

FIGURE 13.5: LICENSING AT MIT

MIT is a prime example of a university that has focused on licensing existing technology, and is one of the most successful universities in the world at technology transfer. Unlike many universities, MIT has no business incubation activities at all. The strategy of the technology licensing office (TLO) is to encourage as many invention disclosures as possible from faculty members, by minimising the barriers to disclosure. Currently, MIT discloses about 450 inventions per year. MIT's TLO then licenses these inventions as nonexclusive or exclusive licences to industry and local venture capital firms. Rather than getting involved in the complexities of spinout formation, the TLO provides a shop window for industry to view its IP and agrees as many licence deals as possible. This is a strategy that has proved to be extremely beneficial for MIT.

FIGURE 13.6: LICENSING AT OXFORD

As a result of a specific focus on licensing, Oxford University has transferred more IP to the market than any other university in the UK. Oxford University's ISIS is one of the country's most prolific TTOs, when it comes to agreeing licensing deals. Since 1997, it has entered into 160 agreements on university technology. Although it does not prescribe the balance between spin-outs and licensing in any way, over two-thirds of its technologies are licensed to existing firms.

One such licence deal was made with UK-based Hymatic Engineering, involving a new technology for cooling satellite sensors that came from research in the university's Department of Engineering Science. The company has further developed this technology for use in portable detectors for nuclear monitoring at customs ports. Hymatic estimates that the new technology resulting from this licence deal will help it generate around £6m additional revenues.

Company Formation: Start-ups & Spin-offs

Start-ups and spin-offs are the most cited form of technology transfer, as they are direct manifestation of such activity and provide a basis for measuring the direct impact of technology transfer activities (for example, numbers employed, revenues, value of equity). Roughly 12% of university-assigned inventions are transferred to the private sector through the founding of new organisations, according to AUTM (2002). Much policy attention has been drawn to the role in spin-offs and start-ups, given their potential role in employment generation and in stimulating economic growth. Although the terms are often used interchangeably, it is useful to distinguish between the two: a spin-off is a company that includes among its founding members a person affiliated with the university, while a start-up firm is one that is not founded by a staff member of the university but develops technology originating at the university (for example, licensed technology).

The frequency of TTO start-up and spin-off activity varies significantly across countries and between universities. Some universities routinely transfer their technology through the formation of new firms, while others, such as Columbia University, rarely generate start-ups. Moreover, rates of start-up activity are not a simple function of the magnitude of sponsored research funding or the quantity of inventions created. For example, Stanford University, with sponsored research expenditures of US$391 million, generated 25 TLO start-ups in 1997; whereas Duke University, with sponsored research expenditures of US$361 million, generated none. A study by Di Gregorio & Shane (2003) compared explanations for cross-institutional variation in new firm formation rates from TTOs and found that important influences with respect to company formation activities included intellectual eminence, which makes it easier for researchers to start-up companies exploiting their inventions, and TTO policy on equity and royalties.

FIGURE 13.7: UNIVERSITY OF LOUVAIN LA NEUVE

The R&D Liaison Unit of the University and the Promotech, a Business & Innovation Centre (BIC) located in the Nancy region of France, developed a project that used intermediaries, such as BICs, to help the commercialisation of university research. One particular area of co-operation is in providing a link between potential university spin-offs and venture capitalists. At this stage, speed is considered important, in case the spin-off locates outside the region or fails to get off the ground, as a result of delays in putting financial resources together. Other areas of co-operation are in the field of effective project identification, determining the most effective exploitation and commercialisation route for research, and in improving patenting and licensing services. The project has also helped to develop a wider and more supportive regional framework for university research commercialisation, which has allowed the university to interact better with local business and technology agencies and intermediaries.

FIGURE 13.8: SUPPORTING SPIN-OFFS: UNIVERSITY OF TWENTE

As part of an initiative to help new university-based spin-offs, the University of Twente in the Netherlands created the Temporary Entrepreneurial Post scheme. This scheme is centred on graduate engineers and seeks to provide a bridge or support for the key transition period when the new graduate is setting up the company and testing the market for their idea. To do this, the university offers a part-time research assistant post to the potential entrepreneur to provide the person with a basic income, as well as to allow some spare time for the person to set up their enterprise. The potential entrepreneur is also eligible for grants to help set up the company itself, and advice and guidance is also provided through the university's Industrial Liaison Office, together with information and introduction to venture capital firms. The university offers 20 such posts each year and the drop out rate is less than 25%. It is estimated that some 300 spin-off companies have been created since the scheme was established in 1979.

COPYRIGHT

Applying for patents is only one of a range of actions that TTOs can take to help protect and exploit their institution's IP. Some TTOs are also involved in registering copyright to protect creative works such as software, databases, educational materials (papers, books, courses) and multimedia works (for example, on-line courses, digital text books). Whether the TTO is involved in copyright registration may have to do with local laws and rules regarding the ownership of copyright material. It is only recently that universities in some countries have begun to claim rights to copyrighted works. Two sorts of *sui generis* protection – industrial design registration and plant breeder's rights – may also be managed by the TTO.

Unlike patent inventions, ownership of copyright works is often neglected. Yet universities generate a lot of their IP in the form of literary or artistic works that can be protected by copyright. Ownership of copyright for publicly-funded databases and other universities has become an important issue, because there are increasing demands by firms and the public for access to such databases. PROs in the US and the UK, but also in Ireland and France, are paying more attention to clarifying copyright ownership of works created by their employees, particularly in light of Internet publication and access.

SOFT METHODS OF TECHNOLOGY TRANSFER

IP management involves carefully managing and diffusing newly-generated knowledge into society. This is often understood simply as patenting and licensing, but some of the best forms of knowledge transfer comes when a talented researcher moves out of the university and into business, or *vice versa*. Given its intangible nature, knowledge is best transferred by people. One program that served to increase university-industry collaboration is the linkage between Edinburgh Crystal, Wolverhampton University and Edinburgh College of Art (**Figure 13.9**).

FIGURE 13.9: CASE STUDY: EDINBURGH CRYSTAL, WOLVERHAMPTON UNIVERSITY & EDINBURGH COLLEGE OF ART

Edinburgh Crystal knew that, to guarantee its long-term survival, it would have to find a younger market. That meant new designs. At the same time, Wolverhampton University's School of Art & Design was looking for ways to develop links with industry. When the School's Head of Glass met Edinburgh Crystal management at a trade event in 1994 it marked the start of a fruitful collaboration. With Edinburgh College of Art also involved, the Edinburgh Crystal Masters Design Scholarship programme was created. The students work at the company full-time on 12 to 15-month placements. The company contributes to bursary funding and academic supervision costs. A three-monthly review process culminates in an external exam leading to the Masters degree. Edinburgh Crystal's operations director said:

'We wanted to get a more contemporary feel to our glass design in a market which was then still very traditional. We felt this programme would impact positively on our design department and stimulate the product development process. This continual stream of students encourages us to push design and production possibilities, keeping us highly competitive.'

Students' work has fed directly into the company's branded range, The Edge, launched nearly three years ago, and several Masters students have gone on to become full-time employees. The School's Head of Glass said:

'It's almost impossible for an academic programme to simulate a commercial creative environment but, in collaborations like this, students are exposed to market realities. They mature quickly as designers.'

INTERNSHIPS

Internships are the most traditional type of linkage, but they often encounter problems unless they are managed and well-organised. BITS in India has developed an innovative programme of so-called 'practice schools', which follow a similar scheme to those offered by MIT. Practice schools are established in a number of enterprises, which agree to collaborate with BITS staff on a regular basis. At the same time, students join practice schools on pre-agreed tasks and they are supervised jointly by BITS teaching staff and staff at the enterprise.

NETWORKS & PARTNERSHIPS

Forums that bring academics and business people together are likely to increase the chance that people with common interests and goals will find innovative ways to develop partnerships (see **Figure 13.10**).

FIGURE 13.10: CONNECT MIDLANDS

In order to gain critical mass, a novel approach to a 'companies fair' was initiated in the Midlands of England. Run by Warwick University, it involved all of the major 12 universities in the area pooling their technology spin-off companies into a network that could more efficiently seek investors and expertise. Based on a Californian model, the network's mission is 'to nurture the development and growth of technology-related enterprise in the Midlands by connecting entrepreneurs to the resources they need to succeed'.

The main advantage of such a programme is that it creates an effective marketplace, where companies can show their wares to potential investors. Warwick University needs this critical mass to make its spin-off companies appeal to investors (as an investor might not be interested in going to Warwick to look at just one company), and benefits also from funding it receives for running the network.

CONSULTANCY ACTIVITY

Consultancy takes the form of expert advice or analysis services. In practice, the difference between consultancy and contract research is blurred – but the general distinction is that, in consultancy, the academic provides advice to the business rather than actually conducting research. Universities have freedom to determine their own policies and, consequently, there is a wide variation in current practice. Institutional limits on the time academics are allowed to spend on consultancy range from 20 days (Oxford Brookes) to 50 (Aston and Swansea) per year. Some of the more research-intensive universities set their limits at 30 days (Imperial and Leeds), while others do not have a precise figure (King's College London and Bristol) but make it clear that academic duties and the university's interests must be put first.

Other mechanisms of softer technology transfer include academics taking places on company boards, leveraging existing alumni networks. Other efforts include educational offerings such as the California Institute of Technology (**Figure 13.11**).

FIGURE 13.11: AN ENTREPRENEURSHIP COURSE AT THE CALIFORNIA INSTITUTE OF TECHNOLOGY

California Institute of Technology provides a course on entrepreneurship, open to both undergraduate and postgraduate students. Essentially, the course contains all the elements critical to building a business and to understanding the language of business. The topics covered include:

◊ Caltech's disclosure and patent policies.
◊ Caltech's incentives and grants, technology transfer, and deals.
◊ Patents and intellectual property.
◊ Strategic role of patents and litigation.
◊ Marketing in technology-based enterprises.
◊ Formation of corporations and types of partnerships.
◊ Options and other financial instruments; vesting.
◊ Accounting and financial reports.
◊ Venture capital.
◊ Financial control.
◊ Initial public offerings.
◊ Human resources issues, job descriptions, and compensation.
◊ Benefits, pensions, and litigation risks.
◊ Business plans.
◊ Mergers and acquisitions.
◊ Corporate finance overview.
◊ Corporate partnerships and strategic alliances.
◊ Dealing with Wall Street.

STIMULANTS TO TECHNOLOGY TRANSFER

In order to appreciate fully the potential for commercialisation activities and to place realistic boundaries on expectations, it is necessary to consider the stimulants to technology transfer. These can be grouped as either macro- or micro-level factors.

MACRO-LEVEL FACTORS

These include:

- **The level of business investment in R&D in the region**: Universities in regions with higher levels of R&D investment are likely to have greater potential and opportunities to develop links with business and to exploit university research. In some cases, the presence of large multinational pharmaceutical or technological companies in a region will serve to enhance investment in university research and commercialisation activities.

- **HEI proximity to industrial clusters:** Clusters of economic activity often facilitate strong networking between businesses, universities and local government agencies..

- **Support of developmental agencies / research councils:** The role and capacity of developmental agencies to support business-university collaboration at a regional level may prove critical in promoting the growth of technology transfer activities through established linkages and offset IP-related costs.

- **Institutional and legislative context:** Goldfarb & Henrekson (2002) found that, when intellectual property was awarded to universities, it was more effective in facilitating commercialisation, as opposed to the Swedish system where the rights are awarded to the inventor.

- **Government support:** Governments can create a supportive context for technology transfer by sponsoring the establishment of one-stop IP centres or networks to serve the smaller public research organisations that lack the resource or critical mass to build their own fully-operational TTO – for example, Belgium's Interuniversity Institute for Biotechnology (VIB).

Attempts at technology transfer are also often impeded by poor information and confusion concerning the arrangements for developing and exploiting IP. In the US, clarity was provided through the introduction of legislation under the Bayh-Dole Act 1980. Implementation of the *National Code of Practice for Managing*

Intellectual Property from Publicly-funded Research (ICSTI, 2004) helps to clarify this issue in an Irish context.

MICRO-LEVEL FACTORS

The historical context of universities shapes their role in the regional / national innovation system, as well as the type of knowledge they generate. Micro-level stimulants that influence the level and extent of technology transfer and research commercialisation include:

- **Research tradition:** Some universities are strongly grounded in a particular research tradition or, historically, have focused on particular channels of knowledge dissemination (Sanchez & Tejedor,1995).

- **Strategy, mission and clear objectives:** The OECD (2003) notes that effective commercialisation of research requires a specific strategy, in order to ensure the appropriate balance of income generation with the adequate protection of intellectual assets.

- **Top-level leadership and commitment:** Universities should co-ordinate the efforts of the various offices that support university researchers in their work with companies and, where appropriate, should consider co-locating them.

- **Quality of TTO:** Mechanisms for technology transfer will be shaped by the resources, reporting relationships and incentives of technology transfer offices. The Lambert Report (2003) in the UK noted that many businesses report problems with the professionalism of some TTOs and that some universities find it difficult to acquire certain resources such as marketing skills, market research, licence negotiation expertise and spin-out experience.

- **Age and experience of TTOs:** Developing expertise in commercialisation activities can take a significant amount of time. AUTM (2002:) notes: 'this is a significant factor in comparing performance, because of the time needed to develop a portfolio of intellectual property to license, build up a body of expertise and develop a culture of technology transfer within the institution – as well as giving licenses the time needed to develop and market products'.

- **Scope of commercialisation initiatives:** Some institutions have implemented schemes to foster an entrepreneurial environment and encourage relationship management, including outreach programmes, lunches for inventors and annual recognition events.

- **Documented policies:** Clear and well-documented, written policies on technology transfer are of real benefit in encouraging commercialisation.

- **Educational offerings:** Many TTOs now offer workshops and presentations to increase awareness of technology transfer and to enhance understanding of the processes in place in their institutions.

- **Knowledge of research and relations with faculty:** Motivating and helping researchers to locate potential collaboration partners requires a sophisticated understanding, not only of how researchers operate but also of individual researchers' focus areas, and of the companies that share their research interests. When technology-transfer, sponsored programmes, or corporate relations officials are knowledgeable about faculty research interests, they can play a key role in pre-screening companies with which the faculty might wish to collaborate. Deans, department chairs, and vice presidents of research are well-positioned to coordinate these efforts.

- **Networking and informal relations:** Most TTOs surveyed by the OECD (2003) stressed the importance of both the TTO's and the researchers' informal relations.

- **Trust and common expectations:** A minimum level of trust is a precondition for effective technology transfer (Lundvall, 2002). To achieve successful co-operation agreement, both parties need to be aware of each others' interests and objectives, as well as each others' complementary strengths (Fassin, 2000).

- **Inventor involvement:** Increasingly, it is acknowledged that transfer of knowledge from the university to the commercial sector generally requires the active involvement of university inventors (Goldfarb & Henrekson, 2002; Meseri & Maital, 2001).

- **Motivation, incentives for researchers and university culture:** These are a major stimulus and critical input to technology transfer. Faculty involvement or buy-in to technology transfer is crucial, as one cannot assume that invention disclosures will be made, but must be encouraged, and the validity of this process for research findings must be actively promoted.

BARRIERS TO COMMERCIALISATION

There are a number of identified barriers to technology transfer at an institutional level and at an operational level, including:

INSTITUTIONAL BARRIERS

These include:

- TTO organisational structure and supporting infrastructure.
- Resource constraints and expertise deficiencies.
- Poor internal relations.
- Lack of clarity over ownership of IP.
- Perceived conflict of interests.
- Overestimating the value of IP.
- Partners may lack understanding or trust.
- Lack of support for SME technology transfer.
- Complicated technology transfer policies.

OPERATIONAL BARRIERS

These include:

- Lack of space.
- Lack of investment in R&D by companies.
- Lack of funding for prototype development.
- The 'research treadmill'.
- Availability of researchers to pursue research fellowships.
- Lack of full-time research positions.
- Lack of confidence in commercial merits of the research.
- Constraints for researchers, including perceived publishing constraints; age of academic and contract researchers; and salaries.

One of the more significant barriers is cultural, as business and universities are not natural partners: their cultures and their missions are different (see **Figure 13.12**). Academics value their freedom and independence, resent their reliance on public funding and feel their efforts are not properly appreciated (Lambert, 2003). Reflecting this, the most frequently cited barrier to commercialisation, both in the literature and from our research, was the cultural barriers that exist between the TTO, the university scientists and industry. Naturally, different stakeholders will have differing expectations but, in the university context, such differences are magnified.

FIGURE 13.12: CULTURAL DIFFERENCES: UNIVERSITIES *VERSUS* INDUSTRY

University Values	Industry Values
New invention	New application
Advancement of knowledge	Added value
New means for further research	Financial returns
Basic research	Applied research
Long-term	Short-term
To know how? What? Why?	Product / service-driven
Free public good	Secrecy
Publication	Protection / patents
Academic freedom	Commercial approach
Supply-side model of action	Demand-side model of action

Technology transfer will only occur when university faculty and representatives from business and industry work together for mutual gain and find mechanisms to manage the inherent conflict between openness, characteristic of the scientific community, and privacy / secrecy, which belongs to the world of business. Therefore, industry-university collaboration cannot be forced and cultural differences must be understood.

CONCLUSION

The need to increase technology transfer activities from third-level institutions to industry is an essential prerequisite to becoming a knowledge-based economy. This chapter identified the technology transfer process, the main mechanisms for technology transfer, namely patents, licensing, company formations and soft methods of technology transfer, which included internships, networks and partnerships and consultancy activities. There are both macro and micro stimulants and barriers to technology transfer.

The most effective manner in which to facilitate and encourage technology transfer from third-level institutions to industry is to have:

- Clarity in the frameworks and procedures of exploitation and commercialisation policy.
- Transparency in decision-making concerning exploitation and commercialisation activity.
- Good information and contact provision to academic personnel regarding intellectual property and commercialisation procedures.
- Streamlined decision-making procedures.

QUESTIONS

1. Outline the different theoretical perspective with respect to technology transfer. Do you agree that the relationship perspective is the best perspective to view technology transfer in the current Irish context?

2. Describe the technology transfer process and discuss what issues makes technology transfer more complex.

3. What is intellectual property (IP) and how can it be protected?

4. Describe the process used by TTOs to negotiate licensing agreements and discuss the merits of exclusive licensing.

5. Outline the soft methods of technology transfer.

6. Discuss the stimulants that impact on the level and frequency of technology transfer .

7. What are the main barriers to technology transfer?

PROFILE: PROFESSOR BARRY SMYTH & PAUL COTTER, CHANGING WORLDS

Changing Worlds was founded in 1999 by Professor Barry Smyth and Paul Cotter who commercialised their research from UCD's Smart Media Institute. Changing Worlds is a provider of intelligent personalisation technology for mobile telecommunication operators, which has been deployed to over 30 mobile operators, including Vodafone, O2 and Swisscom Mobile. The technology allows mobile operators to increase revenue streams from mobile Internet usage. Changing Worlds' vision is:

'...*to tackle the many problems associated with mobile Internet, enabling operators to enhance usability and increase mobile Internet revenues. Our vision is a mobile Internet that is user-friendly and an integral part of daily life. We aim to help operators achieve this goal and grow their revenues from mobile data.*'

Deployments of Changing Worlds' technology on mobile networks have shown an ROI from active users ranging from 75% to 103%, increased user satisfaction and a user preference for mobile portals with personalisation. Other reported benefits included reduced click distance, increased mobile Internet usage, increased average revenue per user, increased conversion of browsers into buyers and increased user loyalty and reduced churn.

In 2000, before the dot.com bust, the company raised IR£3.5million, the main investors being Trinity Venture Capital and Flanders Language Value, based in Belgium, in addition to a number of small investors, valuing the company at IR£12.5 million. In 2005, the company established an R&D centre in NovaUCD and began to collaborate further with researchers at UCD's Smart Media Institute. Changing Worlds' chief executive, Luke Conroy, described this development as:

'*The synergy with such a renowned institution as UCD has proved to be a key differentiator for Changing Worlds when competing in the global mobile telecommunications market. Establishing this research centre in the NovaUCD innovation and technology transfer centre further strengthens our links with UCD and will secure Changing Worlds' future market leadership and competitive advantage.*'

In 2005, the company was the overall winner of the DHL Exporter of the Year Award and it was one of the finalists in the Ernest & Young Entrepreneur of the Year competition in 2006.

14

ENTERPRISE EDUCATION[29]

A fundamental re-ordering of how economies function, and of how organisations are structured and managed, has created a new imperative for enterprise education. National competitive advantage is increasingly dependent on the skill-base of the workforce and, more specifically, on the ability of both firms and individuals to engage in innovative activity and in new economic activity. This has created an imperative for both general skills, since these, it is suggested, are related to innovation, and for specific enterprise skills, which are related to new venture creation. Consequently, in many countries, enterprise education has become an important part of both industrial policy and of educational policy. This has resulted in increased institutional support, in terms of both formal institutions and informal norms and values, for enterprise education and training. This societal and institutional interest in entrepreneurial activity values entrepreneurship as:

- The specific activity of business formation and small business management.

- A new style of managerial behaviour in established organisations.

- A more general, and loosely defined, new attitude to the worlds of work and leisure.

It is for these reasons that enterprise education programmes are being promoted in many countries, with programme objectives including the specific objective of creating more entrepreneurial individuals who will act as independent entrepreneurs, and the more general objective of preparing individuals for a world where they will increasingly need to manage their own careers and lives in an entrepreneurial way.

However, there still is a limited understanding of how best to achieve these quite diverse objectives, even though, paradoxically, entrepreneurial education, particularly in the US, reflects high levels of homogeneity in terms of teaching

---

[29] This chapter is based on Hytti & O'Gorman (2004). The paper was winner of the Literati Club Awards for Excellence, outstanding paper for 2004 for the publication *Education & Training*. The research project was carried out with the support of the European Community (project FIN/00/C/P/RF/92650). The content of this project does not necessarily reflect the position of the European Community, nor involve any responsibility on the part of the European Community.

pedagogy (Katz, 2003). In particular, it has been argued that many enterprise programmes assume, either explicitly or implicitly, that the teaching input of improving the individual's knowledge-base and skills relating to 'how to start a business', will be associated with:

- Increased entrepreneurial motivation, capability and understanding.
- A higher propensity to start a new venture.
- More enterprising and innovative persons.

However, traditional approaches to education, in fact, may inhibit the development of the requisite entrepreneurial attributes and skills.

In this chapter, we explore what is understood to constitute enterprise education. We profile some enterprise education initiatives to identify the objectives and the models, initiatives and programmes that exist under the broad heading of enterprise education.

TOWARDS A CONCEPTUAL SCHEMA OF OBJECTIVES FOR ENTERPRISE EDUCATION

There has been a rapid proliferation of enterprise education. For example, there has been an increase in the number of 'entrepreneurship' teachers and academics; a proliferation in the number of courses and programmes offered at all levels of the education system; the emergence of a supporting infrastructure in the educational system (for example, new professorships); and an increase in the number of private providers of enterprise training. Despite the proliferation of enterprise education, there is still considerable conceptual confusion as to what constitutes it. This confusion has its origins in the fact that it is difficult to define precisely what enterprise education is, what it aims to do and what may be achieved through it. Existing literature has sought to define enterprise education as a distinct activity, by identifying the boundaries between entrepreneurship studies and 'traditional' management studies (Gibb, 1999). However, the boundaries between enterprise education and other forms of education are being blurred, with 'enterprise education' overlapping with other concepts, such as work-related learning, action learning, experiential learning, and entrepreneurial learning.

This conceptual confusion as to what constitutes enterprise programmes is also partly due to the diverse sets of objectives that are included under the broad 'enterprise education' heading. In much of the writing and research on entrepreneurship teaching, there is an insufficient understanding of the different possibilities enterprise education offers. Existing research and practice tends to interpret entrepreneurship education very narrowly – typically understanding it as the need to provide students with 'how to start your own business' and SME management skills. However, in seeking to design and evaluate enterprise education programmes it is necessary, as a first step, to have a precise understanding of the objectives of such educational interventions.

Broadly speaking, there are three sets of aims that may be achieved in enterprise education programmes (see **Figure 14.1**). Enterprise education programmes typically have some combination of these three objectives. The first is to develop a broad understanding of entrepreneurship and, specifically, of the role entrepreneurs and entrepreneurship plays in modern economies and societies; the second is 'learning to become entrepreneurial' and deals with the need for individuals to take responsibility for their own learning, careers and life; and the third is to learn 'how to be an entrepreneur' by learning how to start a business.

FIGURE 14.1: THE ROLES OF ENTERPRISE EDUCATION

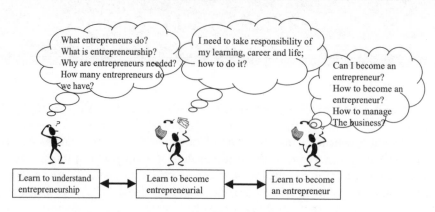

Source: *Elaborated from Gibb (1999).*

First, the objective of increasing the understanding of what entrepreneurship is about typically is associated with interventions targeted at the general population and at groups specifically interested in entrepreneurship. This objective is usually operationalised by providing information through media campaigns and / or seminars and lectures to students across all levels of the education system (primary, secondary and higher) and to the broader population through open *fora*. This type of awareness-building is also presented as the first ladder in preparing people for entrepreneurial careers, as it is argued that an individual's propensity to pursue alternative employment paths is greatly influenced by knowledge of the existence of alternative options – that is, in order to be able to make the choice of becoming an entrepreneur in the later stages of one's career, one has to see that this option exists.

Second, the objective of equipping individuals with an entrepreneurial approach to the 'world of work' frequently is presented in terms of the need for individuals, as part of the workforce, to play an increasingly active role in creating value in existing organisations and professions. This need has become more prominent as working life changes due to the emergence of new 'boundary-less' or 'portfolio' careers. In these new careers, individuals accumulate skills and personal reputations as key career resources through frequent movements between firms, movements into and out of self-employment, and even through movements to new opportunities within a single employment setting. The decision to hire is less concerned with filling positions within an organisation but rather depends on whether an individual offers the skills required to accomplish specific organisational tasks. The economic security of the individual in the 'new world of work', it is argued, increasingly will depend on the individual's ability to learn and to cope with change (see, for example, Handy, 1984). In order to survive in flatter, decentralised, and 'leaner' organisations, individuals need to take increased responsibility for their own learning, continuously updating their own skill-base. Often, this objective is fulfilled by providing information through education and training interventions, with an emphasis on some form of direct experience of both the entrepreneurial process and of two components essential to 'new' organisations – team work and project work.

The third objective of enterprise education is to prepare individuals to act as entrepreneurs and to manage a new business. Often, this is realised by facilitating experimenting and 'playing' with an idea and by trying entrepreneurship out in a controlled environment – for example, by setting up mini-businesses in a classroom setting, and by providing basic skills and information on how to start and run a small firm and how to act as an entrepreneur. This third objective is most often targeted at determined starters, nascent entrepreneurs and, in some cases, newly-started firms.

Despite these varying objectives of enterprise education, there appears to be a consensus as to the appropriate objectives and methods of enterprise education. For example, Katz (2003) argues that, at least in the United States, there is increased homogeneity as to what constitutes appropriate content of enterprise education. He suggests that there are two widely adopted approaches to entrepreneurship education in the US:

- Entrepreneurship courses that focus on wealth creation.
- Small business courses.

In the literature on enterprise education, there is an emerging consensus that enterprise education should take the entrepreneurship process as the starting point and be based on action-learning. Essentially, it is argued that enterprise needs to be understood 'as a science and as an art'. In practice, it seems that the need for action-learning methods has been over-interpreted in educational institutes (primary, secondary and higher) as the need to run mini-businesses or virtual companies in the school curricula.

However, critics of enterprise education argue that:

- 'Individuals can learn but are unlikely to be taught'.
- Too many enterprise education programmes focus solely on what skills and know-how a small business needs.
- Business schools need to need to change both their content and process of learning.
- Students need more than SME management skills.
- Enterprise education will fail when it is conceived narrowly as setting up businesses as part of vocational education and training and, consequently, is not integrated into the student's overall studies.

KEY SUCCESS FACTORS IN ENTERPRISE EDUCATION PROGRAMMES

In a study of 50 programmes from four European countries, Hytti & O'Gorman (2004) identified three sets of issues that impact on the success of enterprise education initiatives. The first set of factors relates to the aims and objectives of enterprise programmes; the second relates to how various methods adopted in enterprise education can be improved; and the third relates to the 'training the trainers', an issue perceived by many involved in enterprise education as *the* critical constraint to effective enterprise education.

It is important to note that there are three important limitations to measuring effectiveness of the methods adopted in enterprise education programmes. First, it is very difficult to establish positive relationships between initiatives and methods and their outcomes, as there is a significant time lag between the educational input and the subsequent output, however measured. This means that other intervening factors, such as an economic recession, might have a larger effect on outputs (Westhead *et al.*, 2000). Second, it is unclear how to measure the output of enterprise education: for example, should it be starting a new business, entrepreneurial activity during one's career, venture performance, or the entrepreneur's job satisfaction? Third, it is difficult to compare across the programmes, as there is variety in the aims and objectives of the programmes and in the teaching and learning methods adopted.

SUGGESTIONS FOR PROGRAMME OBJECTIVES

While programme objectives may vary, educators believed that clear objectives were important. In some programmes, objectives and methods required local adaptation to ensure that programmes are embedded in the regional context. In addition, it should be noted that, while the promoters of enterprise education may have specific aims, the participants might have divergent aims.

In the programmes that had the objective of increasing the number of start-ups, programme effectiveness was associated with the provision of detailed information and advice and the use of local role models. Where programmes adopt the objective of developing enterprising skills, which is where they adopt a broad definition of enterprise education, the ability to integrate learning across the educational experience appears to be a critical success factor. In such programmes, enterprise education is understood to involve more than starting and managing a business – that is, it is more than just a business subject, but rather an approach to learning. Ways of achieving this objective include:

- Putting greater emphasis on integrating enterprise education into various other subjects in the curriculum.

- Introducing the 'enterprise' programme as an opportunity to integrate skills and knowledge acquired in the other courses and subjects studied by the student.

In adopting such an approach, it must be noted, however, that the increased integration of subjects needs to be supported by a tight co-ordination of activities in the school, which can be achieved by, for example, appointing a project leader. **Figures 14.2** and **14.3** outline examples of how enterprise education has been integrated into the school curriculum and how this process has been managed.

FIGURE 14.2: INTEGRATING ENTERPRISE EDUCATION INTO THE CURRICULUM: FINLAND

In a Finnish comprehensive school (**Vanhan Vaasan yläaste, Variska**), a special effort has been made to integrate enterprise education into the school curriculum. Since 1990, the school has gradually developed its activities towards its vision of a school that functions in an enterprising way. Enterprise education is not a separate project or activity that takes place once a year but is a part of the school's everyday work. For example, in geography, pupils carry out projects and presentations of different countries and cultures. In these activities the teacher guides and coaches, while the pupil acts. The methods include, for example, pupils teaching other pupils, role-plays, competitions, discussions, use of library and newspapers and interviews. The 'business idea' of the school is to 'support the positive growth of the pupil's personality and to impart the ability for continuous self-development, continuing studies and life management'. In the future, the pupils will be encouraged to take even greater responsibility for their learning, and the school believes that there is a need for increased co-ordination of the projects.

The Entrepreneurship Lapland 2000 project targeted pupils in 29 comprehensive and second level schools, as well as the teachers and parents of these pupils. In the project, enterprise education and tourism were heavily linked, primarily because tourism is a growing industry in Lapland. Therefore, four projects supporting each other and the tourism industry were started through establishing training enterprises (for example, by organising a marketplace at the local railway station) and integrating enterprise education into the school curricula. The project has been successful in developing positive attitudes towards enterprise, including both business activity and also working in an enterprising way in a more general sense. However, the challenge with the activities is the need for a co-ordinator or project leader to avoid overlaps and to limit the workload.

FIGURE 14.3: INTEGRATING ENTERPRISE EDUCATION INTO THE CURRICULUM: THE LEAVING CERTIFICATE APPLIED, IRELAND

The Irish Leaving Certificate Applied was introduced in 1995 into 50 secondary schools. The Enterprise modules form an integral part of the vocational preparation and guidance courses that aim at fostering the decision-making, entrepreneurial, communicative and interpersonal skills of the students. The activities within the different modules include (i) setting up and running a business or mini-company by operating a school bank or shop or manufacturing products for sale; (ii) work simulation through organising school shows, removing graffiti or fundraising; (iii) investigation of local enterprises by conducting local surveys and conducting market research. The students leaving the programme think that participation in the programme helps them to be more innovative and enterprising. These enterprise modules serve as a means of integrating knowledge and skills, thus highlighting the need for increased integration of enterprise education into the school curriculum.

A corollary of setting objectives is to evaluate performance against objectives. Formal evaluation of programmes did not always occur, reflecting both the difficulty of evaluating performance against objectives and a general reluctance to engage in evaluation activity. However, some programmes sought to evaluate performance (**Figure 14.4**).

FIGURE 14.4: SETTING OBJECTIVES & EVALUATING EFFECTIVENESS: JOKILAAKSO PRIMARY SCHOOL, FINLAND

The Jokilaakso Primary School participated in a European Commission Comenius programme with 18 other schools from 13 different countries. The project consisted of a focused enterprise education project that aimed to publish a book in the national language of all the participant countries. The pupils were responsible for developing the content, with a view to creating international contacts and to improving each school's image. The Finnish students decided to write about Santa Claus and his adventures in Europe. As a result, the pupils gained an increased trust in their own abilities and further knowledge about Europe and learned to work together. In this project the emphasis was that enterprise education, on one hand, should be a part of the normal school activities and not an end in itself, and, on the other hand, have clear and measurable objectives.

SUGGESTIONS FOR LEARNING / TEACHING METHODS

Action learning methods

In programmes that adopted an action learning approach (for example, programmes that involved real or virtual businesses), the underlying thinking is usually that the participants / students will take the primary role. In this model, teachers act more as coaches and facilitators of learning rather than performing the 'traditional' teacher role as suggested by constructivist learning theory. A critical difficulty that such programmes face is for the teacher to achieve the correct balance between the role of coach and that of teacher. One problem is that, if students are left to do independent work, they should be given the opportunity to do so with the minimum of teacher supervision and intervention; however if students / participants are not monitored or do not receive feedback during the learning experiences, they may find that they progress slowly, that the experience is frustrating, and that the workload is excessive. This paradox can be resolved, not by emphasising the frequency of interventions by the teachers, but rather by maximising the quality of the interventions. More specifically, the programmes suggest that in their coaching roles, teachers should limit authoritative instructions, focussing rather on providing the students / participants with the necessary questions that allow the student to identify the critical issue and, where it is necessary to provide advice, it should be presented in the form of suggestions and options, with the student making the choice of how to proceed (**Figure 14.5**).

FIGURE 14.5: ACTION LEARNING METHODS: MANAGING THE WORKLOAD & MANAGING THE 'LEAVING & RETURNING' PROCESS: AUSTRIA

The Junior project was introduced in Austria in the 1995/96 school year as a voluntary project. In the project, 5 to 15 students at the secondary level set up and manage Junior firms for one school year. The project is based on the principle of learning by doing and the teacher's role is that of a 'coach'. The teams process the business ideas and make the decisions. The emphasis is on teamwork and social competencies. The project has been successful in creating a practice-oriented learning environment, increasing motivation of the students and improving school-enterprise contacts. However, the Junior projects are seen to involve a heavy workload in terms of coaching students with different levels of commitment and motivation as well as problems related to co-ordination of the courses. Teachers suggested two approaches to overcoming these problems:

◊   Training for the teachers in project management skills (group dynamics, conflict management, coaching) as well as basic business knowledge.

◊   The opportunity to engage in an exchange of information with the other teachers.

Training firms are run within the curricula of the business-oriented secondary schools and colleges through a simulation of economic reality, where virtual products and services are produced, sold and traded. The students who are the employees simulate tasks associated with the management of an enterprise, including marketing, accounting and finance, distribution, and personnel management. The training firm requires both teamwork and independent working initiative from the students. In the future, more emphasis will be placed on preparing the students to work in the training firms, promoting an independent working style as well as capabilities for team work, and on implementing measures to assure students' reflection on their experiences with the training firm – for example, enabling efficient learning through reflection.

Furthermore, where action learning projects require students to leave the school / educational environment – for example, to work in a training firm or in an established business – student preparation prior to leaving and 'after-care' for the students / participants while away from the school / educational establishment, are necessary elements to effective student / participant learning.

A further problem in action learning programmes is the size of the workload for both the teachers and the students. This problem is of particular concern when programmes are run as an extra subject or an extracurricular activity. One approach to overcoming this problem is to better integrate enterprise education across the curriculum and, in higher education institutes, there may be the option of introducing voluntary seminars or assignments rather than compulsory ones.

'Traditional' methods

In programmes that apply more traditional methods (for example, lectures and assignments), the benefits to the students / participants are typically described in terms of a better understanding of entrepreneurial activity rather than an understanding of how to act as an entrepreneur. In many cases, there is a suggestion that programmes need to create strong links with the business community in order to achieve their aims. The suggestions for best practice in such programmes relate primarily to how to create, for the student / participant, a realistic image of the working life of an entrepreneur and of the work environment in an SME. From the perspective of participants / students, this often translates into having more entrepreneurs in the classroom. However, there are other ways in which a realistic image of the entrepreneurial experience can be brought into the classroom (**Figure 14.6**).

FIGURE 14.6: CREATING A REALISTIC IMAGE OF THE ENTREPRENEURIAL EXPERIENCE IN THE CLASSROOM

The Big Changes for Small Firms project was a national programme in Ireland that targeted companies, students and individuals. In the Entrepreneurship Education & Awareness module, individuals accessed a website, watched a television series and availed of a training pack. An average of 13,000 people watched each of the six programmes in the TV series. During the broadcast of the series, the website received between 5,000 and 6,000 visits a week. All universities and colleges in Ireland also received a copy of the training pack. As a result, the programmes were deemed successful in portraying a realistic picture of the problems experienced by SMEs.

SUGGESTIONS FOR 'TRAINING THE TRAINERS'

The training of teachers is a critical element to the development of effective enterprise education initiatives (**Figure 14.7**). It appears, not surprisingly, that teachers who are more familiar with entrepreneurship and the entrepreneurial process possessed the best prerequisites for the teaching of this phenomenon. In programmes that are primarily related to start-ups and running small businesses, it is often suggested by programme reviews that teachers / educators lacked the information and skills required to teach the business subjects relating to entrepreneurship. It is also argued, in some cases, that the culture and values of schools could be a greater hindrance to carrying out enterprise education than the values, attitudes and skills of any individual teacher.

This might suggest that teachers need in-career continuous training to support the introduction of new teaching methods. Programmes targeted at training teachers, in most cases, are highly appreciated by teachers, supporting the argument that there is a demand for teacher education. Such programmes appear effective at informing teachers of approaches that can be taken to enterprise education, and of the existence of appropriate teaching and learning resource materials. Other ways of supporting the teacher included peer groups, where experiences can be exchanged among different teachers; and by having a support person for the teacher from outside the school – for example, from the business community.

FIGURE 14.7: TRAINING THE TRAINERS

The Primary Enterprise programme was introduced in 1989 in the UK and was designed for use by teachers and pupils of primary schools, particularly the 7 to 10 age group. The programme consists of resource materials and teacher training programmes. Teachers are trained, in active workshop sessions, to teach in an enterprising fashion, as opposed to the traditional didactic teaching style. Throughout the workshop, teachers are introduced to teaching methods that they will be expected to use with their students. The aim of the programme is to help pupils to become more enterprising as individuals and to help teachers develop the required teaching approach. The programme has been well-received, as a highly practical means of helping teachers develop enterprise education within the primary school classroom.

CONCLUSION

At the outset of this chapter, we suggested that enterprise education has become an important part of industrial policy and educational policy in many developed countries, but that there is considerable conceptual confusion regarding what constitutes 'enterprise education'. Broadly speaking, it seems that, from the policy perspective, the need for enterprise education is most commonly interpreted as the need to train or develop more entrepreneurs. Thus, programmes are typically targeted at an audience believed to be in 'demand' of enterprise education. However, this chapter suggests that there is diversity in the objectives that enterprise education programmes can seek to achieve. Enterprise education can achieve a broad array of objectives – that is, it can be much more than simply preparing people to be entrepreneurs. In addition, there is significant variety in approach in terms of the methods used in enterprise education programmes.

Learning / teaching methods used in enterprise education can be improved by adopting best practice from other initiatives. By way of example, we draw attention to a free web-site (www.entredu.com) that documents the programmes discussed in this chapter.

What are appropriate enterprise education interventions? Should enterprise education be offered as a broad subject, that is, 'little bit of it to everyone', or as an elite choice, that is, 'a lot of it to just a few selected'? (Autio, 2002). What are the implications of the ideas in this chapter for policy-makers and those who develop, fund and promote enterprise education initiatives?

First, enterprise education programmes can achieve a number of diverse objectives. Second, whatever the objective, an appropriate method should be chosen and progress towards this should be measured. Third, the learning / teaching methods used in enterprise education can be improved by adopting best practice from other initiatives. Finally, a critical constraint to developing effective enterprise education is the development of appropriately-trained trainers. Therefore, enterprise education needs to be linked to extensive in-career development for teachers / trainers.

QUESTIONS

1. Outline the main objectives of enterprise education?

2. What are the factors that determine the effectiveness of enterprise education initiatives?

3. Can entrepreneurship be taught?

4. Describe and critique an enterprise education initiative.

PROFILE: ANGELA HOPE[30]

Angela Hope became an entrepreneur the day she graduated from Manchester University with a degree in Fashion Textiles. She always knew that she would work for herself and believed that it was almost in her blood, as her Dad had always been self-employed.

Her first venture was with a group of four other design graduates; between them, they had two retail outlets in Bristol and in Bath that they stocked with their designs. Each of the design team was responsible for a different area, with Angela specialising in women's clothing.

Over time, Angela has had different ventures, retaining her passion for self-employment, even during those short periods when she found herself employed. Along the way, she acquired an MA in marketing which complements her technical and creative skills.

From her home in Bristol, Angela and her partner, Martin, often came to Ireland on holidays and fell in love with the beauty of the landscape. They decided to follow their dream and to move permanently to Ireland. Initially, they located in County Mayo and subsequently moved to County Leitrim. Angela loved County Leitrim with its wonderful light, open spaces and green fields, all of which she found were much more conducive to her creativity than the more urban concrete environment of Bristol.

The move to County Leitrim coincided with Angel's first foray into the making of handbags. Describing herself as someone who is more often seen with a rucksack than with a handbag, Angela explains how she found herself making handbags and fell by chance across a very promising opening for a new business:

> *I had a good friend in the London fashion PR scene who had been asking me to make her a handbag for some time. I eventually gave in to my friend's persistence and posted the bag off to London, expecting to hear nothing more. The bag was much admired and many orders came through just word-of-mouth from people who had seen the bag.*

When she began to think further about building a business around limited edition handmade handbags, Angela received encouragement from Anne Marie O'Rourke in Leitrim Design House, a part of the Leitrim County Enterprise Board:

> *Anne Marie spurred me on and gave me the self-belief to go for it. She also gave me practical assistance and helped me to participate in Showcase that first year. The Enterprise Board also provided an employment grant, which I used to renovate an existing outhouse store close to the cottage where I was living. I made the money go a long way as I and my partner did all the work*

---

[30] This profile appeared in Fitzsimons & O'Gorman (2006).

ourselves, including the wiring, plumbing and carpentry. This gave me the space I needed for cutting and storing the fabrics.

From this start in 2002, Angela has travelled to Showcase, which is run by the Crafts Council of Ireland, each year as this is her main shop window to the major buyers. Her bags are now sold in 75 / 80 outlets throughout Ireland, the UK, the Netherlands, and the United States.

The bags are made from wool sourced from Irish and Welsh mills. These are made into blankets from which the material for the bags is cut. They are lined in velvet and Irish lavender is placed between the velvet and the wool to add to the bag's unique charm. Angela describes the bags as classic and timeless, but with a modern feel. The demand for her bags is growing and Angela's main concern is not attracting more buyers but retaining a balance between her creativity, her lifestyle and her work.

Angela is cautious about recommending entrepreneurship to others:

They would really have to want to do it. On the one hand, there is great freedom and flexibility in being your own boss, you reap the rewards fully of your own hard work, but on the other hand, it is really hard work. And the sheer hard work should not be underestimated.

Asked if she would do it all over again, Angela replies without hesitation:

Absolutely!

REFERENCES

Acs, Z., Arenius, P., Hay, M. & Minniti, M. (2004). *Global Entrepreneurship Monitor: 2004 Executive Report*, Boston / London: Babson College / London Business School.

Amabile, T.M., Conti, R., Coon, H., Lazenby, J. & Herron, M. (1996). 'Assessing the work environment for creativity', *Academy of Management Journal*, Vol.39, No.1154.

Aram, J.D. & Cowan, S.S. (1990). 'Strategic planning for increased profit in the small business', *Long Range Planning*, Vol.23, No.3, pp.63-70.

Ardagh, J. (1994). *Ireland & the Irish, Portrait of a Changing Society*, London: Hamish Hamilton.

Association of University Technology Managers (2002). *Licensing Survey FY 2002 – Survey Summary*, Northbrook, IL: Association of University Technology Managers (http://www.autm.net).

Austretch, D. (2004). 'Sustaining innovation & growth: Public policy support for entrepreneurship, *Industry & Innovation*, Vol.11, No.3, pp.167-192.

Autio, E. (2002). Keynote Speech, *12th Nordic Conference on Small Business Research*, Kuopio, 26-28 May.

Baker, T., Miner S. & Eesly, D. (2003). 'Improvising firms: Bricolage, account-giving & improvisational competencies in the founding process', *Research Policy*, Vol.32, pp.255-276.

Barry, F. (2003). 'Irish economic development over three decades of EU membership', *Finance a Uver*, Vol.53, 9/10, pp.394-412.

Barry, F., Bradley, J. & O'Malley, E. (1999). 'Indigenous & foreign industry: Characteristics & performance', in Barry, F. (ed.), *Understanding Ireland's Economic Growth*, Basingstoke: Macmillan.

Bennis, W. (1999). 'Rethinking leadership', *Journal of Public Inquiry*, Spring/Summer, pp.57-61.

Bhide, A. (1986). 'Hustle as strategy', *Harvard Business Review*, September/October.

Bygrave, B. with Hunt, S. (2005). *Global Entrepreneurship Monitor 2004 Financing Report*, Boston / London: Babson College / London Business School.

Campbell, J. (1949). *The Hero with a Thousand Faces*, London: Fontana.

Cooney, T. (ed.) (2004). *Irish Cases in Entrepreneurship*, Dublin: Blackhall Publishing.

Cooper, A. & Gascon, J. (1992). 'Entrepreneurs, processes of founding & new firm performance', in *State of the Art of Entrepreneurship Research*, Sexton, D. & Kasda, J. (eds.) Boston, MA: PWS-Kent.

Culliton, J. (1992) – see Industrial Policy Review Group (1992).

Cunningham, J. & Harney, B. (2006). *Strategic Management of Technology Transfer: The New Challenge on Campus*, Cork: Oak Tree Press.

Cunningham, J. & Lischeron, J. (1991). 'Defining entrepreneurship', *Journal of Small Business Management*, Vol.29(1), pp.45-61.

de Bono, E. (1973). *Lateral Thinking: Creativity Step-by-Step*, New York: Harper & Row.

Department of Enterprise, Trade & Employment (2006). *Strategy for Science, Technology & Innovation 2006-2013*, Dublin: Government Publications.

Di Gregorio, D. & Shane, S. (2003). 'Why do some universities generate more start-ups than others?', *Research Policy*, Vol.32, pp.209-27.

Drucker, P.F. (1985). *Innovation & Entrepreneurship*, New York: Harper & Row.

Drucker, P.F. (2002). 'The discipline of innovation', *Harvard Business Review*, Vol.80, Issue 8, pp.95-103.

Fassin, Y. (2000). 'The strategic role of university Industry Liaison Offices', *Journal of Research Administration*, Vol.1(2), pp.31-41.

Fitzsimons, P. & O'Gorman, C. (2005). *The Global Entrepreneurship Monitor 2004: The Irish Report: How Entrepreneurial is Ireland?*, Dublin: Department of Business Administration, University College Dublin.

Fitzsimons, P. & O'Gorman, C. (2006). *The Global Entrepreneurship Monitor 2005: The Irish Report*, Dublin: Department of Business Administration, University College Dublin.

Fitzsimons, P. & O'Gorman, C. (2007): *The Global Entrepreneurship Monitor 2006: The Irish Report*, Dublin: Department of Business Administration, University College Dublin.

Forfás (1998): *Broadband Investment in Ireland*, Dublin: Forfás.

Forfás (1998): *Telecommunications: A Key Contribution in Competitiveness & Electronic Commerce*, Dublin: Forfás.

Forfás (1999): *E-Commerce: The Policy Requirement*, Dublin: Forfás.

Forfás (2006): *SME Finance Equity*, Dublin: Forfás.

Forfás (2007). *Report of the Business Regulation Forum*, Dublin: Forfás.

Friedman, J. & Silberman, S. (2003). 'University technology transfer: Do incentives, management & location matter?', *Journal of Technology Transfer*, Vol.28, No.1, pp.17-30.

Gibb, A. (1999). 'Can we build effective entrepreneurship through management development?', *Journal of General Management*, Vol.24, No.4, pp.1-21.

Goldfarb, B. & Henrekson, M. (2002). 'Bottom-up *versus* top-down policies towards the commercialisation of university intellectual property', *Research Policy*, Vol.32, pp.639-58.

Gomes-Casseres, B. (1996). 'Alliance strategies of small firms', *Small Business Economics*, Vol.7. No.3, pp.183-204.

Goodbody (2002). *Entrepreneurship in Ireland*, Dublin: Goodbody Economic Consultants.

Hambrick, D. & Crozier, L. (1985). 'Stumblers & stars in the management of rapid growth', *Journal of Business Venturing*, Vol.1.

Handy, C. (1984). *The Future of Work: A Guide to a Changing Society*, Oxford: Oxford University Press / Basil Blackwell.

Harmon, E. (1995). 'Mapping the university technology transfer process', *Babson Conference*.

Henderson, R., Jaffe, A. & Trajtenberg, M. (1998). 'Universities as a source of commercial technology: A detailed analysis of university patenting, 1965-88', *Review of Economics & Statistics,* Vol.80, No.1, pp.119-127.

Henry, C. & McGowan, P. (eds.) (2007). *Irish Cases in Entrepreneurship*, 2nd Edition, Dublin: Blackhall Publishing.

Hisrich, R. & Brush, C. (1984). 'Women entrepreneurs: Strategic origins impact on growth' in *Frontiers of Entrepreneurship Research,* Kirchhoff, B., Long, W., McMullan, W., Vesper, K. & Wetzel, W. Jr. (eds.), Wellesley, MA: Babson College.

Hisrich, R. (1988). 'The entrepreneur in Northern Ireland: Characteristics, problems & recommendations for the future', *Journal of Small Business Management*, Vol.26, No.3, pp.32-39.

Hytti, U. & O'Gorman, C. (2004). 'What is 'enterprise education'? An analysis of the objectives and methods of enterprise education programmes in four European countries', *Education & Training,* Vol.46, No.1, pp.11-23.

ICSTI (2004). *National Code of Practice for Managing Intellectual Property from Publicly-funded Research*, Dublin: ICSTI.

Industrial Policy Review Group (1991). *A Time For Change: Industrial Policy for the 1990s*, *Report of the Industrial Policy Review Group* (J. Culliton, Chairperson), Dublin: Government Publications.

Johnson, B.R. (1990). 'Towards a multidimensional model of entrepreneurship: The case of achievement motivation & the entrepreneur', *Entrepreneurship: Theory & Practice*, Vol.14, No.3, pp.39-54.

Katz, J. (2003). 'The chronology and intellectual trajectory of American entrepreneurship education 1876-1999', *Journal of Business Venturing*, Vol.18, No.2, pp.283-300.

Kilby, P. (2003). 'The Heffalump revisited', *Journal of International Entrepreneurship*, Vol.1, No.1, pp.13-29.

Kinsella, R. & Mulvenna, D. (1993). 'Fast-growth firms: Their role in the post-Culliton industrial strategy', *Administration,* Vol.41, No.1, pp.3-15.

Kinsella, R. (1994). *Fast-growth Small Firms: An Irish Perspective*, Dublin: IMI.

Lambert, R. (2003). *Lambert Review of Business-University Collaboration: Final Report*, London: HM Treasury.

Leach, E. (1970). *Lévi-Strauss*, London: Fontana.

Levitt, T. (1967). 'Innovative imitation', *McKinsey Quarterly*, No.4, pp.35-45.

Lundvall, B.-A. (2002). 'The university in the learning economy', *DRUID Working Paper No.02:06*, Copenhagen: Copenhagen Business School.

McCarthy, B. & Leavy, B. (2000). 'Phases in the strategy formation process: An exploratory study of Irish SMEs', *IBAR*, Vol.21, No.2, pp.55-80.

McClelland, D.C. (1961). *The Achieving Society*, Princeton, NJ: Van Nostrand.

Meseri, O. & Maital, S. (2001). 'A survey analysis of university technology transfer in Israel: An evaluation of projects and determinants of success', *Journal of Technology Transfer,* Vol.26(1), pp.115-27.

Mitra, J. & Formica, P. (eds.) (1997). *Innovation & Economic Development, University-Enterprise Partnership in Action*, Dublin: Oak Tree Press.

Murray, J. & O'Gorman, C. (1994). 'Growth strategies for the smaller business', *Journal of Strategic Change*, Vol.3, No.127, pp.1-9.

National Economic Social Council (1982). *A Review of Economic Policy* (Telesis Report), Report No.64, Dublin: NESC.

National Institute of Standards & Technology (2002). *A Toolkit for Evaluating Public R&D Investment Models & Methods* (http://www.atp.nist.gov).

National Institute of Standards & Technology (2002a). Annual Report on Technology Transfer: Approach & Plans, FY 2002 Activities & Achievements, Washington DC: US Department of Commerce.

Nicholson, L. & Anderson A. (2005). 'News & nuances of the entrepreneurial myth & metaphor: Linguistic games in entrepreneurial sense-making & sense-giving', *Entrepreneurship Theory & Practice*, March.

O'Farrell, P. (1986). *Entrepreneurs & Industrial Change*, Dublin: IMI.

O'Malley, E. & O'Gorman, C. (2001). 'Competitive advantage in the Irish indigenous software industry & the role of inward FDI', *European Planning Studies*, Vol.9, No.3, pp.303-321.

OECD (2001). *Regulatory Reform in Ireland*, OECD: Paris.

OECD (2003). *Turning Business into Science: Patenting & Licensing at Public Research Organisations*, OECD: Paris.

Olson, P.D. (1986). 'Entrepreneurs: Opportunistic decision-makers', *Journal of Small Business Management*, Vol.24, No.3, pp.29-35.

Porter, M. (1985). *Competitive Advantage*, New York: Free Press.

Quinn, C., O'Reilly, P. & Cunningham, J. (2006). 'Crafting strategy & strategy absence in SMEs in culture industries: Evidence from SMEs in the Irish independent television production sector', *Institute of Small Business Conference*.

Reich, R.B. (1987). 'Entrepreneurship reconsidered: The team as hero', *Harvard Business Review*, Vol.65, May-June, pp.77-83.

Reynolds, P., Bosma, N., Autio, E., with Hunt, S., De Bono, N., Servais, I., Lopez-Garcia, P. and Chin, N. (2005). 'Global Entrepreneurship Monitor: Data collection design & implementation 1998-2003', *Small Business Economics*, Vol.24(3), pp.205-231. – cited p27.

Reynolds, P., Bygrave, W. & Autio, E. (2004). *Global Entrepreneurship Monitor: 2003 Executive Report*, Boston / London: Babson College / London Business School.

Rotter, J.B. (1966). 'Generalized expectancies for internal *versus* external control of reinforcement', *Psychological Monographs*, 80: No. 609.

Sanchez, A. & Tejedor, A. (1995). 'University-industry relationships in peripheral regions: The case of Aragon in Spain', *Technovation*, Vol.15(10), pp.61.

Schumpeter, J. A. (1934). *The Theory of Economic Development: An Inquiry into Profits, Capital, Credit, Interest & the Business Cycle,* Cambridge, MA: Harvard University Press.

Schumpeter, J. A. (1942). *Capitalism, Socialism & Democracy*, New York: Harper & Brothers.

Schumpeter, J.A. (1948). *Economic Theory & Entrepreneurial History, Change & the Entrepreneur*, Cambridge, MA: Harvard University.

Sexton, D.L. & Bowman-Upton, N. (1991). *Entrepreneurship: Creativity & Growth*, New York: Macmillan.

Shapiro, M. (1993). 'The entrepreneurial individual in the large organisation', in Beckman, J. (ed.), *Entrepreneurship & the Outlook for America*, New York: The Free Press.

Small Business Forum (2006). *Small Business is Big Business, Report of the Small Business Forum*, Dublin: Forfás.

Stevens G.A. & Burley, J. (1997). '3,000 raw ideas – 1 commercial success', *Research Technology Management*, Vol.40, No.16.

Storey, D.J. (2006). *Understanding the Small Business Sector*, London: Thomson Learning.

Sweeney, B. (2005). *Making Bread*, Dublin: Liberties Press.

Task Force on Small Business (1994). *Report of the Task Force on Small Business* (S. Brennan, Chairman), Dublin: Government Publications.

Timmons, Smollen & Dingee (1985). *New Venture Creation: A Guide to Entrepreneurship*, Homewood, IL: Irwin.

von Hippel, E. (2005). *Democratizing Innovation*, Cambridge, Mass.: MIT Press.

von Oech, R. (1990). *A Whack on the Side of the Head: How You Can Be More Creative*, New York: Warner Books.

Weiss, A. (2003). 'To the digital age: Research labs, start-up companies & the rise of MOS technology (review)', *Enterprise & Society*, Vol.4, No.4, pp.740-41.

Westhead, P., Storey, D. & Martin, F. (2000). 'The Shell Technology Enterprise Programme: Student outcomes', *Education & Training,* Vol.42, No.4-5, pp.272-281.

Wycoff, J. & Wycoff, J. (2003). 'The "Big 10" innovation killers: How to keep your innovation system alive & well', *Journal for Quality & Participation*, No.26, pp.17-48.

Yeats, W.B. (1904). 'Preface', in Gregory, L., *Gods & Fighting Men*, London: John Murray Publisher.

INDEX